The Hamlyn Cookbook

The Hamlyn Cookbook

250 imaginative recipes, from basic soups to elegant desserts

Hamlyn

The Hamlyn Cookbook

First published in Great Britain in 1995
by Hamlyn
an imprint of Reed Consumer Books
Limited
Michelin House, 81 Fulham Road,
London SW3 6RB
and Auckland, Melbourne, Singapore
and Toronto

ISBN 0 600 58827 0

A CIP catalogue record for this book is
available from the British Library

Produced by Mandarin Offset
Printed in Hong Kong

Art Editor: Mark Winwood
Designers: Margaret Sadler
          Louise Leffler
          Leigh Jones
Managing Editor: Anne Johnson
Editors: Maggie Ramsay
        Elsa Petersen-Schepelern
        Isobel Holland
Reference Text: Janet Smy
Recipe Contributors:
        Mary Cadogan
        Sally Mansfield
        Annie Nichols
        Ingeborg Pertwee
        Louise Pickford
        Lyn Rutherford
        Jeni Wright
Production Controller: Melanie Frantz
Nutritional Consultant:
        Michael van Straten
Black and White Line Illustrations:
Coral Mulla
Indexer: Hilary Bird

Notes

Both metric and imperial measurements have been given in all recipes.
Use one set of measurements only and
not a mixture of both.

Standard level spoon measurements
are used in all recipes.
1 tablespoon = one 15 ml spoon
1 teaspoon = one 5 ml spoon

Eggs should be size 3 unless otherwise
stated. Some recipes contain raw eggs.
Readers are reminded of the advice
from the Department of Health that it
would be prudent for readers, particularly those who are more vulnerable,
such as pregnant women, invalids, the
elderly, babies, young children, to
avoid eating uncooked eggs.

Milk should be full fat unless otherwise
stated.

Pepper should be freshly ground black
pepper unless otherwise stated.
Fresh herbs should be used unless
otherwise stated. If unavailable use
dried herbs as an alternative but halve
the quantities stated.

Ovens should be preheated to the
specified temperature – if using a fan
assisted oven, follow the manufacturer's instructions for adjusting the time
and temperature.

For barbecuing, cooking times are
approximate. They have been estimated using a charcoal-fired barbecue and
will vary according to the size and type
of grill, weather conditions and the
intensity of heat.

When barbecuing food: before using
wooden skewers or string soak them in
water for 30 minutes to avoid burning.

Vegetarians should look for the 'V'
symbol on cheese to ensure it is made
with vegetarian rennet. There are
vegetarian forms of Parmesan, Feta,
Cheddar, Cheshire, dolcellate and
many goats' cheeses.

To test if poultry is cooked, pierce the
flesh through the thickest part with a
skewer or fork – the juices should run
clear, never pink or red.

Do not re-freeze poultry which has
been previously been frozen and
thawed. Do not re-freeze a cooked
dish which has been previously frozen
and thawed.

Photographic Acknowledgements

Divertimenti, 45/47 Wigmore Street,
London W1H 9LE, ph: 0171-935
0689, 139/141 Fulham Road, London
SW3 6SD, ph: 0171-581 8065,
Divertimenti Mail Order ph: 0171-386
9911, fax: 0171-386 9393: 67 top
left, 67 bottom right, 67 centre left,
67 top right, 72 top left, 72 bottom
left, 74 right centre, 74 top right, 74
top left, 75 bottom left, 75 top right,
75 centre, 75 left centre, 76 left, 76
bottom right, 76 top right, 77 bottom
left, 77 top right, 77 centre, 77 top
left, 77 top centre, 77 bottom right,
78 centre left, 79 bottom left, 79 right
centre bottom, 79 centre, 79 top centre, 79 centre left, 80 top right, 80
bottom right, 80 left

David Mellor 4 Sloane Square, London
SW1W 8EE, David Mellor Country
Shop, The Round Building, Grindleford
Road, Hathersage, Sheffield S30 1BA:
6 bottom, 66 bottom centre, 66 bottom right, 66 bottom left, 66 top
right, 67 top left centre, 68 top left,
68 centre, 68 top right, 68 bottom, 69
bottom right, 69 top right, 69 bottom
left, 69 top left, 69 bottom centre, 70
bottom left, 70 top, 70 bottom right,
71 top, 71 bottom, 72 left centre, 72
centre, 72 right, 72 top right, 73 bottom left, 73 top, 73 bottom, 74 bottom, 75 right bottom, 75 right centre,
75 top left, 78 centre, 78 top left, 78
bottom right, 78 top right, 79 top
right, 79 bottom centre left, 79 bottom right

Reed International Books Ltd/Bryce
Attwell 64 above right, 64 above left,
64 bottom left, 65,/Steve Baxter 114,
123 above, 130/1, 148 below, 191
bottom right, 210/1,/Mitchell Beazley
6 above, 8, 9, 10, 11, 12, 13, 14
above right, 14 above left, 14 below
right, 14 bottom right, 14 top right,
14 below left, 15 above right, 15 cen-
tre/bottom right, 15 above left, 15 top
right, 15 top left, 15 bottom left, 16
top left, 16 below right, 16 bottom
right, 16 above left, 16 below left, 16
top right, 16 bottom left, 17 above
right, 17 below right, 17 above right,
17 below left, 18/19, 22/3, 25 above,
27 centre, 34/5, 38/9, 38 below centre, 38 below left, 38 below right, 40
above, 41 above, 53 below,/Nick
Carman 128, 201 above, 201 below,
212/3, 230,/Joe Cornish 217,/Mick
Duff 11 bottom left,/Alan Duns
232,/Laurie Evans 56, 58/9, 82, 90,
96 below, 116/7, 129 below, 130, 134
right, 134 left, 139, 175 left, 180 bottom, 196, 197, 210 below, 214, 216,
230/1,/Gus Filgate Gatefold 1 (5),
Gatefold 1 (4), Gatefold 3 (11), 57,
164 bottom, 164/165, 195 above,
198 below, 198 above, 199, 200
below, 204 below, 208 below, 209,
212 below, 214/5, 221,/GGS
Photographics 36, 40 below, 42 left,
42 right, 46 right, 46 left, 47 below,
49, 50 left, 50 right, 51 top right, 51
left, 51 centre, 110 left, 110 right, 188
top left, 188 top right,/Hamlyn Group
Picture Library 234 above, 234 below,
235, 236 above,/Norman Hollands 24,

226/7,/Jeremy Hopley 2, 7 below, 52,
81, 113 above, 125 below, 138/9,
158, 169 top, 184, 193 bottom right,
202/3,/Tim Imrie Gatefold 3 (7),
Gatefold 3 (3), Gatefold 3 (6),
Gatefold 3 (4), Gatefold 3 (9),/James
Jackson 220 above,/James Johnson 7
above centre, 7 above right, 7 above
left, 219 left, 219 centre, 219
right,/Paul Kemp 242, 243,/Graham
Kirk Gatefold 1 (1), Gatefold 2 (5),
2/3, 25 below left, 27 below, 47
above, 86/7, 86 top, 86 below, 86
centre, 92 below, 94, 95 left, 95 right,
96 above, 97, 102, 103, 104/5, 109
above, 112 above, 113 below, 115
below, 115 above, 118 below, 129
above, 135, 143 below, 154 bottom,
155, 159 right, 169 bottom, 170 left,
172, 173 top, 173 bottom, 174 bottom, 176 bottom, 177 bottom, 178,
179 bottom, 180 top, 185 top,
188/189, 190, 193 top left, 202, 203,
208 above, 226 above,/Duncan
McNicol 220 below,/James Merrell
Gatefold 3 (2), Gatefold 3 (10),
Gatefold 3 (1), Gatefold 2 (4),
Gatefold 2 (3), Gatefold 3 (8),
Gatefold 2 (7), Gatefold 2 (2),
Gatefold 3 (5), Gatefold 2 (1),
Gatefold 2 (6), 44, 142, 143 above,
144/5, 144, 146 below, 148 above,
150/1, 150, 151 below, 151 above,
152 below, 152 above, 153, 170/171,
206, 215,/Diana Miller Gatefold 1 (3),
54, 55, 82/3, 84 above, 84 below, 85
above, 88 below, 88 above,
236/7,/James Murphy Gatefold 1 (2),
5, 26, 37, 85 below, 98 centre, 98
below, 98 top, 99, 100, 105, 110/1,
112 below, 124, 125 above, 137, 140,
141 above, 141 below, 156, 157, 166
top, 166 bottom, 167, 174 top, 176
top, 177 top, 182/183, 186/187, 187
bottom, 191 top left, 200 above, 204
above, 205, 212 above,/Peter Myers
236 below,/Alan Newnham 13 bottom, 39 below, 41 below, 90/1, 92
above, 101, 104 above, 116, 118
above, 119, 120, 120/1, 122, 123
below, 133, 146 above, 147, 149, 154
top, 168, 175 right, 179 top, 181, 185
bottom, 186 top, 192, 194, 195
below, 222, 222/3, 226 below, 228/9,
233,/Roger Phillips 62 bottom
left,/John Sims 225,/Charlie Stebbings
224 left,/Roger Stowell Gatefold 1 (7),
Gatefold 1 (6), Gatefold 1 (8), 62
above right, 62 above left, 63, 89, 93,
108, 109 below, 126/7, 127, 132/3,
132, 159 left, 160/161, 161 bottom,
162, 163 bottom, 163 top, 206/7, 210
above,/Phil Webb 106/7, 106, 107,
136 right, 136 left,/Paul Williams 224
right,/Trevor Wood 25 below right

Tesco Stores Ltd 228 top, 229 top

Waitrose, Food Shops of the John
Lewis Partnership 53 top right, 60
right, 60 left

Foreword

Over the past years I have written many cookery books for Hamlyn Publishing. These covered a wide range of subjects and gave up-to-date information on various foods, cooking techniques and carefully tested recipes. The hugely enjoyable years of working with Hamlyn Publishing made me appreciate the expertise with which their books are prepared and the time and effort spent in producing both colourful and inspiring photographs. That is why I am delighted to write this foreword to their new and very exciting Hamlyn Cookery Book.

This comprehensive book offers a fresh approach to everyday cooking. It will give the user confidence to cook all kinds of dishes from pasta to an elaborate dinner party menu. It begins with an illustrated reference section and an introduction to kitchen skills, together with a detailed look at important ingredients. Basic cookery techniques are explained with step-by-step spreads and cook's tip boxes. Foods like stocks, sauces, pastry and breads are examined in detail. There is helpful information about cooking equipment with sections on the best use of your microwave and freezer. The detailed look at different wines will be invaluable.

The second part of the book contains an extensive collection of 250 beautifully illustrated easy-to-follow recipes, many with interesting variations. Each recipe includes an at a glance guide to nutritional content. You will find classic dishes such as Coq au Vin, Tournedos en Croûte, Lasagne and Crème Caramel, with many modern recipes for such things as Linguine with Mussels and Tomato Sauce, Roasted Autumn Vegetables with Garlic Sauce, Baby Aubergines with Herbed Greek Yogurt and a delicious Peach, Apricot and Blueberry Gratin.

In an exciting design innovation, there are three self-contained editorial features that open out to two double pages: The Great Outdoors – which looks at barbecues; Saturday Night Fever – featuring cocktails and drinks for those special occasions and That's Entertainment which describes the way to plan a meal successfully.

I am sure you will find this a most valuable book in your kitchen. If you are a beginner it will give you great confidence; if you are an experienced cook its clear, concise recipes and magnificent photographs will soon be a regular source of inspiration.

Marguerite Patten

Contents

Vegetables

Season by season, the range of vegetables available for consumption is always plentiful, not to mention colourful and delicious. Today's constantly improving marketing techniques ensure they can be bought at the peak of freshness.

Asparagus
The tips should be tightly closed and the stems firm. Cook the spears in a tall pan with the heads in steam and the bottoms in water for 10 minutes.

Avocado
The avocado should yield to gentle pressure at the stalk end but should not be squashy. Eat raw or make into a dip. Once cut, always brush with lemon juice to prevent discoloration.

Beetroot
Young beetroot can be eaten raw, peeled, grated, and mixed with a dressing. To cook avoiding the vegetable bleeding into the water, choose those that do not have damaged skins and cut off the tops, leaving 5 cm/ 2 inches above the root. Boil in lightly salted water for 30–40 minutes, cool and peel. Serve either hot or cold.

Aubergine
The skin should be firm and bright. Some people cube and salt the flesh, leave it to drain and then dry it before cooking, others say this not necessary. Particularly suited to Mediterranean styles of cookery, the aubergine can be stewed, roasted, made into fritters or stuffed.

Broad bean
Early in the summer season, the young bean can be eaten lightly cooked, pods included. As it matures the skin becomes tough and should be rubbed off halfway through cooking.

Buying

Choose vegetables that really are good enough to eat without needing much preparation. Look for the following qualities:

• Leafy varieties, such as spring cabbage, celery and lettuce, should have a fresh appearance, with no sign of browning, wilting or slime.

• Root vegetables, such as carrots, should be firm and have no sign of damp or shiny patches or any surface damage. Avoid potatoes with dry wrinkly skins or if they are turning green or sprouting.

Broccoli

Calabrese has densely packed heads, sprouting broccoli has smaller, looser heads and is leafier. It should look firm and healthy, with no sign of yellowing. It is best lightly steamed or microwaved. Before cooking, trim the stems and cut the florets into even-sized pieces before boiling or steaming.

Cabbage

Use shredded red or white cabbage in salads, dressed with a well-flavoured vinaigrette. To prepare hearted cabbage, halve and then quarter, cutting out and discarding the hard core, and shred finely. Rinse well and cook gently in a covered pan with only the water that clings to the leaves, and some butter or olive oil, or stir-fry. Red cabbage is braised for 1–2 hours with sliced onion, apple, and a little red vinegar and stock.

Carrot

An inexpensive source of vitamins A and C, mineral salts, trace elements and fibre, carrots can be eaten grated raw in salads or cooked. New carrots need only scrubbing, older ones should be lightly peeled. They can be boiled, braised, steamed, or used in soups or stews.

Cauliflower

Eat this all-year vegetable raw or lightly cooked. When cooked the florets should be just soft and the stem should be fairly crunchy.

Chinese cabbage

This has long, white, slightly ribbed stalks and is often called Chinese leaves. It is best cooked by steaming or stir-frying; it is also used for stuffing and in salads.

Cucumber

Select one that is straight and firm with a slight bloom on the skin. It will be at its best when fresh and crisp, and loses these qualities after a few days. Use in salads or cube and fry quickly in butter to serve with chicken or fish.

Celery

At its best during the winter months, celery may be used raw in salads or served with cheese at the end of a meal. It can also be made into soup, added to stews and casseroles or braised.

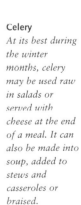

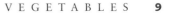

Globe artichoke

Boil or steam for at least 30 minutes. It is ready when a leaf pulls away easily from the base. Dip the base of the leaf into a sauce and scrape off the flesh with your teeth. Discard the hairy choke, and eat the heart with the sauce.

Storing

It is not good value to buy lots of vegetables which languish in the refrigerator for weeks before you get round to using them – the fresher they are the more flavour and nutrition they have to offer. Any close-fitting packaging should be removed to prevent moisture building up.

● Firm vegetables, such as cauliflower or cabbage, can be stored for up to a week in the refrigerator's salad drawer.

● Root vegetables will keep in a cool dark place for a couple of weeks. Remove from polythene bags and keep in strong brown paper bags with the top folded over.

● Leafy and salad vegetables will keep for several days at the bottom of the refrigerator.

Fennel

This bulb is white with overlapping leaves and has a mild rather sweet flavour similar to aniseed. Use it raw in salads, tossed in lemon juice to prevent the cut slices browning, or steam, poach or boil and serve with cheese sauce.

French bean

At its best, this should be bright to darkish green in colour and the skin should have a slight bloom. Boil or steam whole, or broken into even lengths, until just tender. Serve with fish, poultry or meat, or in salads.

Kohlrabi

When fresh and firm, this root vegetable has a crisp, delicate, turnip-like flavour. Choose small ones and do not peel but scrape away any blemishes and drop into acidulated water. Steam or boil whole for just about 15–20 minutes, or slice and stir-fry very small ones, or serve raw in salads.

Leek

Avoid older leeks with woody stems. Use the white part, reserving the green tops for soups. Leeks are best kept loosely wrapped in the bottom of the refrigerator. Lightly cook by boiling or steaming and serve with a sauce, or slice finely and stir-fry.

Lettuce
Varieties divide into three groups: round, like Iceberg; long, like Little Gem or Cos; loose-leaved, like Oak Leaf or Lollo. Wash and dry in a salad spinner or on a clean tea towel. Use in salads, make into soups, or braise.

Mushroom
Button and flat mushrooms are widely available and other varieties appear on a seasonal basis. Simply wipe the stalk and cap with kitchen paper. Use raw in salads, cook in melted butter or add to casseroles, soups and stews. Best eaten on day of purchase.

Marrow
This is best eaten when about 30 cm/ 12 inches in length, when it can be cooked quickly in a microwave oven, or sliced and cooked in butter or olive oil, steamed, boiled or stir-fried. When dealing with a bigger one, peel and halve it, remove the central pithy flesh and seeds, then stuff and bake.

Okra (ladies' fingers)
The five-sided pods of the okra give a silky finish to curries, soups or stews and can be sautéed in butter. To prepare for cooking, wash and dry, being careful not to break the seed pod.

Onion
A wide choice ranges from small pickling onions through to the large bulbous Spanish onion, with red and spring onions in between, both essential in salads, and of course the pungent garlic-flavoured shallot. Use in casseroles, soups, sauces, stews and savoury tarts.

Pea

Pea pods should be round and full but not hard. When young, peas may be eaten raw in salads, but as they mature they should be steamed or boiled in lightly salted water. Older peas (the pods will no longer be bright green) can be made into soups or puréed.

Pepper (capsicum)

A brightly coloured vegetable (red, green, black, white or yellow) which can be used raw in salads, or stuffed and baked, stewed or stir-fried. To prepare, remove the core and seeds. Peppers keep well in the refrigerator.

Potato

This is one of the most versatile of all vegetables and when plain boiled, steamed or baked is low in calories. Peel potatoes for chipping, for other methods cook in their skins. There are many potato varieties that are well worth trying.

Pumpkin

This winter squash is a good source of vitamin A, it has dark yellow fibrous flesh and a sweet flavour. To prepare, remove the seeds and central pithy part, cut off and discard the skin and cube the flesh. Steam or boil until soft (allow about 20 minutes), drain and purée. Use for savoury and sweet dishes.

Radish

The small, round, red and white variety is the most common. Others may be elongated or have white, black or violet skins, but all are eaten raw in salads. Choose those that are firm and glossy. Large ones have no flavour.

Sorrel

This mid-summer vegetable has small, fleshy, light green rounded leaves. It looks like spinach and is prepared in the same way. Serve raw in salads, steam or cook in the water remaining on the leaves after washing.

Sweetcorn (corn on the cob)

This should be creamy yellow and firm. Remove leaves and silk and boil in unsalted water for about 5 minutes until the kernels are soft. Drain and serve hot with melted butter or use in salads, casseroles and soups. Baby sweetcorn can be stir-fried or lightly steamed for salads.

Spinach

Wash the dark green leaves very carefully in several changes of water to get rid of any grit or soil. Young spinach can be used raw in salads. For cooking, allow 250–300 g/8–10 oz per person and steam or cook in the water remaining on the leaves after washing, drain and press out excess liquid.

Turnip

Small young turnips can be eaten raw in salads, or finely sliced and cooked in butter. Older ones should be peeled before they are added to soups and stews.

Tomato

Varieties range from the tasty sweet cherry to the large beef tomato, which can lack flavour. In summer, the rather more expensive marmande from France, and plum tomatoes are both a delight.

Fruit

Always refreshingly appetizing, fruit plays an essential part in a healthy balanced diet, providing energy in the form of sugar (fructose), dietary fibre, minerals and vitamins. The wonderful colours of fruit add brightness to savoury dishes and fruit salads, and it is a perfect palate cleanser between courses.

Apple
A very good source of vitamin C and water-soluble dietary fibre, apples are available in a wide variety. Always take the opportunity to savour home-grown varieties of dessert apples when they are in season. Popular dessert apples are Braeburn, Discovery, Cox's Orange Pippin and Red Delicious. The best varieties for cooking include Granny Smith, Cox's Orange Pippin, Sturmer Pippin; for purées and sauces, use Bramley's Seedlings.

Banana
Use unripe fruit with a pale skin for baking or frying. For eating, choose bananas with a rich yellow skin mottled with brown. Do not refrigerate, as the skins will blacken and the fruit will become squashy.

Apricot
Eat these raw, poach for pies, crumbles, fools and jams, or add to meat dishes. Use the stone's kernel to add an almond flavour to the cooked fruit. Under-ripe apricots will be pale, or tinged with green. At their best the skin will have a warm golden colour. Eat quickly after purchase.

Berries
Eat or cook on the day of purchase. Cultivated blackberries can be eaten raw, the wild fruit gathered from hedgerows is best cooked. Raspberries are best served fresh with cream or in a fruit salad, flan, ice cream or in sauces. The elongated deep red loganberry is very juicy and has a tart flavour. Eat it fresh with sugar and cream, puréed, cooked in sorbets, ice creams, mousses, fools, pies and preserves.

Cherry
weet dessert cherries are delicious eaten raw. The sour cherries, like morello, are best cooked and served with poultry and game. Cooked sweet cherries can be used for flans, pies, ice cream, preserves or made into purées

Buying

● Fruit that is firm, plump and unwrinkled will be fresh and its juice content will be good.

● The fruit skins should not be split, broken or bruised in any way.

● There should be no insect damage.

● Fragrance is a good way of selecting fruit at its very best.

● Berries should look dry and full with no signs of mould or wetness. Always check the base of wrapped berried fruit, there should be no sign of juice leakage.

● Buy soft berried fruit for immediate consumption.

● Store fruit in a cool place – at room temperature it will quickly deteriorate.

Coconut
Puncture 3 indentations at the top of the nut to pour out the colourless juice. Crack open the nut by hitting it with a hammer one-third of the way from the top. Use the flesh raw, or dried and shredded.

Currants – black, white, red
To strip the picked fruit off the stems, hold over a bowl and slide a fork down the length of the stem. Poach lightly in syrup and serve with ice cream, or use to make pies, flans, tarts, ice cream, sorbets, preserves and jellies.

Fig
Sold either fresh or dried. Figs range in colour from pale green to deep purple. The skin is edible. Eat raw with cheese, ham or in fruit salads, or poach lightly in syrup.

Gooseberry
The dessert variety has a red skin with sweet juicy flesh. The cooking types, which are green and hairy, are used for pies, flans, fools, mousses, ice creams and preserves. Gooseberry sauce is often served with grilled mackerel or roast pork.

Date
Fresh dates, available in winter, should have a shiny brown skin and soft, sweet flesh. Use with other fruit in tarts, eat with cheese at the end of a meal, or stone and stuff with nuts, either chopped or whole.

Grape
Grapes are usually eaten raw. If they are used to make open tarts, they should be peeled and any pips removed. Small seedless grapes are sometimes cooked with meat. The best flavour of all is that of the Muscat grape.

Grapefruit
Use either white- or pink-fleshed grapefruit for first course salads with fish and shellfish, squeeze for refreshing juices or make into marmalade. Choose heavy fruit with plump skin and a sharp perfume.

Kiwifruit
Best eaten raw – either remove the peel and slice, or cut off the top and scoop out the flesh and seeds with a small spoon. The kiwifruit has a very high vitamin C content and its high level of acidity will dissolve aspic and gelatine.

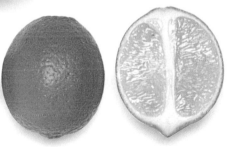

Lemon and lime
Use a few drops of lemon juice to enhance the flavour of smoked salmon and fish dishes, cooked green vegetables, mayonnaise and salad dressings, and fruit salads. To prevent discoloration, apply it to the cut surface of an avocado or banana or to a bowl of water for apple slices. For lots of juice, choose thin-skinned lemons, for peel and pith pick the knobbly ones. Add the grated zest to crumbles, soufflés, sponges and tarts. Use limes as a substitute for lemons. You can use less lime juice because their flavour is stronger.

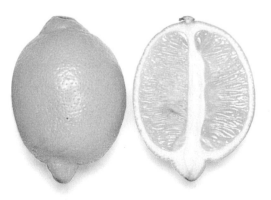

Mango

The inedible skin, which can be dark green, yellow, orange or red, should be shiny and the mango will yield slightly when held. The fruit should be pale orange, juicy and full of flavour. To stone, cut a thick slice lengthways down each side and scoop out the flesh with a spoon. Cut the flesh off the stone section. Slice and serve with ham, or add to fruit salads, purée for ice creams and mousses, cook in vegetable curry, tarts and pies. Use ripe or unripe for chutney.

Orange and tangerine

Dessert oranges can be sliced and added to savoury and fruit salads, the juice used for jellies, sorbets and ice creams, and the zest used to flavour cakes. The bitter Seville oranges are used to make

marmalade. Small 'easy-peelers' include tangerines, clementines, satsumas and mandarin oranges. Sweet and juicy, they are best eaten raw. They can also be used in fruit salads and to make jams and preserves.

Melon

There are many varieties but good ones for eating will feel dense and heavy for their size. The melony perfume should be detectable from the top end, and in some varieties the top end will yield when pressed. The water melon is the largest member of the family. Cover cut fruit in the refrigerator to contain its fragrance. Serve melon, chilled to intensify its flavour, for breakfast or at the end of a meal, and add to fruit or savoury salads.

Pear

There is a wonderful range of pears, and they are best eaten for dessert with cheeses such as Parmesan, Lancashire or Gorgonzola. Use cooked in tarts and puddings, and with game recipes.

Peach

The furry peach skin conceals flesh that can be white, yellow or pink, depending on the variety. Peel the skin with a sharp knife for eating raw, or immerse in boiling water for 30 seconds. The smooth-skinned nectarine is very juicy and has fragrant yellow or white flesh. To stone, slice around the groove and twist the two halves against each other. Use cooked in pies, tarts and preserves.

Pineapple

When it is ripe, a leaf can easily be pulled from the centre and the flesh will have the distinctive pineapple fragrance. It contains an enzyme that breaks down protein, so is good to serve at the end of a meal. Avoid using with gelatine because it will not set.

Pomegranate

The size of an apple, with a tough, brown, leathery skin. The flesh is bright reddish-pink, packed with seeds and very juicy. Slice in half and spoon out the flesh. Use as a dessert or add to sauce. Extract the juice with a lemon squeezer and use for water ice or jelly.

Rhubarb

This is really a vegetable, and only the stems are used. There are two types, the forced or early with pink thin stalks and yellow leaves, and maincrop with thick reddish green stems and dark green leaves. Steam, poach or stew with sugar and use for pies, tarts, crumbles, fools and preserves.

Strawberry

There are many different varieties, but for eating they should all be bright red and firm, with a bright green calyx. Are usually cultivated but can also be wild. Eat strawberries on the day of purchase. Wash gently before removing the calyx. Usually served simply with cream or yogurt, but also used to make flans, pies, tarts, ice cream and preserves.

Pulses

The edible seeds of peas, beans and lentils are known as pulses. Highly nutritious, they can be used in soups, stews, curries, or as an accompanying vegetable. Their only drawback – long soaking and cooking times – is avoided by using canned beans.

Adzuki beans
Also known as aduki beans, these small red, shiny beans are popular in China and Japan. They have a sweetish flavour and are often made into 'red bean paste' as a filling for pancakes and dumplings. The dried beans can be ground to a flour to make cakes and bread. Use in soups, salads, or with other vegetables, or grow as bean sprouts.

Black-eyed beans
Also known as black-eyed peas or cowpeas, these cream-coloured beans with a black spot are similar in shape to kidney beans, but smaller. Widely used in spicy African, Caribbean and Indian cooking.

Borlotti beans
Kidney shaped, speckled and ranging in colour from creamy pink to deep brownish pink, these are the beans traditionally used in Italian cooking. Use in rustic salads, soups and pasta dishes, or substitute them in recipes using kidney beans. Pinto beans look rather like borlotti beans, and are a typical Mexican ingredient.

Butter beans
Large, flattish, creamy white beans with a mild flavour and floury texture, which tend to turn mushy if overcooked. They are good added to mixed beans salads or used in rich stews, where they absorb other flavours.

Chickpeas
Also known as garbanzo beans, these look rather like small hazelnuts, and have a nutty flavour. They are popular in the Mediterranean region, the Middle East, India and many other countries. They are added whole to salads, chunky soups, curries and stews, puréed in dips, toasted with spices as an appetizer, or ground and made into flour (sometimes called besan flour). Chickpeas need a long soaking and cooking time.

Flageolet beans
Pale green or white, very tender young haricot beans with a delicate flavour. Add them to other beans for a salad, or serve in a creamy, garlicky sauce as an accompaniment to roast lamb.

Haricot beans
Creamy white and oval shaped, the familiar 'baked beans' are ideal for dishes which need long slow cooking – with sausages, meat, tomatoes or herbs – such as the cassoulet of France, because they readily absorb other flavours. They can be used in salads, soups or as purées. Cannellini, Soissons and navy beans are all types of haricot.

Preparing and cooking

Store dried pulses in an airtight container in a cool, dark place. Do not keep them for too long, as they dry out during storage. After cooking they can be frozen or kept in a covered container in the refrigerator for 2–3 days.

All dried pulses, except lentils and split peas, need to be soaked before cooking. First, rinse them well to remove dust and grit. There are three soaking methods:

- Cover the beans with 2–3 times their volume of cold water and leave in a cool place for about 10 hours or overnight.
- Cover with plenty of boiling water and leave for 2–3 hours.
- Bring a pan of beans in water slowly to the boil, boil fast for 2 minutes, remove from the heat and leave for 1–2 hours.

After soaking, drain the pulses and rinse well in fresh water. Put them into a large saucepan and cover generously with stock or water. Bring to the boil, then reduce the heat and simmer until the beans are tender, allowing 20 minutes–1 hour for lentils and split peas; 1–4 hours for chickpeas and other beans, depending on their size and age. Top up the pan with boiling water if necessary. When the beans are tender to the bite, drain and use. Some recipes call for pulses to be cooked for a shorter time, and then added to the dish while it cooks, so they take on the flavour of herbs and other ingredients. A pressure cooker will cook soaked pulses in a third of the time taken by conventional methods. To prevent froth clogging the pressure valve add 2 tablespoons of oil to the cooking water.

Bean sprouts

Most bean sprouts are from the small green mung bean, but other beans and lentils can also be sprouted to use in salads and stir-fries. You can buy a special sprouter, with two or more layers, but a large jam jar will do. Rinse the beans and place in the jar or sprouter, cover and keep in a light place (not direct sunlight) at a constant temperature of 13–21°C (50–70°F). Rinse the beans twice a day with fresh water; tip off excess water. After 3–6 days, pale green shoots will appear, which are best when about 2.5–5 cm/1–2 inches long.

Lentils

Lentils need no soaking, just rinsing. Red and yellow lentils, often sold split, cook quickly to a purée. They are used in Indian cooking for soups, rissoles, and to thicken curries. Brown and green lentils keep their disc shape when cooked and have a distinctive earthy flavour, which goes well with sausages, ham and bacon, and makes a delicious winter vegetable.

Peas

Available as yellow or green split or whole peas, these need only 1–2 hours soaking, and cook in less than 1 hour. Split peas become a purée as they cook, and do not need to be mashed or blended. The large whole green marrowfat peas are used to make the traditional English dish, mushy peas.

Red kidney beans

The 'meaty' flavour and texture of these beans makes them a popular choice for salads, soups, casseroles and hot, spicy dishes such as chilli con carne. They hold their shape well and should always be boiled fast for at least 15 minutes at the beginning of their cooking time. Black kidney beans are traditional in many South American soups and stews. They can be substituted for red kidney beans in most recipes – or use half and half for a stunning colour contrast.

Soya beans

Small, round and yellowish-brown, these have the highest protein content of all pulses and are used to make tofu (bean curd), soya milk, soy sauce and miso – a fermented bean paste used in Japanese cooking. Soya beans are also ground to make flour and play an important part in TVP (textured vegetable protein) foods. They are bland in flavour, so always use them in combination with strongly flavoured herbs and spices. They need long soaking and cooking.

Warnings

After soaking, kidney beans (black and red), adzuki and black-eyed beans must be put in a saucepan with plenty of cold water, brought to the boil and then boiled fast for 15–20 minutes to destroy the toxins on the outer skin. Soya beans should be treated in the same way, but boiled fast for 1 hour to destroy a substance that prevents the body absorbing protein.

Salt will toughen the outer skin of pulses, so add it only about 10 minutes before the end of cooking. Bicarbonate of soda destroys some of the vitamin content if added to pulses during cooking.

Herbs

The colours and flavours of herbs will transform your cooking. Many are easy to grow in a garden or windowbox, but they are widely available from greengrocers and supermarkets, either in packets, growing in pots or freeze-dried in jars. Herbs are best when freshly picked, but will keep for a few days in a jug of water, or in the salad drawer of the refrigerator.

Basil
Its warm, spicy flavour goes well with tomatoes and pasta and it is the main ingredient of Italian pesto sauce. Shred – rather than chop – the leaves to retain maximum flavour and add towards the end of cooking time.

Bay
Bay has a strong flavour, but usually needs long cooking to bring out its qualities. It is included in all kinds of savoury dishes – casseroles, pâtés and stocks – and adds fragrance to white sauces.

Chervil
The mild flavour is similar to parsley, with a hint of aniseed, and it combines well with egg and fish dishes and delicate sauces. The lacy leaves are often used as garnishes, but they wilt soon after picking.

Chives
The mildest member of the onion family and best added to dishes just before serving. Snip chives to give colour to potato salad, vichyssoise soup, scrambled eggs or sprinkle on salads. The purple flower-heads can also be added to salads.

Coriander
An essential ingredient of curries and other spicy dishes, coriander looks rather like flat leaf parsley and is very aromatic. It goes well with meat, fish and vegetable dishes and is added towards the end of cooking. Also good in salads.

Dill
The feathery leaves are most often used with fish, such as the Scandinavian marinated salmon dish gravad lax, but dill also goes well with cream or mustard sauces, chicken and vegetable soups. Use it also to garnish cucumber salads.

Fennel
It is easy to confuse this herb with dill, because both plants look similar, with fine feathery leaves, and both of them also have an aniseed flavour. The flavour is stronger in fennel. Chop the leaves and add to sauces and fish dishes. The stalks are often laid over barbecues to flavour fish while it cooks.

Garlic
Essential in Mediterranean dishes, cloves of garlic are used to season sauces, soups, casseroles and salads. The flavour becomes milder as it cooks, and if you fry it, do not allow it to brown as this tends to make it bitter. In order to remove the outer skin, squash a clove under a flat knife and then chop the flesh very finely. Garlic can be white, pink or purple. The purple variety keeps for longer than the other two.

Horseradish
The root of this plant goes down deep into the soil, so it is not much liked by gardeners. The grated root is traditionally used with roast beef.

Majoram and oregano

The traditional flavouring for pizza tomato sauces and Greek salads, marjoram also goes well with fish and lamb dishes, omelettes and vegetables. Oregano is wild marjoram and has a more powerful flavour. The leaves retain their flavour during cooking.

Mint

Spearmint is the common variety, but mints such as apple, ginger, pineapple, Bowles and lemon are all worth trying. Use mint to flavour ice cream, fruit salads, summer drinks, salads, new potatoes and peas. Fresh mint is wonderful used with bulgar wheat in tabbouleh.

Parsley

There are two varieties of parsley, both of which are commonly available – curled and flat leaf, which is becoming more popular. Use in salads, stocks and sauces, with vegetables and in fish dishes. It forms an effective part of a bouquet garni.

Rosemary

This bushy shrub has ever-green needles and a robust overpowering flavour. Chop and use sparingly in stuffings for meat dishes, or add sprigs to flavour lamb, pork or game. Remove the sprigs after use.

Sage

The leaves of this plant retain their powerful flavour even during long, slow cooking. Use sparingly with pork and game birds, or in a tomato sauce.

Tarragon

Another herb used in bouquet garni and fines herbes mixtures. French tarragon is preferred to the coarser-flavoured Russian. Chop the leaves and add to salads, or use in sauces, with chicken, fish and vegetables, or infuse in vinegar. Best used fresh.

Rocket

This is traditionally used in salads and in pasta dishes. It is now widely available in the salad section of supermarkets and is increasing in popularity.

Thyme

This is used in bouquet garni, and to flavour meat casseroles. The lemon thyme combines particularly well with fish and chicken dishes.

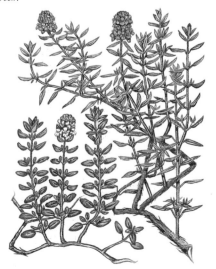

Bouquet garni and fines herbes

The classic bouquet garni is made up of a bay leaf, a sprig of thyme and then 2–3 sprigs of parsley, which can either be bound together with string or tied into a small muslin bag. It is used to flavour almost any savoury dish that needs long cooking, and is removed before the dish is served. Celery, or other herbs such as fennel or dill, can be included.

The mixture known in French cooking as fines herbes – used in omelettes and chilled butter to top fish and meat – is traditionally made from chopped fresh chervil, chives, parsley and tarragon.

Spices

Spices come to us from the aromatic parts of plants, generally the seeds, pods, berries and bark. Their warm fragrant scents add a special aroma and flavour to all forms of cooking. For the best flavour, buy them whole, store them in tinted glass jars away from sunlight, and grind them with a pestle and mortar just before you use them.

Allspice
The berries are similar to large peppercorns. It has the flavour of cloves, cinnamon and nutmeg. Grind it for cakes and pies, use whole in marinades or add to casseroles. It is good ground with peppercorns.

Caraway
The seeds are small, oval, and ribbed and are strongly aromatic. Their warming peppery undertone is used in German and Austrian cooking to flavour breads such as pumpernickel, and in goulashes and sauerkraut.

Cayenne and chilli
Cayenne has an affinity with fish and seafood and goes well with cheese and egg dishes. It comes from the hot chilli pepper and appears in Indian, North African and Latin American food. It should be used sparingly. Chilli can be mild or very hot, so use it in small amounts to begin with. It is ground from different kinds of chilli pepper and is sometimes mixed with other herbs and spices. You can use it as a flavouring for many meat, egg, poultry and fish dishes.

Cloves
These can be used in savoury or sweet dishes, but with restraint because their aroma can swamp other tastes. Push cloves into an onion to flavour sauces and meat stews, stud a ham with them, and add to apple dishes or mulled wine.

Cinnamon
Use the stick form of cinnamon for meat and vegetable casseroles, for curries and rice dishes, and in syrup for poaching fruit, but buy it ready ground for cakes, pies and puddings.

Cardamom
An essential ingredient in Indian cooking, but also used in cakes and pastries in northern Europe, the pods come in green, white and black. The first two have a finer flavour than the black which has an earthy flavour best suited to long cooking. Use the small black seeds in the pods to flavour vegetable dishes, curries such as biryanis, pilaus and dhal, and as a flavouring for ice cream. It is delicious in spiced tea and black coffee.

Ginger
Familiar to us in Chinese and Indian dishes, fresh root ginger is very easy to use. Peel off the outer skin, and grate or finely slice. Add it to cakes, poultry and shellfish dishes, vegetables and fruit crumbles.

Coriander
The small seeds have a mild, slightly savoury flavour and can be used whole or ground in quite large quantities. It is used extensively in chutneys and pickles, curries, meat and vegetable stews and goes well with fish.

Cumin
The mildly aromatic cumin seeds are small, ridged and greenish brown in colour. They have a pleasantly sweet, warm flavour. Use them ground in vegetable stews, in shellfish dishes, and in mildly spiced curries.

Dill
Use these with fish, potatoes and in pickles, vinegars, marinades and salad dressings, especially in the winter months when the fresh herb is not available. The flavour is similar to that of caraway seeds.

Fennel
Fennel is best known as a herb, salad ingredient and vegetable, but its seeds are also valuable in cooking. The seeds are sweet and can be used instead of aniseed in fish soups and stews, with grilled sardines or pork.

Other spices

There are several more exotic herbs which are perhaps less commonly used but nevertheless deserve a place in the kitchen, particularly if you do a lot of Indian or Middle Eastern cooking.

Asafoetida, for example, has a very curious smell, but it is an essential ingredient of Indian and Middle Eastern cooking. Used in minute quantities, it has a remarkable ability to enhance the flavour of other foods, and goes well in vegetable, meat and fish stews. It is not easy to find, and is best bought in powder form.

Fenugreek is another spice that is used in Indian dishes, pickles and chutneys. Roast the seeds lightly to bring out their flavour, then grind to a powder.

Mustard seed comes as black, or yellow seeds. They have a strong flavour, and are used in Indian recipes where they are often added to hot oil at which point they pop, adding their taste to the oil. They are also used to prepare mustards and are included in pickles. Dry-fried, they lose their heat and have a warm nutty flavour.

Nigella seeds are important in Indian and Middle Eastern cookery. Ask for them in Indian food stores by their Indian name, kalonfi. They have an earthy, peppery flavour, and also give texture to bread doughs, cakes and pastries.

Juniper
The small purple-black berries, with their spicy pine aroma, are generally used in marinades, casseroles and stuffings, or in robust meat dishes. Crush the berries before using.

Mace
This is the lacy cage that covers the nutmeg seed. The flavour is rather more delicate than that of nutmeg, and it is infused in milk and used to make white sauces and milk puddings.

Nutmeg
The warm sweet flavour of nutmeg is quickly lost, so grate it just before you need it. Use it to flavour sauces, cakes, pies and puddings, cheese dishes, meat, poultry and vegetables.

Paprika
This is milder than cayenne and chilli and is used with meat, fish, and as a garnish. It is widely used in Hungary and is traditional in many Spanish seafood stews. It is affected by light, so buy small amounts and store in airtight containers away from light.

Pepper
Black peppercorns are stronger than white, red have a nutty flavour, and green have a mild, fresh taste. Use them whole in marinades and stock, and grind as needed. An unusual use for black peppercorns is freshly ground over sliced strawberries.

Poppy seeds
The pretty opium poppy is not only the source of the highly narcotic drug, opium, but also of the delicious poppy seeds used in cooking. It is popular in Jewish baking, decorating many types of bread and rolls, including bagels and platzels.

Vanilla
Use two pods to flavour a jar of sugar. For milk puddings, infuse the pod in scalded milk. Wash, dry and re-use for sugar.

Saffron
This comes from the crocus and the filaments are generally infused in boiling water to extract the colour. Use it in rice dishes, or with seafood stews.

Turmeric
The light, warm spicy taste and pungent aroma are best appreciated apart from ready-prepared curry powders. Learn to use its fragrance in Indian recipes such as pilau. It gives a golden glow to pickles.

Sesame seeds
The seeds have a strong nutty flavour and are best dry roasted until golden or fried in a little oil before use. In their ground form they are made into tahini paste. Sesame seeds are popular in Chinese, Japanese and Indian cookery.

Star anise
This has a spicy aniseed flavour, and is widely used in Chinese dishes. It is used in the Chinese five-spice powder and is often used to decorate finished dishes. The small grey-green ribbed seeds of aniseed have a spicy/sweet flavour and are used in sweet and savoury dishes, with fish and meat and in pastry and bread. In India it is used to freshen the palate at the end of a meal. It is also used in the drinks pastis, ouzo and anisette.

Pasta

Infinitely variable, quick and easy to cook, economical, satisfying, a storecupboard standby, pasta is all these things and more. You can dress it up in an extravagant sauce or toss it in a simple rustic sauce and make a meal in moments. Pasta is not a fattening food, although the sauces that go with it might be. In its home country of Italy, it is served as a first course but elsewhere it is frequently the main part of the meal, followed by salad, fruit or cheese.

Cooking methods

If you love pasta, it is worth investing in a big pan which will easily take at least 4 litres/7 pints of rapidly boiling salted water. This is the amount you need to cook 500 g/1 lb pasta – it allows the pasta to cook evenly and to move about in the boiling water without sticking. Add the pasta to the boiling water, bring it up to a rolling boil and occasionally stir the submerged pasta with a wooden fork. When adding long pasta, coil the strands around the sides of the saucepan as they soften until all the pasta is in the pan, do not break it. Do not cover the pan because the water may boil over. Test the pasta by nibbling a small piece from time to time and when it is elastic and firm, but not hard, turn off the heat and quickly drain it through a colander and turn into a warmed serving bowl.

Cooking fresh pasta

This takes far less time, needing only 5 minutes, or just seconds in the microwave. A drawback of fresh pasta is that it can't be stored like dried pasta. Always buy good-quality fresh pasta: just because it is fresh, it does not always follow that it is good.

Homemade pasta dough

Few people make their own pasta dough, but it's essential for homemade ravioli.
Preparation: 1 hour

What you need:

- 300 g/10 oz strong plain bread flour, sifted
- pinch of salt
- 3 eggs
- 1 tablespoon olive oil
- flour for dusting

1 Put the flour and salt on a work surface. Make a well in the centre and add the eggs. Using your fingertips, gradually draw the flour in from the sides and mix well. Then add the olive oil and continue mixing until you have a soft dough. Alternatively, you can make the dough in a food processor.

2 Turn the pasta dough out on to a lightly floured surface and knead well until it is really smooth and silky. Roll out the dough, giving it an occasional turn and stretching it out, until it resembles a thin sheet of cloth and is almost transparent.

3 Now you have to dry your pasta. Hang it over the back of a chair or a broom handle and leave for 10 minutes to dry. Alternatively, lay it out on a table with one-third overhanging the edge and keep turning it until it dries out completely.

Types of pasta

Bought pasta is factory-produced dried pasta. Made from durum (hard wheat) flour it is the familiar pale straw colour, but it is brown if made from buckwheat or wholewheat flour. Colouring is added by spinach (green), tomato purée (red), beetroot juice (red or pink), saffron or turmeric (yellow), and squid or octopus ink (black).

Durum wheat can be difficult to work with and, to make it easier, it is sometimes mixed with soft wheat flour which reduces the protein content and makes the product more starchy. Look for pasta that is made from 100% durum wheat.

Egg pasta (*pasta all'uovo*) is the pasta of flour and eggs which originated from the Emilia-Romagna region of Italy and is available fresh or dried. This is often used for stuffed pasta.

Storage

- Freshly made pasta should be eaten preferably on the day it is made or purchased, but it can be refrigerated for up to 24 hours.
- Homemade pasta dough can be frozen for up to 3 months.
- Dried pasta is best stored in its original package, or in a dry, airtight container.
- Dried pasta will keep for up to 9 months.

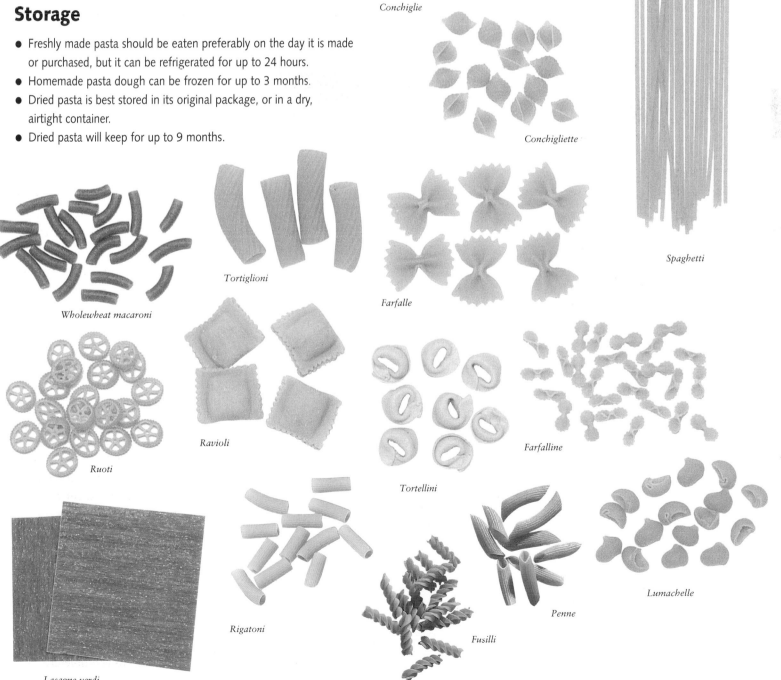

Cannelloni

Conchiglie

Conchigliette

Spaghetti

Wholewheat macaroni

Tortiglioni

Farfalle

Ruoti

Ravioli

Tortellini

Farfalline

Lumachelle

Lasagne verdi

Rigatoni

Fusilli

Penne

Rice

Along with pasta, rice is one of the most useful ingredients in the kitchen. It needs little advance preparation, cooks quickly, is adaptable, goes well with a variety of dishes and is very nourishing. Rice is easy to cook, but there are different kinds of rice and ways of cooking it, so to achieve success every time, be sure that you match the method to the purpose.

Above right: *Fried rice with pork*
Far right: *A Mexican dish known as Green rice, in which rice is mixed with stir-fried green peppers and pimiento-stuffed olives*

Cooking methods
Absorption
For each cup of rice use 2 cups of water or stock, plus ½ teaspoon salt. Wash the rice under cold running water and stir well to separate the grains. Bring the measured water to the boil in a large saucepan, add the salt and rice, return to the boil, reduce the heat and cover with a tight-fitting lid. Cook for 15 minutes (30 for brown), when the rice should be tender and fluffy and the liquid completely absorbed.

Boiling
For 50 g/2 oz rice, use 600 ml/ 1 pint water and ½ teaspoon salt. Bring the water to the boil, add salt, sprinkle in the rice, return to the boil and then simmer for 12–13 minutes (30–40 minutes for brown). A tablespoon of oil will help prevent it boiling over and the grains from sticking together. Rice is cooked when a grain squeezed between the fingers is soft on the outside but still retains its shape and some firmness in the centre. Drain and then serve.

Oven
To cook rice in the oven, preheat the oven to 180°C (350°F), Gas Mark 4. Using 1 cup of washed rice to 2 cups water, put the washed rice in an ovenproof dish with a tight-fitting lid. Then cover with the measured boiling water or stock and ½ teaspoon salt. Stir, cover with foil and a lid. Cook for 30 minutes (1 hour for brown) until the liquid is absorbed and the rice is tender.

Steaming
This Chinese method allows the grains to stay separate. Soak the rice in cold water for at least 1 hour, then drain. Add water to the bottom half of a steamer or large pan. Line the steamer, or a Chinese steamer basket, with muslin. Spoon in rice and cover with the muslin ends. Put on the lid and steam for 25–30 minutes.

Fried rice

Preparation: 20 minutes

What you need:

- 2 tablespoons oil
- 1 garlic clove, chopped
- 2.5 cm/1 inch fresh root ginger, chopped
- 5 spring onions, finely sliced
- 175 g/6 oz prawns
- 1 tablespoon soy sauce
- 175 g/6 oz frozen vegetables
- 2 beaten eggs
- 300 g/10 oz cooked rice
- salt and pepper

1 Heat the oil in a pan. Add garlic and ginger, fry for 30 seconds.
2 Add the spring onions, toss for 30 seconds. Add the prawns, stir for 1 minute. Add the soy sauce and vegetables, stir for 2 minutes.
3 Add the eggs, stir, allow to set, then mix into the prawns and vegetables. Add the rice, toss with the other ingredients until hot and season to taste.

Techniques for success

● When cooking rice by the absorption method, do not increase the amount of water or stock that you cook it in, or the rice will be soggy.

● Avoid removing the saucepan lid and allowing steam to escape when using the absorption method, as this would interfere with the process of absorption.

● Never stir the rice while it is cooking, as this tends to break the grains of rice.

● Rice is cooked when a grain squeezed between the fingers is soft on the outside but still retains its shape and some firmness in the centre.

● Serve freshly cooked rice within 10 minutes of cooking to prevent it from sticking.

● If the rice is to be served cold, put it into a sieve, run warm water through it to separate the grains, and then leave it to drain and cool.

● Dress rice for salads while it is still warm so that the flavours are absorbed.

Preparation

● Long-grain rice absorbs twice its volume in water.

● Brown rice absorbs twice its volume in water.

● 25 g/1 oz short-grain (pudding) rice will absorb 600 ml/1 pint full fat milk.

● Soak Basmati rice in cold water for about 15 minutes and drain well before cooking.

● To prevent grains sticking together wash white rice before cooking to remove the powdery loose starch.

● Allow 50 g (2 oz) of rice per person.

The right rice for the job

● Curries: Basmati, Patna, American long-grain
● Puddings: American long-grain, Java, flaked rice, glutinous rice, pudding rice
● Stuffings: American long-grain
● Rice salads: Basmati, Patna, American long-grain
● Risottos: Arborio rice

Types of rice

Brown rice

Short-grain rice

Wild rice

American long-grain
It used to be called Carolina rice and was grown only there. It is now grown all over the world. The grains, which are hulled and polished, remain firm, fluffy and separate when cooked. Patna is also a long-grain rice.

Brown
The whole grain with only the outer husk removed, leaving the layers of bran. It is available in long-, medium- and short-grain and it needs longer cooking, but it is far more nutritional and has both a nutty flavour and a much chewier texture.

Basmati
Grown in the foothills of the Himalayas, this narrow long-grained rice has a distinctive flavour when it is cooked, especially evident when the absorption method is used.

Glutinous or sticky rice
This is actually a gluten-free rice, despite its name. It is a short- to medium-grain rice and when cooked the grains stick together slightly so that it becomes easy to eat with chopsticks. It is most easily obtained from stores selling ethnic products.

Ground rice or rice flour
This gluten-free flour is used as a thickening agent, sometimes mixed with other flours, to make cakes, puddings and biscuits. In Chinese cookery, it is also sometimes used to make certain types of noodles.

Medium and short-grain
These tend to be stickier kinds of rice and are generally used for savoury dishes where the rice needs to cling or to be moulded or bound together, such as risottos and stuffings. Short-grain pudding rice is used for sweet dishes.

Pre-cooked rice
This only needs soaking in boiling water for 5 minutes following the manufacturer's instructions. It is useful for quick snacks and salads.

Par-boiled or converted rice
Unlike other kinds of white rice, most of the nutrients and vitamins are left in the grains due to the steaming process that takes place before milling. It retains the nutritional value of brown rice without its chewy texture and longer cooking time. It produces plump, fluffy and separate grains.

Pudding
This short-grain polished rice absorbs a great deal of liquid during cooking and becomes soft and mushy. It is used only for puddings and to make rice desserts.

Rice flakes
These are produced by steaming and rolling and can be made from whole or white rice. They are used for puddings, baking, muesli and cereals.

Risotto
This method of cooking is best achieved by using the Italian Arborio rice, which has a roundish grain. When it is cooked, it becomes creamy, while still retaining a slight bite. Costing more than other kinds of rice, it is worth the expense.

Wild rice
This is not actually a rice at all, but is in fact the seeds of a grass that is grown in the United States of America and the Far East. It is a highly nutritious, gluten-free grain, which absorbs about four times its volume of liquid. It has an interesting, slightly nutty flavour. It is often served, mixed with white rice, to accompany various game and poultry dishes and can be combined with other ingredients to make stuffings. Cook it in the same way as you would ordinary rice, allowing at least 35–45 minutes. Soaking it overnight beforehand will slightly reduce the cooking time needed.

Fish

The nutritional qualities, short cooking times, tenderness and adaptability of fish and shellfish make them a popular choice with people who lead busy lives. There are many different varieties of fish, from both sea and river, and there are many ways of cooking them. Unless you can get it at the quayside, always buy fish from a reputable fishmonger to ensure it is perfectly fresh.

Buying and storing

Seafood perishes more quickly than meat and poultry, so take great care, when you come to buy it, that it is fresh. Look for all the following signs:

● Your supplier's shop should be clean, have plenty of ice and display the fish well.

● Freshness is easily seen in a whole fish. It should be stiff and firm, not limp.

● Eyes should be full, shiny and bright, and never sunken or opaque.

● The skin should be shiny, not dry and gritty.

● The gills should be rosy pink, not brownish or dry.

● Fillets should be translucent, not milky-white, firm and spring to the touch with no sign of discoloration. The flesh should be intact.

● Smoked fish should have a bright, glossy surface, a firm texture and a pleasant smoky smell.

● Commercially frozen fish which has been thawed out badly will be unpleasantly watery and woolly.

● Fish should be eaten as fresh as possible, at least within 24 hours of purchase. Otherwise it should be cleaned, gutted and frozen. Fish fillets and steaks can be prepared up to 12 hours in advance, loosely covered in foil and refrigerated.

● To keep fish overnight, wrap in several layers of newspaper and put in coldest part of the refrigerator.

● Fresh mackerel, herrings and sardines should be eaten on day of purchase or put in the freezer overnight.

Preparation

A good fishmonger will trim, scale, skin, gut and fillet for you in a matter of seconds. Flat fish are gutted at sea.

● To remove fish scales from round seafish and some freshwater fish, use the back of a heavy knife. Work on paper to collect the scales, scraping from tail to head. Rinse and pat dry.

● To skin, cut through just above the tail and tear the skin towards the head. Flat fish can be skinned after filleting.

Gutting

● Round fish: slit the belly open, working from the head towards the vent with a knife or scissors. Place the flat of the blade behind the entrails and slide them out, then wrap in paper and discard. Now scrape out the black blood channel down the backbone. Cut off the head and gills.

● Round fish, served whole: gut through the gills by grasping the fish in one hand and twisting its head to one side. Push a finger inside the gills and hook it under the entrails. Draw them out and snip off. Cut off the gills. Rinse and pat dry.

Filleting

You will need a very sharp, flexible knife. Use the discarded head, bones and trimmings to make stock. Remove any tiny bones with tweezers or pliers.

● Round fish: scale, cut off the head, tail and fins, and gut through the belly. Place opened fish flesh down on board and press firmly along the backbone with your thumbs to loosen it. Turn the fish over, release the bone with a knife, and lift out carefully so the rib bones are also removed. Cut along the centre to divide into 2 fillets.

● For small round fish: cut off the heads and gut through the belly. Hold the fish open under running water so that the force of the water separates the fish into 2 fillets and washes out backbone.

● Flat fish: cut off the head and trim away the fins with scissors. Cut through the fish along the backbone. Slip the knife blade under the flesh on one side of the backbone. Then using a sawing motion with the flat of the blade against the rib bones, work the fillet away from the bones and detach. Remove the second fillet in the same way. Turn the fish over and repeat on the other side to divide into 4 fillets.

Marinades

Fish responds well to being marinated before cooking. It should soak in the marinade for anything between a few hours and overnight. Try always to use glass, china, plastic or stainless steel bowls for storing food in marinades. Do not use aluminium foil as a covering, as the acidic marinade will 'burn' into it and taint the fish.

The marinade can also be rubbed into the slashed flesh of the fish just before cooking. This gives it additional flavour.

Soy sauce marinade

This marinade works especially well with any white fish.

What you need:

- 2 tablespoons oil
- 2 tablespoons light soy sauce
- 1 tablespoon lemon juice
- ½ teaspoon ground cumin
- 1 teaspoon chopped chives

Mix all the ingredients together. Allow the fish to marinate in this mixture for at least 30 minutes, or overnight.

Spicy marinade

This marinade works especially well with a strong-flavoured fish such as halibut or bream.

What you need:

- pinch of saffron
- 2 garlic cloves, crushed with salt
- pinch of ground coriander
- 1 tablespoon finely chopped parsley
- 150 ml/¼ pint wine vinegar
- 2 tablespoons tomato ketchup
- 1 tablespoon lemon juice
- salt and pepper to taste

Soak the saffron for 30 minutes in 1 tablespoon boiling water. Mix all the marinade ingredients together, including the saffron. Marinate the fish for several hours, then drain, dry and grill.

Herb marinade

This works particularly well with any fish that is going to be grilled or barbecued, such as tuna and mackerel.

What you need:

- 4 tablespoons olive oil
- 4 garlic cloves, crushed
- 125 ml/4 fl oz dry white wine
- 1 small onion, finely chopped
- 1 sprig each of fresh rosemary, thyme and parsley

Mix all the ingredients together and then marinate the fish for several hours or overnight, or for as long as 24 hours.

Court bouillon

This is the poaching liquid in which to cook large, whole fish, such as salmon and salmon trout.

What you need:

- 2–3 small onions, sliced
- 3 carrots, sliced
- 2 bay leaves
- small bunch of parsley
- 2–3 slices lemon
- 15 g/½ oz butter or 2 tablespoons olive oil
- 5–6 black peppercorns
- 2 litres/3½ pints water
- 300 ml/½ pint wine vinegar or 600 ml/1 pint white wine

Put all the ingredients in a large pan, bring to the boil, cover and simmer for 20 minutes. Allow to cool to blood temperature before you put in the fish.

Cook's Tip

When the fish is cooked, the cooking liquid can then be strained and used as a basis for a sauce. The liquid will lend extra flavour to them.

Flat fish

Dover sole
Blunt-nosed body is dark brown on the back with a white underside, flesh is firm, white and delicate. Can be used for most cooking methods, goes well with sauces. Best cooked on the bone and served with butter, parsley and lemon; serve poached fillets in sauce.

Turbot
Large, round flat fish with a small head. Sandy or dark brown with small hard nodules but not scales and a white belly. Flesh is firm and delicate in flavour. Sold whole, or in fillets and steaks. Suits any cooking method, but best poached or grilled and served with parsley or hollandaise sauce.

Plaice
Dark brown with russet spots on its back with white under-side. Best deep-fried in batter or egg and breadcrumbs, or poached and served with parsley or cheese sauce.

Halibut
The largest of all the flat fish. Grey to olive-green back, and white underside. Good flavour, fresh is better than frozen. Sold in steaks, cutlets and fillets. Best poached or baked, served with sauce or melted butter.

Lemon sole
Plump oval body, sandy-brown back with mottled markings, small head, white underside. Not related to Dover sole. At its best when very fresh. Use it for Dover sole recipes.

Witch
Oval shape with pale or medium-brown, slightly mottled back and a white underside. Good-quality white flesh which needs to be well seasoned. Best cooked using Dover sole recipes.

Megrim
Sandy-brown body with faint spots, white underside. Can be watery, substitute for any flat fish. Best served in well-seasoned dishes.

Haddock

Smaller than cod, with dark grey back, silver underside and marked black lateral line. Usually sold in fillets. Best deep-fried and served with chips, or use cod recipes.

Hake

Long, dark grey, tapering body with large head, black mouth. Flesh is white, soft and creamy. Best deep-fried in batter, pan-fried, baked or poached. Hake is best eaten very fresh since it can become tasteless after a few days.

Whiting

Slim, silver-grey fish, silver sides and white belly. When very fresh, has sweet flaky flesh. Best poached, fried, or flaked and used in fish cakes.

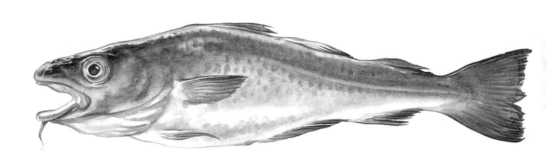

Cod family

Cod

Greenish-grey back with mottling, paling to light grey on the sides and a white belly. Firm white flesh with good flavour, sold as steaks and fillets. Combines well with other fish in pies and stews, can be used for fish cakes. Can be baked, poached, grilled and fried.

Bass, bream, grouper

Grouper

Large species, identified by deep body, large head and a mouth that looks upwards. Flesh has a good flavour and texture. Cook as for bass.

Bream

Small narrow fish with greenish-yellow, silver body, big eyes on a small head. Sardine-like flavour. Best barbecued, grilled or baked.

Bass

Attractive fish with streamlined body, steel grey through to silver. Good texture and flavour. Best cooked by steaming, poaching or baked in salt, also good in salads.

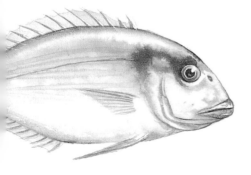

Oily fish

Mackerel

Glistening green-blue back with dark wavy lines and white underbelly. Buy very fresh, and do not buy if it looks dull. Rich flesh has good strong flavour and firm texture. Best grilled or barbecued and served with gooseberry sauce. Also, good stuffed, baked or poached. Roll fillets in oatmeal and fry.

Herring

Dark blue-green back becoming silver on sides and belly, reddish tint around the eyes. Flesh is fragile, has strong flavour and creamy texture. Best cooked patted with seasoned oatmeal and fried in lard or butter, or scored, brushed with fat and grilled.

Sardine

Actually a young pilchard, smaller than herring, with blue-green back paling to silver. Best fried in olive oil or grilled over charcoal.

Whitebait

Young herrings, pilchard and sprats, bright, silver and slender. Very good flavour. Best cooked dipped in milk, shaken in a bag of flour and deep-fried.

Sprat

Similar to herring. Good flavour, but small and bony. Best cooked tossed in well-seasoned flour and fried in bacon fat with fresh thyme.

Great fish

Tuna and bonito

Deep streamlined body, pointed snout and fast-tapering tail. Flesh is not attractive but improves during cooking. Best cooked by grilling, barbecuing or baking.

Swordfish

Large fish with sword-like upper jaw. Creamy-beige flesh with sweet flavour. Best grilled, barbecued or made into kebabs, having first been marinated.

Freshwater fish

Salmon trout

Similar to salmon, but the body is thicker, the head blunter, and the tail not as forked. Flesh is pale pink, but not as rich as salmon. Correctly called sea trout. Best cooked as for salmon.

Salmon

Streamlined silvery body with scattered black markings. When really fresh, has a creamy substance between the flakes of flesh which sets to a curd when cooked. Avoid steaks that look soft, grey, oily or watery. Best cooked whole by poaching in court bouillon in a fish kettle, or baked wrapped in foil. Grill or bake steaks and cutlets.

Trout, rainbow

Similar to salmon, but with a trim body, blunt head, olive green-blue back, finely spotted. Delicate flavour with white or pink flesh. Responds well to freezing. Best cooked by poaching, grilling or frying.

Assorted fish

Skate and ray
Flat, kite-shaped body, pointed snout for skate, blunt for ray. Sold mainly as wings. Any slight odour should disappear on cooking – if it doesn't the fish is unedible. Best poached and served with browned butter. Also good grilled or deep-fried.

John Dory
Grey body, large ugly head. The firm white flesh is moist and sweet. Best cooked by steaming, baking or frying. Use small ones in soup.

Monkfish
Enormous horny head with huge mouth, tapering tail and mottled skin. Good flavour, dense firm flesh. Best grilled, poached or roasted.

Red mullet
Deep rose, with faint golden bar along each side; not related to grey mullet. Best cooked with strong flavours such as garlic, rosemary, fennel. Good for grilling and barbecuing.

Snapper
Very large species, some of which are now imported. Names to look for are Bordemar, Bourgeois, Therese, Red Snapper, Job Gris, and Job Jaune. A very versatile fish with well-flavoured juicy flesh. Best grilled, barbecued, baked, or poached.

Shellfish and crustacea

Squid

Long body sac has eight short tentacles and two long, the mottled skin is easily removed. Body, flaps and tentacles are eaten, the sac can be stuffed. Best cooked either very quickly, or for a long time.

Prawn

Frozen prawns in their shells have the best flavour and are good in salads, pasta dishes and risottos. When buying frozen peeled prawns, choose the ones with the least glaze. Those that come from South-east Asia are cheap but have little flavour so use in strongly flavoured dishes such as curries.

Crab

There are many different species of crab across the world. All have a hard shell and ten claws or legs, with both brown and white crab meat. Fresh crabs that you cook yourself will have better flavour than cooked crab meat.

Buying and storing shellfish

- Shellfish deteriorates more quickly than fish, eat when very fresh and discard if they smell at all 'high'. Buy it live when possible, but if you buy it already cooked, it should smell fresh.
- Live shellfish should have all their claws intact and should be quite frisky. A lobster that looks tired is most probably dying.
- Mussels, clams, and oysters are all bought live and, if fresh, they should have tightly closed, uncracked shells. They should not be gaping open, but if they are slightly open, give them a sharp tap against a hard surface and this should make them close. Discard any that don't close.
- Scallops may be sold gaping open.
- Cooked crabs and lobsters should have intact shells. If their shells are cracked, the texture of the meat may also have been damaged during the cooking process. They should also feel quite heavy in relation to their size. Cooked ones that feel light could indicate poor condition. They may contain water, so shake them close to your ear and listen. A strong smell of ammonia means that they are stale and old.

Preparing crab

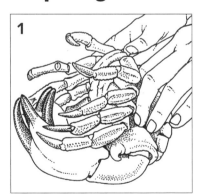

1 *Stand the crab on its head and lever away the back end of the shell with your fingers*

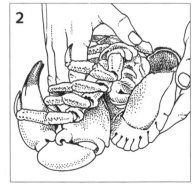

2 *Gently pull the body and legs away from the shell*

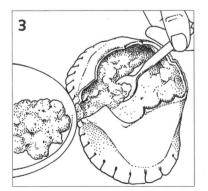

3 *Discard the intestines. Then scoop out the brown creamy meat and discard gills*

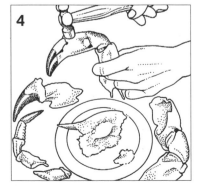

4 *Dig out white meat with skewer; crack open claws and legs and extract meat*

Dublin Bay prawn
Also called langoustine. Shaped like a lobster with slender orange body, long claws. Mainly eaten as scampi (their tails). If raw, cook in their shells in gently boiling water for no more than 10 minutes and eat with melted butter. If pre-boiled, reheat gently but do not recook as they easily toughen.

Mussel
Mussels can be found throughout the world most commonly having a blue-black shell with cream or orange meat. Mussels are most commonly eaten cooked, but some varieties, like the date-shell can be eaten raw.

Lobster or crayfish
When alive, dark blue, but then turns a vivid red when cooked. Best boiled, steamed or grilled. Can be eaten hot in sauce, or cold.

Clam
There are several varieties: including cherrystones or razor-shell. Cook quickly in chowders or eat raw.

Preparing lobster

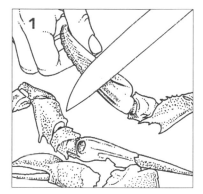

1 *Crack the legs and claws with the back of a knife, a hammer or a nutcracker*

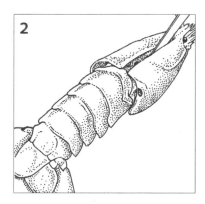

2 *To split lobster in half, draw a sharp knife up through head, then down through body*

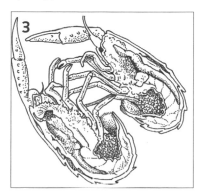

3 *Pull halves apart to expose flesh, which should include red coral and dark roe*

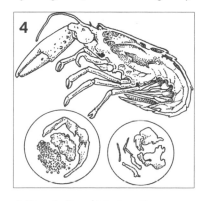

4 *Discard gills and intestines. Creamy green liver should be reserved to make a sauce*

Preparing shellfish

● Shelling cooked prawns: pinch off the legs and take out any roe. Remove the shell by peeling it back from the underside and discard. Pull the meat away from the head and discard the head. Remove intestinal tracts from large prawns, but not if pale and barely noticeable. To make a delicious shellfish stock, place shells and heads in a pan, cover with water, bring to the boil, and simmer for 30 minutes. Strain and reduce the stock to a good flavour. The stock can then be frozen in small quantities and used, as required, to enrich sauces.

● To open an oyster: grip firmly using a coarse cloth. Push an oyster knife into the hinge and twist to lever open. Be careful not to cut your hands, which can easily happen if the knife slips.

● To prepare live lobsters: put them in the freezer for 5–10 minutes prior to cooking, where they will quietly fall asleep. They can then be killed quickly during the cooking process by boiling.

● To prepare mussels: scrub them, removing any beards and barnacles. Tap them sharply against the work surface and discard any that don't close. Steam them quickly, shaking the pan continuously, until they open. Discard any that do not open.

Poultry

There are many different types of poultry and game that can be used by the enthusiastic cook. Chicken, duck, turkey and goose are all available for the table all year round. Autumn is the season to appreciate wild game, although some – to protect the species – is now farmed specially for the table.

Buying and storage

● Remove from the plastic covering, refrigerate and use within four days. For longer storage, freeze on purchase.

● Freezer burn on a frozen chicken will make it dry and tasteless.

● Chunks of ice between the poultry and bottom of the wrapping indicates partial thawing and refreezing. The flesh will be poor quality.

● Thaw deep-frozen birds thoroughly. There should be no ice crystals on the inside or undue coldness before cooking begins.

● Thaw slowly in the refrigerator, at room temperature, or in a bath of cold water. Never use warm water, as this will spoil the texture of the meat.

● As soon as possible remove the giblet bag so that air can get to the cavity.

● To counteract hardening and drying out of poultry, spread a thin layer of margarine over the skin to form a seal and cover loosely with foil.

Right: sautéeing chicken joints seals them and prepares them for the casserole
Far right: chicken is a mild-tasting meat, which readily absorbs the flavours of herbs and spices, as in this Thai recipe for stuffed chicken wings

Types of poultry

● Poulet: immature spring chicken. Allow 1 for 2 people.

● Poussin: baby chicken. Allow 1 per person. Fiddly and bony, eat with your fingers.

● Capon: neutered rooster fattened on corn. Very succulent because the flesh is marbled with fat. They are illegal to produce in this country.

● Boiling fowl: an old bird, tough and cheap. Use for dishes requiring a long gentle simmer.

● Roasting chickens: use for most chicken recipes. Allow 1.75–2 kg/3½–4 lb bird to feed 4–6 people.

● Turkey: for best flavour, choose a hen, hung for 3 days, with moist skin tinted pearly white. Frozen turkey takes at least 48 hours to defrost; let it thaw gradually in the refrigerator

and finally at room temperature for a few hours. Once thawed, cook as soon as possible. It must be cooked through to the centre. Allow 500 g/1 lb dressed weight per person.

● Goose: choose a young bird, with pliable lower beak and breastbone and a plump, well-filled plump breast. A gosling weighs up to 2 kg/5 lb; at 8–9 months old it becomes a goose and weighs 2.5–5.5 kg/6–12 lb. Thereafter it becomes much fatter and tougher, and therefore needs longer cooking.

● Duck: duckling describes birds aged up to 6 months. If too young, the bird will not have enough meat to be worth eating. Look for a breast that, when pinched, feels meaty. Duck freezes well because of its high fat content.

Preparing poultry and game

● Game birds are lean and need to be barded or protected by a cover before roasting.

● Feel game birds with your fingers and ease out any lead shot.

● Poultry is trussed to keep a stuffing inside or to give a good shape to the bird. When the strings are removed the bird can be easily carved.

● Before roasting, wipe poultry and game with a damp cloth. Pat dry with kitchen paper.

● Stuff large birds to provide a contrast flavour to the flesh and make them more interesting.

● Boned birds can be reshaped by careful stuffing and are then simple to carve.

● Tiny game birds can be flavoured with a grape, a pinch of fresh herbs, or a clove-studded onion.

● Weigh poultry after stuffing and calculate the cooking time

Approximate cooking times for poultry

	Fast roasting	Combined high and low heat roasting	Slow roasting
		Sear at 220°C (425°F), Gas Mark 7, then reduce the heat to 160°C (325°F), Gas Mark 3	160° (325°F), Gas Mark 3 for total roasting time
Chicken 1–1.5 kg/2–3 lb 1.5–2.5 kg/3–5 lb		Sear 30 mins, then 15–30 mins Sear 30 mins, then 30–60 mins	1¼ –2 hours
Goose 3.5–4.5 kg/8–10 lb 4.5–5.5 kg/10–12 lb		Sear 45 mins, then 1¾–2 hours Sear 45 mins, then 2–2½ hours	
		Sear at 220°C (425°F), Gas Mark 7, then reduce the heat to 180°C (350°F), Gas Mark 4	
Turkey 3.5–5.5 kg/8–12 lb 5.5–7 kg/12–15 lb 7–9 kg/15–20 lb		Sear 50 mins, then 1½–2 hours Sear 50 mins, then 2–2½ hours Sear 50 mins, then 2½–3 hours	3½–4 hours 4–4½ hours 4½–5 hours
Duck or duckling 1.5–3 kg/3–6 lb		Sear 30 mins, then 50 mins–1½ hours	
Guinea fowl 750 g–1.5 kg/1½–3 lb	220°C (425°F), Gas Mark 7; 30 mins–1 hour		
Poussin 500–750 g/1–1½ lb	220°C (425°F), Gas Mark 7; 20–30 mins		
Squab 500–750 g/1–1½ lb	220°C (425°F), Gas Mark 7; 20–30 mins		
Quail	220°C (425°F), Gas Mark 7; 15 mins		

to be sure that the stuffing will be cooked right through.

● Duck is seldom stuffed; it gives off too much fat. Add flavour to it with a clove-studded apple or onion, and discard before serving.

Cooking poultry and game

● Steaming: suitable for chicken breast and for small whole quail. Place on a piece of muslin, lower on to steamer bottom and cook over gently boiling water, allowing 8 minutes per 500 g/ 1 lb weight.

● Roasting: chicken, turkey and poussin should be draped with

fatty bacon, muslin soaked in butter or oil, or rubbed with butter and basted frequently. Duck and goose need to be pricked all over so that their fat can both escape and baste at the same time.

● Roasting: game birds are very lean and do not require a great deal of cooking. They do, however, need barding with a thin layer of bacon fat, tied in place and removed for the last 10 minutes so that the top of the bird can brown.

● Light-fleshed game birds are roasted until well done, those with darker flesh are usually served underdone.

● Cooking times depend on the size, type, weight and age of the bird that is being cooked.

● Goose and duck give out a lot of fat during roasting so cook them on a rack.

● Birds for spit roasting should be stuffed, trussed and secured on a roasting fork.

● Testing for doneness: a meat thermometer, placed in the thick-

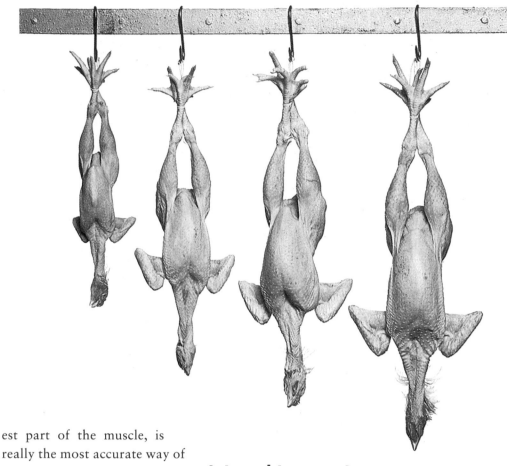

est part of the muscle, is really the most accurate way of testing. Poultry is ready when a skewer in the thickest part of the thigh releases absolutely clear juices, tinged with gold, and without any trace of pink (uncooked meat) in them.

Internal temperatures

All poultry should be cooked to an internal temperature of not less than 70°C (155°F) to eliminate the risks of bacterial and parasitic infection.

Above: this assortment of different types of poultry, most of them already plucked, cleaned and ready for the pot, hangs from the hooks in a butcher's shop. They offer the cook a wide choice for cooking. The birds shown here, from left to right: a young poulet; a roasting chicken, suitable for most recipes; a boiling fowl, which requires long slow cooking; a turkey, the traditional bird for many of life's celebrations; a goose; a duck; and two guinea fowl

Trussing a chicken

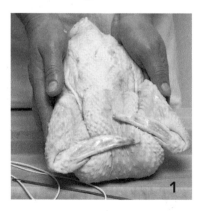

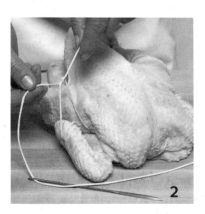

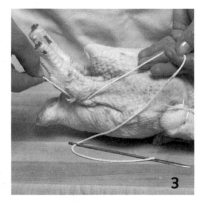

1. Stretch the neck flap firmly under the bird and fold back the wing tips to secure the flap firmly in place.

2. Push threaded trussing needle right through body just above the wings. Return it through the body, this time piercing wings. Tie and trim loose ends of string. Re-thread the trussing needle.

3. Push the needle through the skin just underneath the drumstick joint, then through the gristle on either side of the parson's nose and bring it out through the skin under the far drumstick. Return the needle through the bird, just to one side of the original path. Tie securely and trim the ends.

Carving a chicken

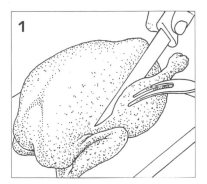

1. Place the bird breast side up, remove the legs and wings on each side. If the chicken is large, separate drumsticks from thighs.

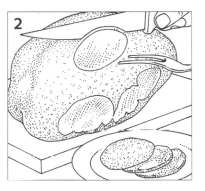

2. Carve thin slices diagonally from each side of the breast.

Carving

Use a sharp knife, which is much safer than a blunt one. If you are unsure about it, carve in the kitchen, keep the meat warm and serve it all at once. Always use a fork fitted with a safety guard. At the table, keep the cut side towards you, presenting the uncut side towards the guests.

● Duck: difficult to carve, so use poultry shears. Insert shears into vent and cut through breast. Open up and cut along each side of backbone and remove. Place each half skin side up on a board, cut between wing and leg to give 2 portions.

● Game birds: as for duck.

● Turkey and goose: carve as for chicken.

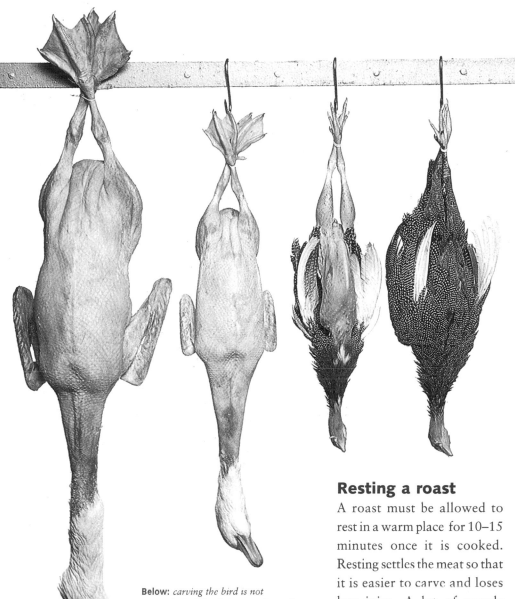

Below: *carving the bird is not particularly difficult but you do need to know something of the bird's anatomy to make sure you are doing it right, and it does require some practice. If in doubt, practise in the kitchen and bring it to the table once carved*

Resting a roast

A roast must be allowed to rest in a warm place for 10–15 minutes once it is cooked. Resting settles the meat so that it is easier to carve and loses less juice. A lot of people worry that the meat will get cold, but a cooked bird has a lot of heat stored in it and would take hours to get cold.

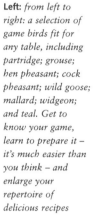

Left: *from left to right: a selection of game birds fit for any table, including partridge; grouse; hen pheasant; cock pheasant; wild goose; mallard; widgeon; and teal. Get to know your game, learn to prepare it – it's much easier than you think – and enlarge your repertoire of delicious recipes*

Buying game

● Young birds generally have pointed flight feathers at the tip and edge of wings, downy feathers on the breast and under the wing, soft pliable feet and short rounded spurs on the legs.

● The best test is to insert a matchstick into the small opening that young game birds in feather have just above the vent. This is smaller or may close in mature birds. In young pheasant it will open to a depth of 2.5 cm/ 1 inch; in partridge or grouse it will be 1 cm/½ inch.

Right: *a duck is a very fatty bird which, when it is roasted, produces a lot of fat. This then needs to be separated from the lean meat juices in order to make a good gravy*

● Ripeness is judged by smell and the condition of the bird round the vent. This becomes moist and fragile when the bird is well hung. A high bird smells gamey, a rotten one smells bad.

● Hanging tenderizes meat, retains moisture and develops the gamey flavour.

● If game is smelly once plucked, wipe with a cheesecloth dampened in diluted vinegar.

● After hanging, it is plucked, drawn and trussed.

Plucking and drawing game

After game has been hung, place on a newspaper-covered bowl or board. Pull out the body feathers first, then the remainder with fingers or tweezers.

When all the feathers are out and before drawing, singe any stubborn quills using a lighted candle, a taper or low gas flame. Cut off the head, roll back the neck skin and cut off the neck. Slit neck skin, loosen windpipe and gullet with the fingers. Make a slit above the vent to enlarge it, slide in your fingers and remove innards. Do not break the gall.

Types of game

● Grouse: this is the most popular game bird. The meat is dark red, rich and gamey, yet delicate. A young bird can be roasted for 15–20 minutes and

Warnings

● Wash your hands thoroughly before and after handling poultry. Wash all utensils between handling raw and cooked food.

● Prepare raw poultry on white non-porous boards which can be washed in hot water with a little bleach.

● Avoid any contact between cooked and raw foods, during both storage and preparation.

● Cool poultry that you have cooked for eating later as quickly as possible. Cover and refrigerate as soon as possible.

served slightly underdone. Allow 1 per person. Older birds are best marinated and casseroled.

● Partridge: the grey-legged or common partridge is generally regarded as the best for eating; the red-legged is slightly larger. Best eaten when young, weighing about 500 g/1 lb and needing little hanging. Allow 1 per person. Use older birds in pâtés, pies, casseroles and soups.

● Pheasant: the hen is often the plumper, juicier bird. Feel the width of the breast to see if it is plump, the legs should be smooth and the feet soft. One bird will make 4 servings.

● Pigeon: wild woodpigeons are gamier than those bred for the table, squab are the young ones. The most tender bird will be a young one which has soft, supple feet without scales. Marinate older birds in red wine prior to cooking them.

● Quail: the smallest game bird, which is now usually farmed for the table. The game flavour is very faint. Allow 2 per person.

● Venison: the meat is fine textured, dense and dark red, with little marbling or fat. Roast young venison, and casserole or stew older venison.

● Wild duck: this is rated highly for its characteristic fishy flavour. Drakes tend to be tougher than ducks, and are therefore best marinated. Eat within 24 hours of killing.

Below: *Peking duck – served with wafer-thin pancakes, cucumber matchsticks and plum sauce – is one of the most most interesting and delicious ways of serving duck, popularized in Chinese restaurants the world over*

Meat

Meat is an important source of food. In this chapter you can find out many ways of making the most of inexpensive cuts of meat, and achieving the best with those that cost a bit more. Enjoy creating different flavours from the same cuts of meat and explore the enormous versatility of the many different varieties.

Choosing

● All the cuts of meat, at a good store, should look appetizing, silky, but not wet. Boned, rolled joints should be neatly tied, bones should be sawn smoothly, meat should be neatly trimmed with excess fat removed.

● The best meat of each animal comes from the hindquarter and loin, the tenderest comes from the parts that have had least exercise. Exercise develops muscle fibre and the connective tissue that holds muscles together. Connective tissue is mostly responsible for toughness.

● Tough meat can be prepared so that it arrives at the table full of flavour and juice by marinating in a marinade which includes wine, lemon juice, vinegar, yogurt, or pulped tomatoes. These acids break down connective tissue. Lengthy cooking completes the process.

● Oil used in marinades adds succulence to the meat.

● Pounding or cutting also breaks up the connective tissue, while flavourings – such as chopped onions, garlic, herbs, spices and seasonings – add taste.

● Ageing (the hanging of carcasses) tenderizes beef and lamb. Mature beef is a dark red colour, its fat will be pale gold. White fat and bright red meat indicate that it is immature. Pork, veal and kosher meat are not aged.

Cooking beef

● Per person, allow about 100–175g/3½–6 oz lean meat off the bone; 250–375 g/8–12 oz on the bone.

● Use dry heat – roasting, frying, grilling – for tender cuts; and moist heat – braising, pot roasting, stewing and simmering – for tougher cuts.

● Grill small, reasonably thick pieces of best-quality meat. Brush the meat on both sides with oil to prevent it drying out,

sear the meat on both sides and rest after cooking for a few minutes to acquire an even texture.

● Fry good-quality flat cuts in a little hot oil or butter in a large shallow frying pan, turning the meat once or twice. Do not pierce it while cooking, keep a fairly brisk heat going, do not overheat the fat or it will burn.

● Steak doneness (per 500 g/1 lb for a 2.5 cm/1 inch steak): blue, inside almost rare: 5 minutes; rare, red inside with the juices running freely: 7 minutes; medium rare, fewer juices, paler centre: 12 minutes; medium, pink in centre, juices set: 14 minutes; well done, centre beige, flesh still juicy: 15 minutes.

● Stir-fry both rump steak and fillet steak.

● Roast joints from the back, ribs, fillet or sirloin. Small joints shrink more than the large ones, choose a joint larger than you actually need and use the leftovers for other dishes, such as curries and salads. If roasting on the bone, allow 20 minutes per 500 g/1 lb plus 20 minutes extra, at 200°C (400°F), Gas Mark 6. If off the bone, allow 25 minutes, plus 25 minutes extra.

● Boil silverside and brisket slowly with vegetables. Allow 15–20 minutes per 500 g/1 lb.

● Braise any small lean joints of topside or silverside, blade or chuck steak.

● Stew or casserole cuts such as shin, leg, chuck, blade, neck, skirt and flank.

Right: *frying some tender fillet steak*
Far right: *marinating the meat before cooking*

Storing meat

● Store meat in a film-covered plastic tray on a plate in the refrigerator.
● Any meat that is not pre-packed should be wrapped in foil or greaseproof paper and then refrigerated.
● Chops deteriorate faster than joints.

Approximate maximum storage times for meat

Uncooked meat	In a refrigerator	In a freezer
Beef	3–5 days	12 months
Veal	3–5 days	12 months
Lamb	3–5 days	9 months
Pork	2–4 days	6 months
Minced beef	1–2 days	3 months

Internal temperatures of meat

This is extremely important and all meat should always be cooked to an internal temperature of at least 60°C (140°F) – more for medium and well-done meat. This eliminates all risks of both bacterial and parasitic infection.

Internal temperatures of meat

	Rare	Medium	Well done
Beef	60°C/140°F	70°C/155°F	80°C/175°F
Veal		75°C/165°F	80°C/175°F
Lamb	60°C/140°F	65°C/147°F	80°C/175°F
Pork		70°C/155°F	80°C/175°F

Warnings

● Wash hands before and after handling meat. Wash knives and utensils between handling raw and cooked food.
● Prepare raw meat on white non-porous boards which can be washed in hot water with a little bleach.
● Carefully but loosely cover meat in a shallow container or if pre-packed leave in tray and refrigerate.
● Avoid contact between cooked and raw foods during storage and preparation.
● Cool meat cooked for eating later as quickly as possible, cover and refrigerate.
● Meat should be thoroughly cooked.

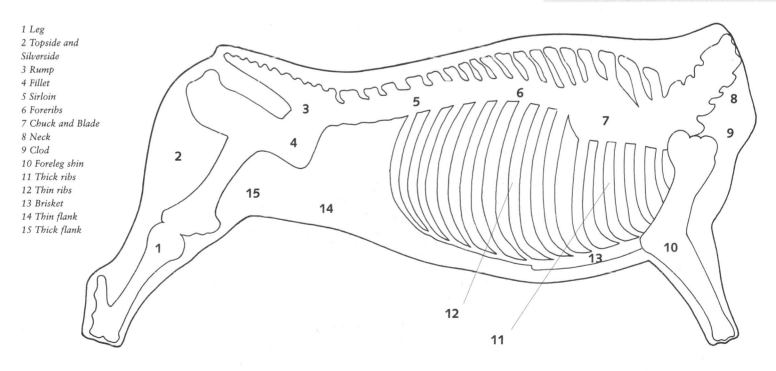

1 Leg
2 Topside and Silverside
3 Rump
4 Fillet
5 Sirloin
6 Foreribs
7 Chuck and Blade
8 Neck
9 Clod
10 Foreleg shin
11 Thick ribs
12 Thin ribs
13 Brisket
14 Thin flank
15 Thick flank

Approximate cooking times for meat *(minutes per 500 g/1 lb and temperatures)*

Meats and cuts	Roasting	Pot roasting/braising	Boiling
Beef			
Tender cuts: rare	15 minutes plus 15 minutes in a hot oven	30–40 minutes on stove top	
Tender cuts: medium	40 minutes in a warm oven		
coarser cuts	20 minutes in a fairly hot oven		1 hour at a steady simmer
Boned/rolled	30 minutes in a fairly hot oven		
Veal			
Thin cuts and on the bone	25 minutes plus 20 minutes in a fairly hot oven		
Thick and boned and rolled cuts	35 minutes in a warm oven	40–50 minutes in a warm oven	
Lamb			
Tender cuts	20 minutes in a fairly hot oven (plus 15 for large cuts)		
Smaller cuts for casseroles and stews		Total of 2½ hours in a warm oven	30 minutes
Pork			
Small, thin cuts	30 minutes plus 20 minutes in a moderate oven	60 minutes on stove top	
Thick cuts	30 minutes plus 20 minutes in a moderate oven	60 minutes in a warm oven	
Pickled cuts			Your butcher will advise

Cooking veal

● Roast leg, loin, rib joints and boned and rolled shoulder. Use a moderate oven at 160°C (325°F), Gas Mark 3 allowing about 35 minutes per 500 g/ 1 lb on the bone; about 40–45 minutes per 500 g/1 lb if boned and rolled. Baste frequently and serve thoroughly cooked.

● Fry or grill chops, fillets and escalopes cut from the leg in butter or olive oil. If grilling baste frequently to stop meat from drying out.

● Braise, pot roast, stew or casserole topside, breast, middle neck and scrag, pie veal, stewing veal.

Right: *grilled lamb noisettes*

Carving a rib of beef

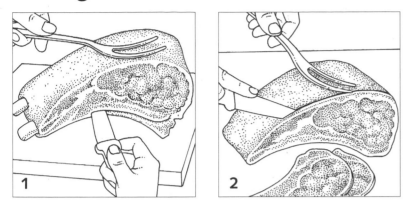

1. Remove the bones at the wide end of the rib before carving, then run the knife along between meat and contours of the ribs.
2. Steady the roast with the back of the carving fork, and then slice the meat vertically, with each slice falling free.

Basic roast beef

Serves 6–8

What you need:

- 2 kg/4 lb sirloin or rib on the bone
- dry English mustard
- 300 ml/½ pint stock
- 150 ml/¼ pint red wine
- salt and pepper

1 Preheat the oven to 220°C (425°F), Gas Mark 7. Weigh the beef and allow 20 minutes per 500 g/1 lb for medium rare meat and 15 minutes for rare.
2 Place the beef, with the fatty side uppermost, on a wire rack over a roasting tin and sprinkle with dry mustard and pepper but no salt.
3 Roast for 20 minutes. Turn the oven down to 160°C (325°F), Gas Mark 3 and time the joint from now. Baste occasionally. Halfway through the cooking time, tip off the dripping and use for the roast vegetables and the Yorkshire pudding.
4 When cooked, sprinkle with salt and leave to stand in a warm place for about 20–30 minutes.

Marinades

A marinade is a mixture of oil, wine and other flavourings which penetrates the outer layer of the meat when left in it overnight in the refrigerator. The acid in the marinade breaks down the tough fibres and the oil prevents moisture evaporation and adds richness.

Lamb kebabs

For 1 kg/2 lb boned lamb for kebabs

What you need:

- 150 ml/¼ pint red wine
- 1 tablespoon lemon juice
- 1 tablespoon oil
- 8 whole allspice
- 1 heaped tablespoon cumin
- 1 sprig of fresh thyme
- ½ onion, sliced
- 6 black peppercorns

Cut the meat into 5 cm/2 inch lean cubes. Mix all the marinade ingredients together. Place the cubes of meat in a shallow dish, pour the marinade over and leave for 8 hours, or overnight, turning the meat occasionally.

Grilled meat

For 750 g/1½ lb meat for grilling or frying

What you need:

- 450 ml/¾ pint olive oil
- juice of 1 lime or lemon
- 1 onion, sliced
- pepper
- 150 ml/¼ pint white wine
- 2 crushed garlic cloves
- freshly chopped basil

Combine all the ingredients in a mixing bowl. Place the meat in a large dish, pour over the marinade and leave for several hours.

Barbecue steaks

For 4 x 175 g/6 oz barbecue steaks

What you need:

- 1 crushed garlic clove
- 75 g/3 oz brown sugar
- 1 teaspoon wholegrain mustard
- 1 tablespoon wine vinegar
- 300 ml/½ pint stout or bitter
- 2 onions, finely chopped
- pepper

Combine all the ingredients for the marinade in a pan and bring to the boil. Reduce the heat and simmer for 10 minutes. Cool before pouring over the steaks. Cover and refrigerate for at least 2 hours – overnight is ideal.

Cook's Tip

Roast meat should be allowed to rest for 20–30 minutes before serving. This makes it easier to carve.

Buying pork

- Look for firm white fat, pink, smooth velvety flesh.
- Bones should be pale with a tinge of blue to them.
- Do not buy any pork that looks damp or clammy or has oily, waxy-looking fat.

Far right: *brushing the pork shoulder with oil before cooking*
Right: *lightly frying the pork noisettes*

Cooking pork

- Roast the belly and foreloin (which can be rolled and stuffed), leg and loin.
- Roast on the bone at 200°C (400°F), Gas Mark 6, allowing 25 minutes per 500 g/1 lb plus 25 minutes extra. Off the bone, roast pork slowly at 180°C (350°F), Gas Mark 4, allowing 35 minutes per 500 g/1 lb plus 35 minutes extra. Add 10 minutes more for a stuffed joint.
- To get good crackling, score the skin in parallel lines right down through the fat. Do not baste or allow it to come in contact with any fat, liquid or cooking juices in the roasting tin.
- Grill and fry loin and leg chops, shoulder and chump end chops.
- Spare ribs come from the belly and can be roasted or barbecued.

- Braise leg chops, hand and spring joints and the blade from the neck end of the shoulder.

Bacon and ham

Cured meat from the pig's back or side, used for bacon, is called 'green' or unsmoked and has a mild flavour. Smoking cured bacon preserves the meat further by retarding bacterial growth, adds flavour and improves colour. Good-quality bacon will be firm and deep pink in colour with white fat, a pleasant flavour and no yellow or greenish stains.

The pig's hind and shoulder are used for ham and cured very much more slowly than bacon. Ham can be eaten in its cured 'raw' state or used for boiling and braising. Hams sold ready for baking are milder cures and do not need soaking first. Other cuts should be soaked for up to 24 hours if traditionally cured. The rind is left on during cooking and keeps the meat in shape and flavours it.

A soaked ham is gently simmered in water for just about 25 minutes per 500 g/1 lb. Keep it covered with water which should not boil. When it is cooked, remove from the heat. When cool enough to handle, remove the rind, score the fat, baste with honey or syrup and bake in a hot oven for about 20 minutes. Small joints, after soaking, can be marinated in cider and braised, casseroled or steamed.

Cuts of bacon
Back bacon

- Short back is the best cut of bacon for rashers.
- Long back is thinly sliced for grilling or frying.
- Back and ribs give rashers and joints for boiling or braising.

1 Leg Shank end
2 Leg Fillet end
3 Chump end
4 Loin
5 Sparerib
6 Head
7 Trotter
8 Blade or Shoulder
9 Hand and Spring
10 Belly

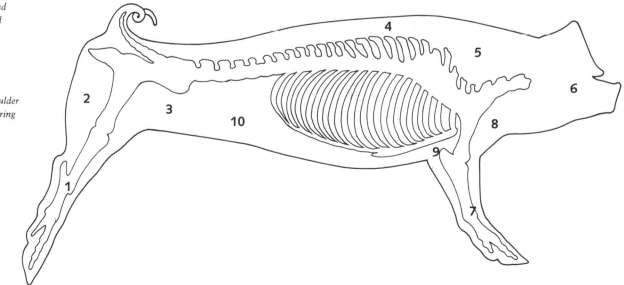

- Top back provides lean bacon rashers and joints for both boiling and braising.

Collar bacon
- Prime collar is the best joint for boiling, whole or cut in pieces.
- End of collar, an economical cut, is first soaked and then boiled or baked.

Flank bacon
Flank bacon can be boiled, or sliced and fried.

Forehock
- Hock knuckle can be boned and minced or used in a stew or a casserole.
- Prime hock is small, fatty and good for boiling.

Gammon
- Slipper is good either for boiling or for roasting.
- Hock can be boiled or partly boiled and baked.
- Middle, the best joint for boiling or roasting, also makes steaks and lean bacon rashers for grilling.
- Corner is a lean boiling or roasting joint, which gives good grilling rashers.

Middle bacon
Middle bacon provides good grilling rashers.

Oyster
The oyster gives rashers for frying or grilling.

Streaky bacon
- Top and prime streaky bacon can be used for boiling joints or for cutting into rashers.
- Thin streaky bacon is used for frying crisply, for wrapping small items before grilling and for lining pâté tins.

Types of ham
Most hams can be boiled or baked after curing and eaten either hot or cold.

Bradenham
With its coal-black skin and deep red flesh, this is another famous English ham. It is cured with molasses and so has a sweet but robust flavour. If it is bought uncooked, it should be soaked for at least a week before cooking, otherwise it will tend to taste very salty.

Jambons de campagne
These are French country hams from the Dordogne area of France. They are farm-cured and often quite salty but delicious sliced and served with unsalted butter and French bread.

Parma
This is dry-cured for part of the time under weights which gives it a flattened shape. After it has matured for about a year, it is soaked in tepid water to soften the rind. After drying and storing, it can be very thinly sliced.

Prague
This is traditionally salted and then mildly brined before being lightly smoked over beechwood embers, from which it emerges as perhaps the sweetest of all smoked boiling hams.

Suffolk
Traditionally cured in brine with spices and honey, this ham is then smoked and hung to mature. It has a full delicate flavour.

Virginia
This is among the so-called 'country-cured' hams that come from America. Pigs destined for

this ham are fattened on peanuts and acorns, and the meat is usually smoked over scented hickory and applewood.

Wiltshire
This is cured as part of the whole pig. It is extremely mild and does not keep so well as most other hams. Like bacon, it is sold smoked or unsmoked.

York ham
Firm and tender, this is the best known of the British boiling hams. It is delicately pink, with fat that is white and translucent. This ham is cured by the dry-salt method. Green York ham is dry-cured, washed and placed in a calico bag to mature for about six months.

Above: *Parma ham and melon makes a simple but delicious summer salad*
Below: *grilled bacon gives flavour to a hearty casserole like Boeuf à la bourgignonne*

Crown roast of lamb

For a crown roast of lamb, curve two trimmed racks of lamb round into a circle, bones up and fat inside. Sew the ends together to form a circle, or tie with string.

For a guard of honour, interlace the bones of two trimmed racks, meat inside, and hold together with some string tied round between the bones.

Carving a shoulder of lamb

1. Place the joint, skin side uppermost, and make a series of parallel cuts in the middle of the joint. Run the knife horizontally along the length of the bone to release these short slices.
2. Turn the joint over, remove all the fat, and then carve the meat in larger, horizontal slices.

Carving a leg of lamb

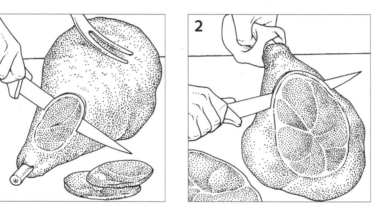

1. Holding the roast steady with the back of the fork, begin carving from the rounded side of the leg. Slice thinly away from yourself, gradually turning the knife to get large slices almost parallel to the bone.
2. Turn the leg over and, holding the bone in a cloth, carve long slices from the opposite side of the leg.

Buying lamb

● It should have a fine grain when cut across the muscle.
● Fat will be white, waxy, firm, yet brittle.

Cooking lamb

● Have as much fat as possible trimmed off before roasting.
● Roast a leg or loin at 180°C (350°F), Gas Mark 4 for 25 minutes per 500 g/1 lb plus another 25 minutes extra for well-done meat. For rarer meat, allow 15 minutes per 500 g/1 lb and remove it from the oven and leave to rest in a warm place for 25 minutes.
● Crown roast consists of 2 trimmed pieces of best end of neck (also called rack of lamb) joined together.
● Roast breast after boning, trimming and stuffing.
● Stew and casserole scrag and middle neck, best end chops.
● Spit roast or barbecue shoulder or leg of lamb.
● Grill or fry chump and loin chops, best end of neck chops and cutlets, neck fillet, medallions cut from the loin.
● Casserole boned shoulder, middle neck and scrag end.

1 Leg
2 Chump
3 Loin
4 Neck
5 Scrag
6 Shoulder
7 Breast

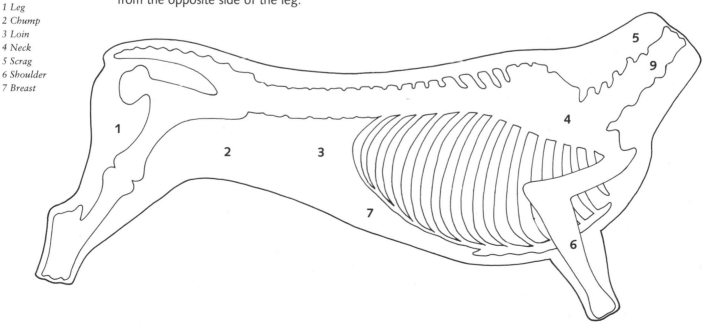

Offal

The collective name for all the edible innards and heads and toes of animals, offal has different distinctive flavours and textures which respond well to careful cooking. It should be bought fresh and cooked as quickly as possible.

Sweetbreads

Veal (not on sale in Britain) is the best, being whiter and larger than lamb's. Sweetbreads are two parts of the thymus gland; those that came from the pancreas gland are coarser. They need a lot of initial preparation before being finally cooked.

Brains

Calf's are better than lamb's. They are first soaked in water, then boiled in lightly salted water before being gently fried or poached until cooked.

Liver

Liver is the most nutritious and widely eaten of all offal. Sold either whole, when the membrane covering should be removed, or in slices. Strongly flavoured pig's or ox should be soaked in milk before cooking.

● Calf's: slice and cook quickly and lightly by grilling or frying and serve while still rosy pink inside. Overcooking will make the liver tough, dry and very leathery.

● Lamb's: deeper colour than calf's and has a less good flavour but can be substituted for it in recipes using liver.

● Pig's: use in pâtés, or braised in one large piece with wine and different vegetables.

● Ox: the coarsest and strongest flavoured, best braised for 1–2 hours with onions.

Kidneys

These should be firm and smell sweet. Skin, halve, remove gristly core and either grill or sauté them briefly, or simmer slowly for a long time – anything in between and they will be very tough and rubbery.

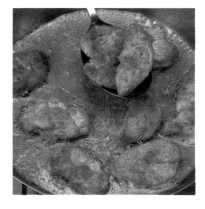

● Calf's: large and pale from milk-fed veal, small and dark from grass-fed veal. Brown briskly in butter, then grill over charcoal or roast encased in their own fat.

● Lamb's: mild and delicious flavour, an essential part of a mixed grill.

● Pig's: larger than lamb's and a stronger flavour. Grill or fry or cook slowly in wine.

● Ox: dark and strongly flavour, best braised. Used in steak and kidney pies.

Tongue

Available fresh, but more often salted or smoked. Choose one that is soft to the touch and soak overnight if salted. Simmer with vegetables and herbs until tender. Skin carefully and serve hot or cold. Ox is best.

Tripe

The lining of first and second stomachs and usually from ox and calf. It comes in a variety of textures – honeycombed (the best), slightly rough and smooth.

Tripe is usually sold prepared and partly cooked, it should always look white and fresh.

Heart

Ox is tough and best sliced and braised. Lamb's, pig's and calf's are more tender, and good blanched, stuffed, wrapped in bacon and roasted.

Heads, tails and feet

Long slow cooking is needed to tenderize and bring out their velvety, gelatinous qualities.

Heads: preparation is a lengthy business.

● Pig's: generally used for brawn, and eaten cold. Cheek is cooked until tender, then shaped and coated in egg and breadcrumbs.

● Calf's: can be cooked, boned and chopped and eaten cold.

● Ox cheek: dark, dense flesh but good when very fresh. Marinate in wine and then braise gently until cooked.

● Calf's and pig's ears: simmer, coat with egg and breadcrumbs and fry.

● Oxtail: needs long, slow, cooking and makes very good soup and stew. Make the day before serving, and remove fat before reheating it.

Feet

● Pig's trotters: simmer until tender and serve hot or cold in their own jelly. When cooked, they can be breadcrumbed and then grilled gently.

● Cow heel: when boiled and skinned and its meat cut into strips, can be added to beef stew to give a velvety texture.

● Calf's foot: cook in stews and casseroles to add richness and texture to the dish.

Left: *gently frying sweetbreads – aficionados consider them a great delicacy*

Basic techniques

Cookery is an endlessly fascinating and rewarding art, but intensely disappointing when things go wrong. Disappointments are fewer and success more easily achieved if you understand how and why things happen. Mastering the basic techniques described below will ensure that you soar more frequently to culinary heights.

Right: *boiling is one of the most commonly used methods of cooking food. Remember, though, that if food is boiled for too long in too much water, it will lose a lot of its nutrients into the cooking liquid*
Far right: *steaming is a healthier way of cooking than boiling because it retains a lot of the food's nutrients, as well as its texture, colour and flavour. Steaming food in a special bamboo steaming basket is a popular way of cooking many foods in China*

Boiling

A form of cooking in liquid at a temperature of 100°C/212°F. The liquid used for this can be stock, salted water or flavoured with wine, herbs or spices.

● Salt added to water raises the boiling point and makes food cook more quickly. It is added at the start of cooking to vegetables, but close to the end for stocks and stews.

● Simmering takes place over a low heat and small bubbles break just below the liquid's surface. Stocks and soups are covered so that as much as possible is extracted from the ingredients.

● Poaching: in which delicate food is cooked in liquid, is a gentler form of simmering.

● Fast boiling – a rolling boil – is used for cooking pasta, reducing liquid and jam making.

● Vegetables such as peas and greens are cooked in an open pan in fast-boiling, well-salted water.

● Root vegetables are simmered in a covered pan.

● Blanching: placing foods in boiling water to loosen skins or, for freezing, to prevent deterioration in colour and flavour. Food is put into boiling water for a set time, then into ice-cold water for the same time.

● Reducing: the liquid is boiled uncovered over a high heat in a pan with a large surface area.

Far right: *stir-frying is a delicious and healthy method of cooking, which is often used in Far Eastern countries such as China and Indonesia. It is suitable for both meat and vegetables, all of which should be cut into thin strips. Food can then be cooked quickly in hot fat until it is tender but still firm to the bite. A great advantage is that it does not require a lot of oil.*

Above: *meat that is being braised is often marinated beforehand in order to break down the tissue. Poultry and game should be braised whole, but treated as joints for casseroling*
Above right: *grilling is one of the healthiest cooking methods because it does not require much fat to be used. Make sure the grill is hot before putting food underneath it*

Steaming

Cooking food in hot vapour over boiling liquid retains a high proportion of flavour and nutrients. Direct steaming uses a tiered steamer, flowered trivet or colander inside a saucepan, or a pressure cooker. Indirect steaming is when food in a covered pudding basin is set in a pan of water reaching halfway up the basin's side. Food such as fish can be placed on a lightly buttered covered plate over a pan of water.

Braising

This is a method of cooking meat on a bed of finely chopped vegetables over gentle heat in a pan with a tight-fitting lid. It is used for meat that is past its prime, or which is low in natural fat (like venison), and for some vegetables. Casseroling cooks meat and vegetables in more liquid than is used for braising. Tight-lidded pots keep in condensation and keep food moist. To stop steam escaping, cover the pot first with foil and then the lid.

● Mirepoix: bed of diced vegetables on which meat or whole vegetables are braised.

Grilling

Select food that is tender, no more than 5 cm/2 inches deep, and marinate drier and leaner cuts of meat, poultry and thick-fleshed fish. Preheat the grill (not the grill pan) at its highest setting for at least 10 minutes. Lightly

grease the grill rack before placing the food on it. Regulate the intensity by lowering the pan rather than reducing the heat. The food to be grilled should be at room temperature.

● Gratin: dishes on which a thin golden brown crust is formed under a high heat from a grill or in the oven.

● Searing: sealing the surface of the food, to retain juices, goodness and flavour.

● Steak doneness: blue, inside almost rare; rare, red inside with juices running freely; medium rare, fewer juices and a paler centre; medium, pink in centre, juices set; well-done, centre beige, flesh still juicy.

● Seasoning: add salt just before putting food under the grill. Salting food in advance tends to draw out the juices, leaving the inside dry.

Frying

A method of quickly cooking or browning food in hot fat or oil. This method is suitable for tender pieces of meat, fish and certain vegetables. Always pay attention when frying, as deep fat will catch fire if it becomes too hot.

● Shallow frying is carried out over medium heat using equal amounts of sizzling oil and butter, or just oil.

● Sautéeing uses very little fat, and the food is moved constantly throughout the process to prevent sticking and burning.

● Pan-frying or dry-frying uses a thick-based heated pan and the food cooks in its own juices.

● Stir-frying uses little oil. The cooked foods are pushed to the side of the wok while fresh food is tossed and turned in the oil.

● Batting out: tenderizing by placing delicate meat between sheets of greaseproof paper and pressing with a rolling-pin, or using a specially designed bat.

● Deep-frying uses very hot oil which seals the outside of the food, preventing moisture escaping and fat soaking in.

● Deep-frying: fat should come only halfway up the pan to avoid overflowing; it should be strained after use and stored covered; if it foams with yellow bubbles and smells unpleasant it should be discarded.

Eggs

Full of nutrition and an indispensable ingredient in all kinds of cooking, eggs deserve a place in every cook's kitchen. They are inexpensive and easy to prepare and cook. A lot of people claim that they are unable to cook an egg properly, but master the techniques of a few simple ways of cooking them and, in no time at all, you will be surprised to learn that you have acquired an enviable culinary reputation.

Cooking techniques

There are many different ways in which to prepare eggs. Most people have their favourites.

Boiling

● The eggs should not be cold, or the shell will crack when you lower it into boiling water.
● If they are to be peeled, they should be a couple of days old,

Below: making a successful soufflé is within everyone's reach

otherwise the white will stick to the shell when you peel it.
● The fresher the eggs, the longer they should be cooked.
● Soft-boiled eggs have a softly set white and a runny yolk. Lower eggs into boiling water and cook for 3 minutes.
● Medium-boiled have a firm white with just soft yolk. Cook for 4 ½ minutes.
● Hard-boiled eggs are firm throughout. Lower into cold water, bring slowly to the boil, simmer and time from this point for 8–10 minutes. As soon as the eggs are cooked, place in a bowl under cold running water. When cool, peel and use at once.

Coddling

A coddler looks like an egg cup with a lid. Place a knob of butter in the base and drop in the egg. Add a little salt and pepper and screw on the lid. Place in simmering water, which should come three-quarters of the way up the coddler. Turn off the heat. Cover the pan and leave it for 8–9 minutes. Remove the coddler from the pan, unscrew the lid and serve the egg in the coddler.

Poaching

● The frying pan method: pour water into the

pan to a depth of 4 cm/1½ inches and bring to simmering point. Break each egg into a saucer and carefully lower it into the water. Cook for 3 minutes, either covering the pan or just basting the egg with hot water. Remove on a fish slice or a perforated spoon.
● Poacher method: half fill the pan with water, place the cups in position and add a knob of butter to each cup. Bring to the boil, lower the heat, break the eggs into the cups and simmer, covered, for 4–5 minutes. Loosen each egg with a knife and tip out.

Scrambling

For 2 people, break 3–4 eggs into a bowl and whisk lightly with a fork. Season with salt and pepper and stir in 2 tablespoons of milk or single cream. Melt about 25 g/1 oz of butter in a pan over a low heat. Pour in the eggs and leave for about 30 seconds before gently stirring with a wooden spoon. Cook for a further 30–60 seconds, stirring, until the eggs are just set. Serve the scrambled eggs at once.

Baking

Eggs are cooked in individual ramekin dishes. Lightly grease the dishes with butter. Place in a roasting pan with 2.5 cm/1 inch warm water, break an egg into each dish and season well. Dot with a little butter or cream and cook in a preheated oven, 180°C (350°F), Gas Mark 4, for about 8–10 minutes, until just set. Remove from the water at once.

Omelette

For 2 people, beat 3–4 eggs very lightly just before using, and season lightly with salt and pepper. Heat a knob of butter in a pan. When it has melted and is just turning colour, pour in the eggs. Tip the pan towards you and lift up a little of the mixture on the far side with a fork, tip the pan so that the unset egg runs into the space. With a little unset egg on the top fold the omelette in half and serve.

Whisking egg whites

● Use the egg white at room temperature, and clean utensils, free of grease.
● Soufflés need the egg whites to be whisked until slightly translucent and holding in soft peaks.
● Meringues require the whites to be whisked until they are opaque and hold in firm peaks.
● Use whisked egg white immediately as it may collapse if left for even a short time.

Folding in egg whites

● Stir in a big spoonful of white into the mixture to lighten it. Then scoop the rest of the egg whites on top.
● Using a metal spoon or a spatula, cut down into the centre of the bowl.
● With a scooping action, bring the spoon up towards you, turning the mixture bottom to top. Continue, turning the bowl and working clockwise.

Uses

● The yolk acts as a binding agent for stuffings, fish cakes and rissoles.
● The yolk emulsifies and will hold butter or oil in suspension (as in mayonnaise).
● Eggs act as a thickening agent for soups, sauces and stews as well as custard where the yolk coagulates as it is heated to hold the liquid in suspension.
● Egg whites aerate, having the ability to hold air and increase volume by many times (as in meringue).
● A whole egg, or egg yolk, is used for coating foods or glazing them.

Quail egg   White hen egg   Brown hen egg   Duck egg   Goose egg

Fresh test

● Break a fresh egg and the white should be translucent and cling to the yolk, if the white runs away from the yolk it is not very fresh.
● When placed in a tumbler of water a fresh egg will sink to the bottom and lie completely flat in the base. If it tilts slightly, it is a little stale. If the egg floats to the top of the water it is not suitable to use for boiling and should be cracked before use. If a pungent smell comes from

Storage

● Buy date stamped eggs in small quantities, and then use them as soon as possible.
● Store eggs, pointed end down, in the refrigerator and bring to room temperature about 30 minutes before using.
● Eggs are enclosed in porous shells so they will easily absorb smells; store them away from strong-smelling food.

Warnings

● Do not use cracked or dirty eggs.
● The egg's shell is porous and can absorb contamination from birds' feed, the laying process or through handling. Always buy where high standards of cleanliness are practised and there is a rapid turnover.

● A certain amount of heat will kill the bacteria in eggs, but often eggs are used raw (in mayonnaise, for instance) or lightly cooked. Pasteurized eggs are available and can be used for most kinds of cooking, but not for mayonnaise or lemon curd.

Stocks

What's the point of making stock? It adds a depth of flavour to sauces and soups and although it may take a while to cook, the results are well worth while and a lot better than the flavour achieved by a stock cube. The finished stock can be reduced by boiling uncovered over a high heat in a saucepan with a large surface and then frozen as ice cubes for later use.

Below: *a good brown stock will enrich many soups and stews*
Right: *ham stock adds flavour to lentil and bacon soup*

Basic techniques

● Do not add salt. When the stock is reduced the flavour will be concentrated, so add salt only to the finished soups, casseroles and sauces.

● Simmer the stock, partially covered, and remove the scum frequently. Adding a cup of cold water to the ingredients will bring froth to the surface.

● Leave to cool in the pan and skim off as much fat as possible before removing bones. Strain into a bowl and remove the remaining fat when cold.

● Raw bones, often available free from a butcher, make a stronger-flavoured stock than the ones that come from the remains of a roast joint.

● Raw meat, with a lot of blood in it, helps to make the liquid rich and clear.

● Veal bones make a stock that sets to a firm jelly, which keeps longer than liquid stock.

● Reboil stocks every two or three days if refrigerated to stop them going bad; every day if kept in a larder.

Fish

Fish stock

Strain and reduce this and use as the basis of a sauce, or make into aspic to glaze fish that is to be served cold. Cod, plaice or salmon can be substituted for fish trimmings, the addition of crab legs and prawn shells will add extra flavour, and 2 glasses of wine can be substituted for some of the water.

Makes 1.5 litres/2½ pints stock

What you need:

● 2–3 sticks celery
● 2 onions
● 1 carrot
● bones and trimmings of 2–3 sole
● 1 bay leaf
● 2 litres/4½ pints water

Skin and slice the vegetables. Add ingredients to a large pan, bring to the boil and simmer, uncovered, for 30–45 minutes.

Meat

Brown stock

Use this for strongly flavoured meat and vegetable soups, add to stews, casseroles, mince dishes and meat sauces. Fry the bones, meat scraps, vegetables until a dark even brown but never let them burn or scorch.

Makes about 1.8 litres/3 pints

What you need:

● 1.5 kg/3 lb beef or veal knuckle bones
● 375 g/12 oz shin of beef
● 3 litres/5 pints water
● 2 sticks celery, chopped
● 2–3 carrots, chopped
● 2 onions, chopped with the skins on
● 2 leeks, chopped
● 2 tomatoes

- 2 cloves
- sprig fresh thyme or ¼ teaspoon dried
- 1 bay leaf
- 1 glass red wine (optional)

1 Brown the knuckle bones in the stockpot, pour off the fat and retain. Add the water and bring slowly to the boil. Simmer for 2–3 hours, skimming frequently.
2 In a separate saucepan, fry the vegetables (including the onion skins) in some of the fat until brown. Drain off the fat and add the vegetables to the stockpot with the remaining ingredients. (Adding the onion skins gives the stock a good colour.)
3 Simmer for 2 hours and then strain and leave to cool. Remove any fat when the stock is cold.

Chicken stock

Use this more delicate stock for risottos and those soups, stews and sauces that need substance but not a strong flavour.
Makes 1 litre/1¾ pints

What you need:

- 2 onions, peeled and chopped
- 1 carrot, chopped
- 2 sticks celery, chopped
- 1 leek, chopped
- handful of parsley stalks
- 1 bay leaf
- 5–6 peppercorns
- 2 chicken carcasses, jointed with skin but not fat
- 1 veal bone
- sprig of fresh thyme or ¼ teaspoon dried
- about 2 litres/4 pints water

1 Put all the ingredients into a large pan. Cover with the water and bring slowly to the boil.

2 Skim off any scum or fat. Simmer for 3 hours, skimming frequently. Strain, cool and take off any fat.

Ham stock

Use this as a basis for soups made with pulses.
Makes 1 litre/1¾ pints

What you need:

- 1 ham bone
- 1 large onion stuck with a clove
- 2 sticks celery, chopped
- 2 carrots, chopped
- 1 bay leaf

Cover the ham bone with cold water, bring to the boil, add the vegetables and bay leaf and simmer for 3 hours. Strain and cool.

Vegetables
Light vegetarian stock

Use this for delicate soups and sauces, risottos and for all vegetarian dishes.
Makes 1 litre/1¾ pints

What you need:

- 250 g/8 oz onions, chopped
- 250 g/8 oz carrots, chopped
- 2 stalks celery, chopped
- 1 clove garlic, crushed
- 1 small turnip, chopped
- cauliflower or broccoli stalks, chopped
- 1.8 litres/3 pints water
- handful of parsley stalks
- 2 sprigs fresh thyme or ½ teaspoon dried
- 1 bay leaf

Put all the ingredients into a saucepan. Bring to the boil and simmer gently for 1 hour. Strain.

Sauces

The basic rule for sauces is that they should have a good flavour and texture and be made from the best ingredients. Defined as 'liquid seasoning for food', they should enhance or complement whatever you are serving. Success comes from knowing your way confidently round the simple methods that are used to make flour-based and butter- or oil-based sauces.

Above: *onions, garlic and different herbs for flavouring sauces*

Flour-based sauces

Most savoury sauces thickened with plain flour incorporate it into the sauce in the form of a roux, a liaison of flour and butter. These are the white sauces like béchamel (made with milk), the 'blond' sauces like velouté (made with white stock) and the sauces made with brown stock.

Béchamel sauce

Makes 300 ml/½ pint

What you need:

- 300 ml/½ pint milk
- 25 g/1 oz butter
- 25 g/1 oz plain flour
For the infusion:
- ½ small onion, halved
- 1 small carrot, halved
- ½ celery stick, cut into small pieces
- 1 small bay leaf
- 1 bouquet garni
- 4 black peppercorns
- pinch of grated nutmeg
- pinch of salt

1 Put the milk and all the infusion ingredients into a saucepan. Slowly bring to the boil. Remove from the heat, cover and leave until cold. Strain the milk through a fine sieve and discard the flavourings.
2 Melt the butter in a heavy-based saucepan over gentle heat. Add the flour and stir well with a wooden spoon to make the roux. Do not allow it to colour. Gradually add one-third of the infused milk, blending well and stirring constantly.
3 Gradually blend in the rest of the milk. Bring to the boil, stirring well, and cook for a further 2 minutes. Season to taste.

Velouté sauce

Makes 300 ml/½ pint

What you need:

- 20 g/¾ oz butter
- 20 g/¾ oz flour

Variations

- *Mornay: off the heat, stir in 50 g/2 oz grated Gruyère or Parmesan. Use with chicken, veal, eggs, fish, pasta and vegetables.*
- *Egg: stir in 1–2 finely chopped hard-boiled eggs and 1–2 tablespoons chopped parsley or chives. Use with fish.*
- *Mushroom: gently fry 125 g/4 oz mushrooms in 25 g/1 oz butter, drain and stir into the sauce with a squeeze of lemon juice. Use with fish, meat and poultry.*
- *Parsley: stir in 2 tablespoons finely chopped parsley, cook for 2 minutes. Use with bacon, fish, eggs and vegetables.*

- 300 ml/½ pint chicken, veal or fish stock
- 1 egg yolk
- 2–3 tablespoons cream
- salt and white pepper

1 Melt the butter in a saucepan until foaming. Stir in the flour and cook for 5 minutes until the roux is straw-coloured.

2 Bring the stock to the boil and gradually stir into the roux. Bring to the boil, season with salt and pepper and simmer for 15 minutes, whisking, until the sauce is the correct consistency.

3 When the sauce is thick and smooth, enrich with egg and cream just before serving. To avoid it curdling, remove the pan from the heat, mix a little of the hot liquid with the egg and cream before stirring it into the sauce. The sauce may be returned to the heat to heat through, but do not let it boil.

Alternative method

An alternative way of making sauces is to use a wire whisk. Use the same ingredients for béchamel and velouté sauces.

Put the liquid into a saucepan and whisk in the flour until thoroughly blended. Continuing to whisk, add the butter and bring gently to the boil.

When it is just bubbling and thick, turn the heat down and whisk well. Season to taste.

Brown sauce

A brown roux is made from oil or clarified butter (melted butter strained through muslin). If the butter is not clarified, it is likely to burn. It is important to use a well-flavoured stock, and always use cold stock as this helps to clear the sauce by causing the

scum to rise. The sauce can be frozen unless you've used frozen stock.
Makes about 450 ml/¾ pint

What you need:

- 3 tablespoons oil or clarified butter
- 1 small onion, finely diced
- 1 small carrot, finely diced
- ½ stick celery, trimmed and finely diced
- 15 g/½ oz plain flour
- 1 teaspoon tomato purée
- 600 ml/1 pint brown stock
- 1 bouquet garni
- salt and pepper

1 Heat the oil in a saucepan, add the onion, carrot and celery and cook for 5–7 minutes, stirring constantly, until they are on the point of changing colour.

2 Stir in the flour, reduce the heat and cook for 15 minutes until the roux is a rich brown, stirring constantly. Remove from the heat, cool slightly and stir in the tomato purée.

3 Return to the heat and gradually stir in two-thirds of the stock. Slowly bring to the boil, whisking constantly. Add the bouquet garni, salt and pepper and half-cover with the lid. Simmer for about 35–40 minutes, skimming the surface frequently. Add half the remaining stock, bring to the boil and skim again. Simmer the stock for 5 minutes, half covered. Whisk in the remaining stock, bring to the boil without stirring and skim again. Strain into a clean pan, bring back to the boil and skim until clear. Season with salt and pepper and use as required.

Variations

- *Aurore: whisk in 2 tablespoons tomato purée, season, remove from the heat and whisk in 35 g/1 ¼ oz butter. Use with eggs, chicken, pork, fish, veal.*
- *Caper: stir in 1 tablespoon lemon juice and 1 tablespoon chopped capers. Use with fish.*
- *Tarragon: put 150 ml/ ¼ pint white wine, 3 tablespoons chopped tarragon and a finely chopped shallot into a pan, and heat to reduce to 1½ tablespoons. Strain into the sauce and simmer for 2–3 minutes. Off the heat, stir in 15 g/½ oz butter and another 3 tablespoons of chopped tarragon. Use with eggs, fish, chicken and vegetables.*

Above left: *Spinach pancake and asparagus in cheesy béchamel sauce*

Butter- and oil-based sauces

Hollandaise, which uses egg yolk and butter and is served hot, and mayonnaise, served cold and made with egg yolk and oil, are thought to be tricky but a food processor or liquidizer makes them foolproof.

● The type of oil used determines the flavour. A vegetable oil will give a blander flavour than olive oil.
● Vinegar also varies the flavour.
● All the ingredients should be at room temperature.

Hollandaise sauce

Makes about 300 ml/½ pint

What you need:

● 250 g/8 oz lightly salted butter
● 3 egg yolks
● 1 tablespoon water
● 1 tablespoon lemon juice
● ¼ teaspoon salt
● pinch of cayenne pepper

Variations

● *Bearnaise: bring a tablespoon of vinegar to the boil with a teaspoonful each of chopped shallot and fresh tarragon. Strain and add the vinegar in place of the lemon juice. Serve this sauce with steaks and with strong-flavoured fish.*
● *Maltaise: substitute the juice of half an orange for the lemon juice. Use with fish, asparagus and other vegetables.*

Melt the butter in a pan with a pouring lip until it begins to foam. Place the egg yolks, water, lemon juice and seasoning into the food processor or liquidizer and blend at high speed for a few seconds. With the motor running, pour the butter, except for the residue at the bottom of the pan, very slowly in a continuous stream on to the egg mixture. When all the butter is amalgamated, the sauce should be thick and creamy. Season to taste and serve with asparagus, broccoli or poached salmon. If you don't want to use butter, you can use yogurt or crème fraîche.

Mayonnaise

Makes 450 ml/¾ pint

What you need:

● 1 egg
● ¼ teaspoon salt
● ½ teaspoon dry mustard
● 1 tablespoon wine vinegar
● 300 ml/½ pint olive oil

1 Crack the egg into the liquidizer or processor, add salt and mustard. Process for 30 seconds, then add the wine vinegar and blend again.
2 With the motor still running, pour in the oil in a thin steady stream. The sauce will thicken after 150 ml/¼ pint oil has been added. Continue to add the oil until it has all been absorbed.
3 Scrape the mayonnaise into a bowl with a rubber spatula and store, covered, in the refrigerator.

Using wine to deglaze the sediments in a pan

Remove the cooked meat or fish and keep warm. Pour off any

Variations

● *Aïoli: mix 3 cloves crushed garlic with the egg, and use equal quantities of olive and sunflower oils. Serve as a dip with crudités, or raw vegetables.*
● *Verte: blanch 25 g/1 oz fresh herbs, 25 g/1 oz watercress and 50 g/2 oz spinach for 2 minutes in boiling water. Refresh under cold running water, dry and pound or liquidize to a purée. Pass through a sieve and stir into 125 ml/ 4 fl oz mayonnaise. Serve this green sauce with cold fish and shellfish.*
● *Tartare: stir 1 tablespoon each chopped capers, gherkins, fresh herbs and 1 finely chopped hard-boiled egg into 125 ml/4 fl oz mayonnaise. Serve tartare sauce with fish, deep-fried mushrooms and shellfish.*

unwanted fat from the pan, but keep the juices. Pour a little dry or medium wine into the pan and over heat scrape up the sediment, dissolving it into the liquid. Reduce the wine down till only a glaze is left on the pan's base. Then add a tablespoon of butter, swirling it round the pan until incorporated, add any residue juices from the meat or fish, season and serve. Or, instead of butter, use fresh double cream or crème fraîche.

Gravy

Skim off all the fat from the roasting pan without losing any of the juices. Use a sheet of kitchen paper to remove the last traces of fat.

Pour in 300 ml/½ pint stock and bring to the boil, scraping

the bottom of the pan to loosen any sediment. Boil for a moment or two and season to taste. If a thicker gravy is needed, add a little arrowroot, slaked with water, or some mustard and whisk well. Strain the sauce into a warm gravy boat.

Tomato sauce

For a quick tomato-based sauce, make use of the ready-prepared passata sauces (sieved tomatoes), or add whole or chopped plum tomatoes. To these, you can add all sorts of other ingredients to make a special sauce, such as fried minced beef (bolognese); gently fried finely chopped baby mushrooms; clams (alle vongole); or peeled prawns. The addition of 1 tablespoon of tomato purée will thicken it slightly, while 2 tablespoons of cream or crème fraîche will make it richer.

Aids to success

- Use a heavy-based pan to prevent scorching.
- Cook the roux thoroughly, stirring well, to prevent a 'raw' taste in the finished sauce.
- Whisking helps to prevent lumps and gives the sauce a shiny glaze.
- Add seasonings during cooking, not at the end, so that maximum flavour is absorbed.
- If the sauce is too thick add, a tablespoon at a time, milk, cream or stock.
- If you are enriching with egg, cream or butter, add off the heat and just before serving to prevent curdling or separating. Do not reboil.
- Always taste before serving.
- If the sauce is made in advance, cover the surface with clingfilm to prevent a skin forming.
- Sauces can be kept covered in the refrigerator for about 3 days.
- To thicken sauces at the last minute, use cornflour (which may taste floury), farina (potato starch) or arrowroot, all of which need to be cooked only very briefly. Mix 1 teaspoon with cold water to make a thin paste. Stir into the sauce a little at a time over heat. It will thicken at once.

Dressings

Salads are a wonderful way of providing the essential minerals or vitamins that are lost in the cooking process. The crunchy texture of raw vegetables, the subtle colours of mixed salad leaves, the contrast between flavour and texture of fruit in a spicy dressing, and the subtlety of marinated beans, rice or pasta all make for interesting meals. Prepare the dressings and store them in the refrigerator so that there is always an interesting one to hand.

Below: *keep a selection of good-quality oils and vinegars in your storecupboard*

Oils

Salads are the best medium to appreciate the greenish-golden colour and beautiful fruity flavour of extra virgin oil that comes from the first cold pressing of the olives. Virgin oil is the next grade down, followed by blended oils from subsequent pressings. Generally Spanish has a strong flavour, Provençal is fruity and Italian nutty, while Greek has a heavy texture.

● Sunflower oil, light, mild and thinly textured, can be used with more expensive oil when making delicate salad dressings and is the best oil for those recipes where a fairly neutral oil is required.

● Walnut oil, cold pressed from dried walnuts, has a deliciously nutty flavour and is expensive. It does not keep well once opened, so buy in small bottles, refrigerate and allow it to warm up before use.

● Hazelnut oil is delicately flavoured, lighter than walnut and particularly good in salads containing fruit.

Vinegars

● Wine vinegar is ideal for salad dressings and can be red or white. If it is stronger than you like, dilute it with a little wine of the same colour.

● Cider vinegar has a strong distinctive taste and in sharpness is midway between wine and malt vinegars. It is good used in dressings for tomato or potato salad.

● Sherry vinegar is made from sweet sherry. Use half and half with lemon juice in a vinaigrette to give a nutty taste, almost like walnut oil. Use in dressings if you don't want to add sugar.

● Herb vinegars are easy to make. Allow 1 tablespoon of fresh herbs to 600 ml/1 pint wine vinegar. Place the herbs – tarragon, mint, basil or thyme – in a jar, cover with vinegar and keep in a warmish place for a week, giving the jar an occasional shake. Decant into a bottle and add a sprig of the herb.

● Garlic vinegar is made by crushing cloves of garlic and leaving in vinegar for 24 hours. Use in salads with anchovies and capers.

Vinaigrette

This is the most commonly used dressing. It can be used with any type of salad.
Makes 100 ml/3½ fl oz

- 1 tablespoon white wine vinegar or tarragon vinegar
- 1 small teaspoon Dijon mustard
- 1 large clove garlic, sprinkled with salt and crushed
- 5 tablespoons extra virgin olive oil
- salt and pepper

Put the vinegar into a small bowl, and stir in the mustard and garlic. Add the oil, gradually beating it in with a teaspoon or fork. It should blend thoroughly with the other ingredients. Season with salt and pepper to taste.

Cider vinaigrette

Use with potato or tomato salad.
Makes 325 ml/11 fl oz

- 4 tablespoons cider vinegar
- 1 teaspoon Dijon mustard
- ½ teaspoon salt
- ½ teaspoon sugar
- 250 ml/8 fl oz sunflower oil

Mix the vinegar, mustard, salt and sugar together until the salt and sugar are thoroughly dissolved. Add the oil and blend or shake until thoroughly mixed.

Herb vinaigrette

Use for green bean salads, or dress warm pasta or rice and leave to cool.
Makes 300 ml/½ pint

- 50 ml/2 fl oz lemon juice
- 50 ml/2 fl oz white wine or cider vinegar
- ½ teaspoon sugar
- 2 teaspoons finely chopped parsley
- 2 teaspoons finely chopped chives
- 2 teaspoons finely chopped basil
- 250 ml/8 fl oz sunflower oil

Put the lemon juice, vinegar, salt, sugar and herbs in a liquidizer or jar and process or shake to dissolve the sugar. Add the oil and process or shake again.

Yogurt dressing

Use for potato salad or coleslaw.
Makes 175 ml/6 fl oz

- juice of 1 lemon
- ½ teaspoon sugar
- ½ teaspoon salt
- 3 tablespoons salad oil
- 6 tablespoons plain yogurt

Mix the lemon juice, sugar and salt until dissolved. Add the oil and whisk in the yogurt. Allow this to stand for 30 minutes before using.

Blue cheese dressing

Use on any mixed salad.
Makes 350 ml/12 fl oz

- 125 g/4 oz Roquefort or Danish Blue cheese, crumbled
- 125 ml/4 fl oz milk
- 4 tablespoons salad oil
- 1 tablespoon white wine vinegar
- 1 level teaspoon sugar
- salt and pepper

Put all the ingredients in a liquidizer or food processor and blend until smooth. If the dressing is too thick, add a little more milk until the mixture is the texture of very thick cream. Season to taste.

Honey and lemon dressing

Use this when making salads containing fruit. It is also good with white cabbage salads.
Makes 275 ml/9 fl oz

- 150 g/5 oz cottage cheese
- 150 ml/¼ pint low-fat yogurt
- juice of 1 lemon
- 50 ml/2 fl oz runny honey
- 1 teaspoon finely chopped onion
- 1 teaspoon paprika
- 1 teaspoon celery seed

Put all the ingredients in a liquidizer or food processor and blend until the dressing is smooth and creamy.

Salad hints

- Always tear salad leaves: if you cut them they go limp.
- All salad stuff should be washed in cold water and then dried in a salad spinner, or with a tea towel or kitchen paper.
- After washing, refresh in the refrigerator for 15 minutes, the leaves will crisp up.
- Prepare salad dressing and toss the leaves in it just before serving otherwise they will go limp.
- Salads of tomato and spring onion and red or white cabbage benefit from marinating in the dressing for an hour or so before serving.
- Add dressings to salads of beans, pasta and rice while still warm so that as they cool they absorb the full flavour.
- A food processor or liquidizer will mix the oil, vinegar and flavourings thoroughly and they won't separate out easily.
- Dressings can be put in a screwtop jar and just shaken until well mixed.
- Make dressings and keep them in the refrigerator for a week or more, using as necessary.

Pastry

The different forms of pastry are given their distinctive texture and taste by the proportions of flour, fat and water and the method of making. The handling of the ingredients and the mixed dough is very important – lightness of touch, speed of work and the coolest of conditions are all essential for successful pastry making combining to make rich yet light pastry.

Below: *Profiteroles*
Right: *Covering, sealing and edging a pie*
Far right: *Peach and honey pie*

Ingredients

● Fats: butter gives a crisp, rich shortcrust pastry with a good flavour. Use cold, straight from the refrigerator, cut into tiny cubes or coarsely grated. Solid vegetable fat has good shortening qualities, works well used in equal quantities with butter. Low-fat spreads do not work well as they contain water. Oil makes the pastry soft to handle but gives it a crumbly texture.

● Flour: use plain all-purpose white flour; self-raising to give a soft, thicker crust; wholewheat will give a nutty flavour but is more difficult to work with so it is often mixed in equal quantity with white flour. Always sieve before using.

● Liquid: the less the better. Water gives crispness and firmness, too much makes the pastry easy to handle but cooks to a very hard crust. Add egg or egg white to give a firm, not hard crust, and egg yolk for a rich, soft, crumbly crust.

Techniques

● Rubbing in: keep everything as cool as possible, including your mixing bowl. Rub the fat into the flour using your fingertips until it is the texture of breadcrumbs. Shake the bowl so that large pieces of fat come to the surface and rub again. Dough should be handled as little and as lightly as possible, as over-rubbing makes large oily crumbs and tough pastry.

● Adding liquid: make a well in the mixture, sprinkle in some liquid and mix in using a fork, add more liquid if necessary. Stop mixing when it holds together in lumps. Lightly flour your hands and quickly gather the pastry into a ball, rolling it around the bowl to pick up any remaining crumbs.

● Kneading: using a light touch bring the outside edge of the dough into the centre, rotate anticlockwise until the bottom and sides are smooth. Turn the dough over, wrap and rest.

● Resting: prevent pastry shrinking by covering it and chilling for at least 30 minutes before rolling out or baking.

● Rolling out: lightly dust the work surface with flour. Roll in short strokes in one direction only, but not to the edge. Rotate the dough 90° after each rolling to stretch the dough evenly. Over-stretching causes shrinkage.

● Lining a flan tin: roll dough to a size that will cover base and sides. Roll round a rolling-pin, lift over the flan and unroll. Ease into the base and up sides.

● Baking blind: this stops the

pastry base from rising. After lining the flan tin, prick the base with a fork to release trapped air. Cover the base with greaseproof paper, fill with ceramic or dried beans. Bake for 10 minutes, remove the beans, return to the oven for 5 minutes. Fully baked cases can be used when a filling only requires reheating.

● Temperature: all pastry needs a hot oven. If the temperature is too low the pastry will be tough and heavy. If too hot, the outside will brown while the inside stays soggy. The usual temperature is 200°C (400°F), Gas Mark 6; puff pastry and filo need a hotter oven, 220°C (425°F), Gas Mark 7.

Variations

- *Sweet shortcrust, add a tablespoon of icing sugar to the flour mixture. Use for sweet pies and tarts.*
- *Pâte brisée: this French shortcrust is crumbly and can be rolled more thinly: 150 g/5 oz plain flour; 65 g/2½ oz butter; ½ teaspoon salt; 1 egg yolk; 1–2 tablespoons cold water. Mix all ingredients together as in the main recipe. Use for both savoury and sweet pies and flans.*
- *Pâte sablée: French sweet shortcrust, as above, use 125 g/4 oz plain flour and add 50 g/2 oz sugar. Use for sweet pies and tarts.*

Types of pastry

Freshly made pastry can give the most wonderful results if you have the time, but many of the ready-made pastries now available work just as well.

Shortcrust

This is the easiest of all pastry doughs and a favourite for both savoury and sweet pies.
Preparation: 15 minutes plus chilling time.

What you need:

- 175 g/6 oz plain flour
- pinch of salt
- 75 g/3 oz butter
- 2–3 tablespoons water

Mix the flour, salt and butter together by hand or in a processor until the mixture resembles fine breadcrumbs. Add the water a tablespoon at a time until the dough binds together. Knead it carefully, wrap in clingfilm and chill for 30 minutes.

Choux

Preparation: 30 minutes
Cooking: 25 minutes

What you need:

- 250 ml/8 fl oz water
- 50 g/2 oz butter
- 150 g/5 oz flour

1 Preheat the oven to 220°C (425°F), Gas Mark 7. Grease a baking sheet.
2 Bring the water to the boil, turn off the heat, add the butter and leave to melt. Put the flour in a food processor and, with the motor running, pour on the water/butter mixture to form a paste. Return the paste to the pan, cook, stirring for 3–4 minutes. Return the paste to the processor bowl, start the motor and add the eggs one by one.
3 Place tablespoonfuls of pastry on the baking sheet and bake for 25 minutes or until golden. Remove and prick each to let the steam out. Split, fill and serve.

Food processor method for shortcrust

Cut the fat into small pieces. Add all the ingredients except the liquid and process for 10–15 seconds. Add the liquid and process until the mixture balls up around the knife. Do not over-process as the paste will become sticky and taste greasy.

Pastry to buy

- Filo: this gossamer thin pastry, used for strudel, samosas and other sweet and savoury fillings, can be bought in packets, either fresh or frozen. When using it, work with a few sheets at a time, making sure to keep the others covered to prevent drying out. Each sheet of pastry should be brushed with melted butter or oil. To fit a dish of a specific size, simply overlap by 2.5 cm/1 inch. Filo can be deep-fried or baked. Frozen filo will defrost quickly, and can be refrozen.
- Flaky and puff: save time and buy these ready-made, either butter or vegetarian based, fresh or frozen. Puff pastry is very similar to flaky pastry. Both pastries are time-consuming to make yourself with difficult techniques to master plus some skill and patience to achieve acceptable results.
- Pastry cases: these come in different sizes and flavours and are worth buying ready-made particularly if you are short of time or planning to feed a large number. Available fresh or frozen, and easy to use.

Bread

There is nothing quite like the warm fragrance of baking bread. It is like riding a bicycle: once learned, never forgotten. The recipes given here are easy and once you have mastered them, you will find that they can be adapted for other breads. The secret is to practise and to understand how the dough reacts as you handle it. You do need time to prove bread, leave it to rise while you get on with other things. And while it is baking, savour the fragrance.

Below: *Flower pot loaves*
Right: *Unrisen and risen dough*
Far right (top to bottom): *Tin loaf, Bloomer, Short baton, Coburg, Cottage loaf*

Ingredients

● Yeast: fresh should be beige, crumbly-soft and also be sweet smelling. Yeast will keep for 5 days loosely wrapped in the refrigerator. Dried yeast must be 'sponged' in some liquid to reconstitute it.

● Flour: strong flour is best for bread-making. Wholemeal, or wholewheat flour produces a heavier loaf which will not keep as well as a white loaf. A mixture of both wholemeal and white flour works well.

Techniques

● Kneading: dough must be pushed and pulled to develop the gluten. Place on a lightly floured surface and stretch the dough using heel of one hand to push away, knuckles of the other to pull towards you. Fold, give dough a quarter turn and repeat. By hand, it takes up to 10 minutes for dough to

become smooth and elastic. A food mixer with a dough hook takes less time.

  ● Knocking back: risen dough is punched with the knuckle to push out air. Punched to its original size, it is then kneaded briefly before being shaped.

  ● Shaping: to make buns knead pieces of dough, cup your hand over the dough and then rotate it, gradually straightening your fingers until the ball is smooth. Loaves can

be made in any shape – to secure the top section, press a wooden handle through to the work surface. Prove the bread on greased baking trays or in tins and then glaze.

● Proving: this second rising is given after the dough has been knocked back and shaped. It is placed on greased tins, covered with oiled polythene or a damp tea towel and left until doubled in size – either in a warm place (not too hot or the yeast will be killed) or overnight in the refrigerator. The more slowly dough rises, the more even the texture of the bread.

● Glazing: beaten egg yolk gives a crusty finish and holds toppings in place. Sweetened milk gives a shiny, sticky surface.

● Baking: bread continues to rise in the oven for a short time. After 20 minutes the loaf's shape will be set and you can glaze this part with egg yolk and return to finish cooking.

● Doneness: turn out of tin, tap the base. If it sounds hollow it is cooked, if not return to tin to finish cooking.

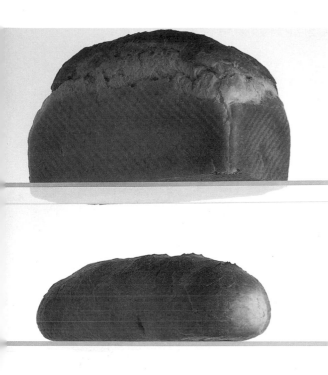

Wholemeal rolls

Makes 8
Preparation 45 minutes, plus rising and proving
Cooking: 20 minutes

What you need:

- 20 g/¾ oz fresh yeast, or ½ sachet dried
- 300 ml/½ pint lukewarm milk
- 1 teaspoon caster sugar
- 250 g/8 oz wholemeal flour
- 250 g/8 oz plain flour
- 1 teaspoon salt
- 50 g/2 oz butter

1 If using fresh yeast, dissolve the yeast with a little of the milk and the sugar in a small bowl. Warm a large mixing bowl and sift the flours, dried yeast if using, and salt into them.
2 Pour in the fresh yeast mixture, all the milk (this applies to both yeast methods) and the beaten egg and mix to a fairly slack dough.
3 When the dough leaves the sides of the bowl, press it into a ball and tip out on to a lightly floured board.
4 Knead for about 15 minutes until it is elastic, smooth and shiny. Put the dough back in the bowl, cover with oiled polythene or a damp tea towel and leave in a warm place for 1 hour until doubled in size. Take the dough out of the bowl, punch down and knead again for 10 minutes.
5 Preheat the oven to 220°C (425°F), Gas Mark 7. Divide the dough into 8 pieces and shape them all into flattish ovals. Put the ovals on a floured baking sheet and allow them to prove for 15 minutes. Bake for about 20 minutes or until firm.

Ciabatta

This Italian-style bread is deservedly popular. You can use the dough for pizza by adding an extra tablespoon of oil at the second kneading. Then divide the dough in half and spread out with your hands on a baking sheet until 5 mm/¼ inch thick all over. Add toppings, prove for 15–20 minutes and bake in a preheated oven, 220°C (425°F), Gas Mark 7, for 15–25 minutes.

Makes 2 loaves
Preparation: 15–20 minutes, plus rising and proving
Cooking: 40 minutes

What you need:

- 15 g/½ oz fresh yeast or ½ sachet dried
- pinch of sugar
- 300 ml/½ pint warm water
- 4 tablespoons olive oil
- 1 teaspoon salt
- 500 g/1 lb strong white flour

1 Cream fresh yeast and sugar with a little warm water and leave for 10 minutes until frothy.
2 Mix oil and salt into flour and dried yeast, if using. Add fresh yeast mixture and knead for 1–2 minutes. Gradually add remaining water, making sure dough does not become too moist.
3 Brush a tablespoon of oil in the bowl, roll dough in it. Cover with a damp tea towel or clingfilm. Let rise for 45–50 minutes.
4 Knock down and knead again, ensuring oil is incorporated. Halve and roll out to 23 cm /9 inches. Flatten on baking sheet, leave to rise for 35–40 minutes.
5 Bake in a preheated oven, 220°C (425°F), Gas Mark 7, for 40 minutes.

Utensils

Left and above:
A stainless steel folding steaming platform which adjusts to fit most pan sizes is a very useful cookware item if you don't have a steamer unit in your saucepan range. Steaming allows you to cook food quickly and retain a high proportion of flavour and nutrients.
This shallow saucepan is made from stainless steel and has a heat diffusing base – a thick layer of aluminium sealed in a stainless steel casing – which ensures even cooking and cuts down on energy consumption. The rim is gently curved to prevent liquids boiling over.

Above:
Vitreous enamelled cast iron cooking pots last a lifetime. Useful ones to have are gratin dishes and casseroles. If used on top of the stove, heat the pan very slowly over low-to-medium heat.

Below:
Stainless steel deep casserole with a 5-layer base which allows food to be steam-cooked without fats or oil. Evaporation is prevented by the heavy weight of the well-fitting lid.

Pots and pans

For long-term wear buy the best saucepans you can afford. Stainless steel with a copper base, or a thick layer of aluminium, is a combination that is hard to beat and will give you a lifetime's service. Buying cheap pans is a false economy – they quickly burn and soon reach the throwing-away stage. Good pans should be well balanced, easy to hold, have welded handles and lids that fit tightly. You will need about 3–4 in the range of 1–7 litres/2–12 pints.

Left:
Pans that do double duty, like this shallow casserole/sauté pans are a blessing to cooks with limited storage space. This comes from the same range as the casserole above and can take a steamer insert or a second pan, which would make it into a double saucepan.

Dry-frying, using a cast-iron grill pan is fast, direct and simple. The pan is heated until very hot and the seasoned food cooked directly on the ridged surface, producing extra flavour where food comes into contact with intense heat. It can be done with no fat or with food that has been marinated.

Above and below right:

Plain steel pans are best for making omelettes and pancakes, and a lidded frying pan with a heat-resistant handle can be used on the stove or in the oven. If you want to use slightly less oil or butter, heat the pan for 2–3 minutes over moderate heat before adding the oil or butter. Do not heat an empty pan over a high heat because this simply makes the pan too hot too quickly and will mean your ingredients dry out and burn. To season steel pans, heat slightly and wash to remove protective coating. Dry and reheat with cooking oil to a fairly high temperature. Run oil over base and up sides to cover whole area. Cool and wipe out surplus. To prevent ingredients sticking to the pan, move them around the pan with a non-scratch implement, handle fragile ingredients with care.

Above:

If you love pasta then you will need a pot that is large enough so that it can cook in plenty of boiling salted water with enough room for it to move without sticking. This 7 litre/12 pint pot is large enough for 7–8 portions and is fitted with a stainless steel draining basket. Its thick base means this saucepan can also be used for making stock, soups and stews.

Cleaning stained pans

● Burned pans: cover burned matter with water, add 2 tablespoons of salt or vinegar, bring to the boil and leave overnight.

● Enamel pan stains: add 600 ml/1 pint water, add 1 teaspoon of bleach and leave for 2 hours. Wash and rinse thoroughly.

● Discoloured aluminium: boil a weak solution of rhubarb, tomatoes or lemon peel in it.

● Stainless steel: clean with a gentle bristle brush, warm soapy water, polish when dry.

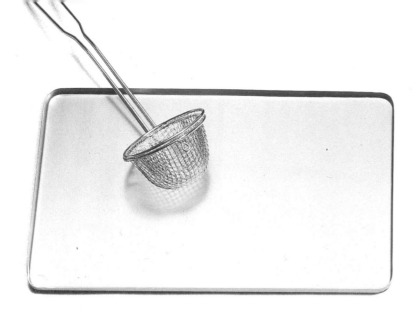

Above and above right:
The biscuit/baking sheet has raised sides which prevent anything sliding off when the tin is removed from the oven. Resting on it is a deep-frying basket for use when you are making samosas, doughnuts or potato baskets. Use the bakepan for cakemaking or as a bain marie when you are baking custards.

Lining tins

Cakes with long cooking times require a greaseproof lining for the sides and bottom. Cut a long strip 5 cm/2 inches higher than depth, fold one long edge in 2.5 cm/1 inch, then make cuts at intervals. Place cut edge down in greased tin, then grease paper. Line Swiss roll tins using one sheet of paper, make 45° angle slits into corners, fold edges in 2.5 cm/1 inch, then raise to make a 90° angle at corners. Secure with paper clips.

Below:
A tin of individual pie shapes can be used for small quiches, fruit tarts or Yorkshire puddings. It has a hard-wearing non-stick finish, nevertheless it is better always to oil the surface lightly before use.

Above:
Roasting tins should be smooth and have no seams or crevices in which fat can collect or germs breed. Those with a rolled top edge or a generous rim are easy to lift. A roasting rack keeps meat or poultry from frying in fat.

Tins and sheets

When food is placed in the dry, hot atmosphere of the oven, it is cooked equally from all directions, and the containers do not have to withstand and conduct heat from an intense source as saucepans do. The function of a baking tin is to mould and contain and to respond as fast as possible to the temperature of the oven. The shape of the tin you use depends entirely on what you are baking and what you want it to look like.

Some baking tins have bright shining surfaces, which deflect the heat away from the contents so they will not scorch, other tins have dark finishes which absorb and hold the heat and need a slight temperature reduction to achieve the same results.

Tin plate is most widely used for baking containers. Aluminium, a good conductor of heat, is more expensive than tin. Non-stick surfaces, applied to either tin or aluminium, are hard-wearing but can easily be damaged by metal implements. Clean by soaking in water and then wipe with a soapy cloth and rinse.

Choose tins that are sturdy, smooth inside with no crevices for trapping food, and with rolled edges that will make them easier and safer to handle. Never use abrasives or steel wool on your bakeware, and see that it is washed, dried and aired thoroughly in a warm dry place and given a light coating of cooking oil before storing. You can expect a lifetime's wear from good–quality tins and constant use will give them a dark protective patina.

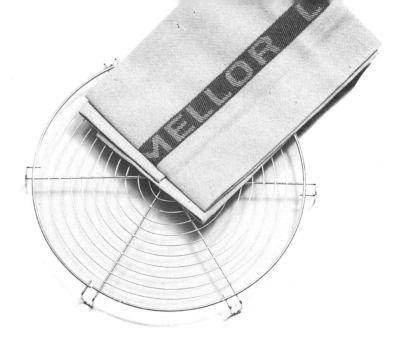

Above right:

Deep quiche tins, in three sizes, have loose bottoms which makes the job of removing the cooked quiche much easier. They also mean that you can put the tin base on to a plate for serving. If you want to lift the quiche off the base for any reason, use two broad turners or egg slices to support the bottom of the flan.

Below:

Flan moulds can be used for sponges or pies, some have fluted edges and a choice between removable or fixed bases, some are deep – like those shown here – others are shallow. Fluted rings can be difficult to clean because food sticks to them, so always soak them in hot water after use. Flan tins are preferable to porcelain flan dishes as they conduct heat very well which prevents soggy pastry.

Above right:

Cooling racks are either circular, specifically for cakes, or rectangular for all types of baked food and are meshed to allow good circulation of air. They are used for cooling cakes and biscuits without allowing them to sweat. It is better to buy one that is larger than you think you need, and it should stand fairly high. If leaving food – especially cakes – overnight, cover with a tea towel to prevent it becoming crusty and dry. Once out of the oven leave the cakes or biscuits in their baking tins for a little time before removing them to a cooling rack. Cakes, biscuits and pies can be very tender and are liable to crumble if handled too soon after removal from the oven. Allowing them to cool for about 20 minutes is usually sufficient but these timings can vary depending on the size of the cake, pie or biscuits and the length of time in the oven.

Below:

A small 12 cm/5 inch tart tin is very useful to have as a standby. Often extra pastry from a baking session can be used to line it, and it is also a good size to freeze as a pastry case, the larger ones take up more room and can be damaged more easily. Small tins are good for individual tarts, and can be ready when the cook needs them for a quick meal! Small tins are also useful when you want to present family or guests with individual portions, which can be attractively garnished or decorated on the plate.

Right:

Cake tins can have loose bases or spring clips. When using the latter, make sure the base fits into the groove at the side and won't move or allow the mixture to escape. Place the base rim side up on the worktop, place round above it and then close clips. Bases can then be greased and floured or based lined.

Above right:

Individual flan pans, 9 cm/3½ inch in size, are just right for baking blind and filling with delicious concoctions for stunning starters or filled with fruit for desserts. You can also use them as buffet party and picnic food pastry cases

Below:
Wooden spatulas and spoons are the perfect tools to use in non-stick pans. The slanted straight end will fit against the sides of pans and bowls, making it easy to remove all the food.

Above, left to right:
A ladle for serving soups and sauces and for jam-making. The kitchen spoon has a pouring lip which can be helpful for pouring batter. The disc skimmer will move over the surface removing fat from liquid and scum from jam and stock.

Metal turners must be able to slide under food without causing damage and be broad and firm enough to support them as they are turned or lifted from the pan. Perforations in the turner will allow excess fat or oil to escape.

A metal fork with long tines will hold meat firmly while it is being lifted from a roasting pan or casserole. A carving fork should have a guard.

Mesh skimmers are better than solid perforated disc ones for scooping food that is being deep-fried because the oil can drain freely through the mesh and mesh skimmers will not lower the temperature of the oil.

Spoons and stirrers

The wooden spoon is one of the most useful tools in the kitchen. It is invaluable for beating, mixing and stirring, it will never burn your hand because wood is a very bad conductor of heat, it will not scratch or wear away saucepans, and it is quiet and strong in use. The best ones to use are those made of a close-grained wood which is not likely to split. The design of wooden spoons has been honed by cooks over the centuries, and you will find shapes for all sorts of purposes but especially useful are those whose bowl has a fairly thin edge that can get right to the bottom corner of steep-sided saucepans.

Metal spoons are used for transferring food quickly from pan to dish, gently folding together delicate mixtures and last-minute taste checks on soups and sauces. Wood should not be used for this because it can retain the flavour of its last use.

Whisks introduce air, emulsify and blend ingredients or thicken those substances containing fat, and they are wonderful for rescuing lumpy sauces. Metal skimmers, ladles, slices and perforated spoons all have their own particular roles to play, and these are the items that you are likely to buy as your needs arise.

Keep all these items close to your hob. Many of them have hooks or loops for hanging and can be kept on racks, but wooden spoons are most usefully kept in a jar where they will be ready for immediate use.

Below, left to right:
Olive wood deep server; tasting spoon; kitchen spatulas; and a selection of stirrers, long handled ones makes the best beaters, use those with short handles for mixing as well as stirring.

Above, left to right:
A large, heavy-duty balloon whisk is the chef's answer to dealing with egg whites, but you need a very strong arm to use it; the classic size whisk is the one most often used for making sauces, but many people prefer to use the flat one next to it. This can be used in jugs and will also whisk egg whites on a plate.

Cut a flourish with this swizzle stick which, used in an up - and - down movement, will froth liquids, but can also be used to mix dressings for salads as well as whisking up cocktails.

The round balloon and the small egg whisks are good for sauces if you are using a small saucepan, but the larger one is better for mayonnaise and for whisking egg whites, it does not need the strength required by the large balloon whisk. When whisking whites start beating from the bottom of the bowl, lifting the whisk high in a circle to incorporate as much air as possible.

You want to take air into your egg whites as you whisk so that they are really light to taste. This will mean the dish you take the whisked egg whites into will be light also. When the whites start foaming increase the size of the circles, using the whole bowl, and whisk as fast as you can. When stiff, whisk down in the whites to stiffen, rather than incorporate air, and continue until a shallow peak holds its shape.

   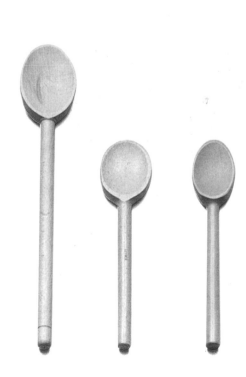

Below left and right:
Almost a classic piece of equipment, this small rotary grater makes quick work of cheese and herbs. Hand-held graters need to be chosen carefully, they should rest firmly on a flat surface or sit in a bowl without slipping or sliding. The different kinds of surfaces should be able to grasp tough or brittle foods and cut smooth slices or slivers from softer cheeses and vegetables. The grated food texture is controlled by the size of the cutting holes. Use them carefully to avoid grating your knuckles.

Below:
Kitchen scissors should be very sharp, strong and made of stainless steel and the lower handle large enough to take the last three fingers of the cutting hand. A serrated edge will give an extra bite to the first cut and blades should cut evenly right down to the tips. Have them professionally sharpened when they become blunt.

Above:
Poultry shears make light work of cutting through gristle and bone, either during preparation or serving at the table. The pointed tips enable the shears to reach and operate effectively in small, awkward places.

Left:
Herbs can be finely chopped in this wooden bowl. It is a version of the pestle and mortar, still the most effective method for pulverizing nuts, garlic, berries, seeds and herbs. Use a wooden bowl for crushing dry food but not for anything that exudes moisture because the pungent juices will impregnate the wood.

Cutting and carving

Essential tools in the kitchen are good sharp knives that are comfortable to hold, they take the hard work out of food preparation making it a keen pleasure rather than a troublesome chore. Six or seven knives will provide you with a good selection that will enable you to deal easily and swiftly with various tasks. All of them should be stored where you can see them, get at them swiftly and return them after use ready for the next time, so a knife box or a wall-fixed rack, inaccessible to children, is ideal. Keeping knives in drawers will damage their blades and you may also cut your hand.

Choose a knife that feels comfortable in the hand, heavy and well balanced. The part of the blade that extends into the handle should run the whole length and be securely riveted in place. Although expensive, high-carbon stainless steel knives are good buys, they last a long time, hold a very fine edge and can easily be cleaned. Carbon-steel knives are quite easy to sharpen but rust and discolour.

Knives should always be kept in razor-sharp condition. A blunt knife is frustrating and dangerous to use – it performs badly, needing a great deal of force, and it can easily slip out of control. One of the best methods for sharpening knives is to use a hand-held steel and draw the blade lightly down it at a shallow angle, between 18–20°. Put the knife first to the front of the steel, then the back. The steel should have a small guard or hilt to protect the hand. A few strokes every time you use the knife will keep it very well sharpened (see illustration opposite).

Chopping boards

It is best to have at least two chopping boards, one made from a hard wood, such as maple, which you can use for most tasks, and the other to be kept for the preparation of raw meat. This board should be made from a white non-porous material which can be cleaned with hot water and a little bleach. Always remembers to wash boards and knives between handling raw and cooked food.

Choose wooden boards at least 4 cm/1½ inches thick, ideally the grain on the main part of the board should run in the opposite direction to that on the reinforced ends. Melamine boards may look attractive when new, but their hard surfaces soon blunt knife blades and may cause knives to slip. Apart from your basic chopping boards, other useful ones are a round board specially for bread, a rectangular cheese board with a slot for a knife and a small cutting board for lemons.

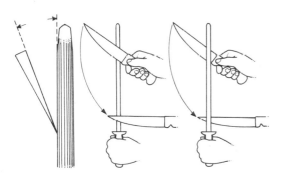

Above: *Sharpening a knife. For full instructions see previous page.*

Below, left to right:
Steel: *The traditional way of sharpening knives is to use a*
sharpening steel. Keep a knife sharpener in the kitchen and use it often.
Bread knife: *choose one with a fairly long blade with deep serrations as this will be most efficient.*

Carving fork: *this is used to lift roast meat and keep it steady while carving. It should have a guard to prevent the knife slipping. The long, straight tines are essential for bigger roasts.*
Carving knife: *used together with the carving fork for cutting thin slices from roast and cooked meat.*
General kitchen knife: *a general-purpose knife usually 15–25 cm/ 6–10 inches long. Use for chopping, slicing, paring and cutting.*
Cleaver or chopper: *this is the heaviest knife, which comes in various sizes. It is used for chopping through*

bone. It has a very broad rectangular blade, which can be used for crushing garlic – place the garlic under the cleaver on a board and hit the blade. It may also be used to flatten sliced meat.
Paring knife: *designed to peel fruit and vegetables. It usually has stainless steel blades 7.5 cm/3 inches long, plain or serrated.*
Other speciality knives
other knives have very specific purposes.
Palette knife: *a knife with a very flexible, round-ended blade in different sizes; used for spreading jam butter-cream and icing over cakes.*

Filleting knife: *this has a flexible, pointed blade to follow the contours of the fish, lifting flesh off the bones.*
Grapefruit knife: *this is a small knife with a double-serrated curved edge for loosening grapefruit flesh.*
Canelle knife: *this has a short flat blade with a U-shaped indentation, used to cut strips of lemon or orange rind or to create patterns in the peel of cucumbers and other vegetables.*
Oyster knife: *this has a very short, broad, pointed blade and usually has a guard. It is used for opening oysters and other shellfish.*

Straining, sieving and measuring

Things that measure and strain liquid, squeeze and purée, sift and shake allow you that extra precision when you are following recipes. At first glance there seems little difference between one kind of strainer, colander or sieve and another, but it is only through use in the kitchen that the cook can discover just how well designed and useful the different types can be. As in other kitchen tools, these items can sometimes double up in function: a colander can be used as a steamer, the asparagus slice (below) for fish, and handsome shakers and jugs will go from kitchen to table.

Measuring jugs are essential in these days of international recipe exchange when it is only too easy to become confused by cups, pints and litres (see opposite page). It has to be said that however casual the addition of ingredients to a recipe might seem, cookery, is in fact an exact science, so care taken in accurate measuring is repaid by the taste and appearance of the cooked product.

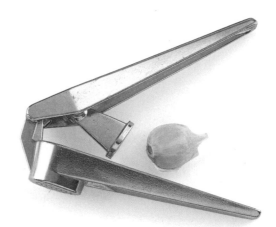

Below left and below:
Stainless steel long handled colander has a stable base and can be held firmly while draining pasta or vegetables. Stainless steel wire colander will look good on the table, but its shape also allows it to be used as a steamer.

Above:
Garlic is an essential addition to many recipes but is very fiddly to prepare. This garlic crusher makes it an easy job, you don't need to peel the clove and when the hammer is released the debris clings to it and can be easily removed.

Below:

Lemon squeezers are often puny little things, with room for the juice of only one lemon at a time. This one, in stoneware, has a nice capacious bowl, is sturdy so you can really apply pressure to the lemon and looks good enough to be taken from the kitchen to the table.

Right:

Storing things in the kitchen can be a real problem. It has recently been fashionable to hang things from the ceiling, but if the items are low enough to be really useful, they are dangerous for the unwary heads of tall people! In the end, it is probably most practical to have a secure rail fitted close to your hob on which things can be hung from sturdy butcher's hooks. Securely attached to a wall, this iron bar is strong enough to take heavy pans.

Below:

Simple traditional French stoneware jugs in two sizes, 900 ml/1½ pint and 1.5 litres/2½ pints fulfil a useful function in storing liquids prior to refrigeration. The glaze will not craze or fade because of the high temperature at which they are fired.

Opposite page below left and this page right below:

Round fine mesh stainless steel strainers can be used for sifting tasks as well as straining and puréeing. For sifting, never fill too full and knock side of frame gently against palm of hand. If you cook asparagus in a shallow pan rather than an upright steamer, a slice will lift it out and drain off liquid. Use it for fish, too. A funnel is good for transferring liquids from one container to another.

Below left:

A light dredging of fine sugar or cocoa powder is often the only finish a cake or sponge needs. To add interest, sift icing or caster sugar over a paper doily and then carefully lift it off.

Right:

A Pyrex measuring jug is the most useful item to have. The toughened glass will withstand boiling liquids and you can see very clearly exactly how much is in the jug. Because it is a poor conductor of heat, the handle remains cool. However, it is also helpful to have plastic jugs which are marked for liquids and solids and in which you can measure small amounts of fluid.

Measuring

American ingredients are measured in cup sizes, a precise volume of 250 ml/ 8 fl oz; Europeans measure dry ingredients by weight, liquids in litres and the English Imperial pints and gallons are not the same as the American measures. It is essential to have an accurate measure in your kitchen and to always follow one set of measurements.

Barbecue equipment

Come the first warm day of spring or summer and out comes the barbecue attended by all its accessories. This most popular form of outdoor entertaining is great for everyone but the cook who spends much of the time getting hot and bothered and spattered with fat. Nevertheless, barbecued food tastes great and engenders everyone with a healthy appetite.

There is no other option than to go about it with good humour and to see if there are ways of making it an efficient operation. The result of which is to be showered with praise and exclamations of, 'What a lovely time we've had, when shall we have another one?'

Barbecuing is a healthy and exciting way of cooking with many inspiring accompaniments and a taste not achieved by any other cooking method.

Left:
A stainless steel barbecue designed to eliminate the need for firelighters and starter fluids. The combination of the chimney, which concentrates the heat, and the ventilation holes, which create a powerful draw present a fail-safe method of igniting charcoal. Simply put crushed newspaper in the chimney, spread charcoal on the hearth, light the paper and start cooking 20–25 minutes later. Slots on the wind-shield make it possible to raise or lower the grill as needed.

Barbecue preparation

Buy good–quality charcoal and store it in a dry place. Charcoal absorbs moisture readily and won't burn well if damp. Line the barbecue with foil to reflect heat and make it easy to clean later. Pile the charcoal in a pyramid and light (never use petrol and never lean over the grill when lighting). Light the fire in plenty of time to get hot. Leave until covered with white ash and then spread the embers. If you can hold your hand over the heat for 10 seconds it isn't warm enough for cooking.

Above:
Well–made turner, fork, knife and tongs with exceptionally long handles keep your hands safely away from the heat. Other useful items would be long flat skewers for kebabs, then food will not be able to skid round them; a bristle brush for basting food (man-made fibres can melt or burn) and a meat grill.

Right:
Fish can fall apart or, if small, can be difficult to turn over on the barbecue. A double-sided grill, like this 66 cm/26 inches long one, has folding legs for standing on the barbecue and easily holds a large fish or several smaller ones, carefully placed within.

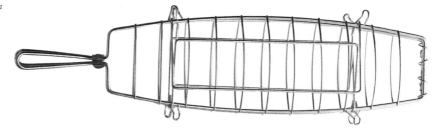

Above:

Care needs to be taken with tablewear taken outdoors, because it is usually placed on the ground and accidents can happen only too easily. Keep an eye on the safety factor when choosing tumblers. These, for instance, are made of tough, chip-resistant Duralex glass.

Above right:

When you are eating outdoors, cheese, butter, meat and anything sweet or creamy needs to be protected from flies and wasps. This food cover, an old-fashioned idea but up to date in its hygiene applications, is made of fine, tinned wire mesh.

Food tips

Marinades tenderize, prevent undue drying and add flavour. Pre-cook food when you can, and finish off on the barbecue. Salt draws out moisture, so save it for last-minute seasoning. Cook beef rare or medium rare; veal and lamb medium to well done; pork thoroughly; poultry thoroughly, the juices should run clear when pierced with a skewer; sausages thoroughly; fish opaque and until the flesh comes away easily from the bone. Be sure to keep raw and cooked food apart and prepare on different work surfaces.

Above:

Grape-decorated earthenware wine cooler with glazed rim, lends a suitable rustic look to outdoor drinking. Soak the cooler in cold water before placing the bottle inside to keep cool. Excellent, too, for riverside picnics.

Right:

When you are cooking outdoors you need a work surface for preparation and serving, the foldaway table solves the problem admirably. The reversible top is made of hardwood and one side is smooth, the other, which has a groove running round it, becomes a large carving board.

Left:
The enjoyment in eating steak goes if you have to battle with a less-than-sharp knife and a fork with unsatisfactory tines. Look for serrated stainless steel blades, resin-impreg-nated wooden handles which are smooth and well-balanced, and a fork with sturdy tines.

Right:
Hurricane lanterns, like this one made of tin-coated steel, provide a safe, easily adjusted flame for hours on one filling of paraffin. Although at night the light might draw the moths, it is generally believed that the smell of paraffin keeps mosquitoes at bay.

Oriental cooking

A Chinese cook has described stir-frying as being like a conjuror , magically changing – in the twinkling of an eye – raw pieces of food into a succulent and fragrant dish. She said there was nothing more therapeutic than stirring away in the wok to get rid of any pent-up emotions or tensions, nor was there anything more gratifying than to have a wokful of goodies to share and enjoy with family and friends.

Oriental techniques appear simple, but they actually require great mastery in order to get them just right. The practice, though – as in so many things that are worth doing right – is sheer delight.

Another advantage of stir-frying is that it is one of the healthiest of all cooking methods, requiring very little oil. Food is cooked until it is still crisp – never mushy – and therfore retains a great deal of its flavour, texture and colour.

On this page are some of the tools that you need for this particular form of cookery.

Above and top:
Non-stick, substantial wok with two handles with a draining rack and chopsticks, and a heavy natural steel one with handle, drainer and bamboo rice paddle. Both measure about 35 cm/ 14 inches which is wide and deep enough for all wok cookery techniques.

A new steel wok has a protective film of grease. Remove the film by filling wok with water and boiling for 30 minutes. Scrub wok with an abrasive, rinse and dry over heat for 5 minutes. When cool, wipe both sides thoroughly with vegetable oil. Clean after each use; wash with water, using a mild detergent if necessary, and a clean cloth or soft brush. Dry and rub off with oil.

Above:
A tava, fry pan, used for cooking Indian chapati. These are made from wholewheat flour and water, rolled out very evenly and then cooked on the smoking hot steel pan and finished over an open fire to make them puff up.

Left:
Wok-turner, based on a classic oriental design, is a cross between a scoop and a stirrer. Cleaver is used to slice, cut, shred and mince vegetables, meat and bones. Porcelain grater minces ginger root.

Above left:
Terracotta baking brick for Indian breads or pizzas retains heat for serving. Chinese scouring brush for cleaning a wok. Oriental ladle for serving soups and a noodle spoon/server.

Above:
Bamboo steamer with slatted steaming basket. Stand the steamer in the wok, add the basket with food wrapped in leaves or on a plate, add boiling water to within 2.5 cm/1 inch of the base and cover with the wok lid. Turn up the heat; fish should cook very quickly.

Gadgets

Every cook has a collection of tools, bought because they seemed a good idea at the time but in fact rarely use. On this page, we share with you some of the 'good ideas' that are in everyday use.

A good collection of kitchen tools is invaluable and will save you both time and money in the long run. It is worth spending as much as you can afford to on good–quality equipment which will perform the necessary tasks quickly and easily at the times you need them most.

There are numerous gadgets to perform every imaginable kitchen task. Before you buy any new equipment think about what you will be using it for: some of tools are versatile enough to be used for a number of tasks. The other consideration is what you will be using the tool for, the more often you think you will be using it, the stronger it needs to be. If you are thinking about buying a big piece of equipment consider where and how you can store it to prevent it being damaged when not in use.

Above:
Citrus squeezer with ample room for pith and pips to prevent overflowing. Base has a lip on both sides.

Right:
Wooden lemon squeezer is just the thing to keep by the hob. Lemon juice is indispensable, just a few drops of juice will bring out the flavour mayonnaise and salad dressings, to smoked salmon, fruit dishes, various kinds of sauces and fish and poultry.

Left:
If you cannot afford a food processor, the next best kitchen aid is the stainless steel Mouli. A classic design, it has been available for generations of cooks. It will purée babyfood and vegetables for soups, make fresh sauces from tomatoes and acid fruit and makes the very best potato purée. It comes with coarse, medium and fine discs.

Below:
Mill for peppercorns has hardened steel grinders that can be adjusted from very fine to coarse. It is simplicity itself to refill and is made of metal alloy. Black peppercorns are mild and aromatic; white ones are hot and less fragrant. A few allspice berries added to your grinder along with black peppercorns will give an extra spicy flavour.

Above:
Apple flans, for good presentation, really need to have apples sliced into neat pieces and it can be quite tricky. So welcome to this little gadget which really does deserve a home. Simply push the slicer which has stainless steel blades through the apple and it will divide it into 14 segments. It also cores it at the same time.

Below:
Can openers are essential kitchen equipment. This design has a butterfly action, and is also fitted with a useful piercer. This makes it possible to drain juices or liquids from cans without losing any of the contents, or having to tip them into a sieve.

Below:
Two fruit utensils. The lemon zester, on the left, cuts slivers from all citrus fruit in a matter of seconds. The orange peeler removes the pith, cuts strips and also peels. The two tools make the preparation of dishes such as caramelized oranges and lemon meringue pie very much simpler.

Below:
Even the design of the humble potato peeler has variations, and here are three of them. Left, swivel-blade for left- or right-handed use. Centre, traditional steel blade. Right, stainless steel blade for left- or right-handed use.

Food processors

These remarkably versatile machines are only worth having if kept on a worktop, with accessories readily to hand. When you buy one make a point of using it in some different way, every couple of days. That is the only way to build up your understanding of how it works and just how time-saving and helpful it can be. Using it in this way will also mean that when there is a real rush on in the kitchen you will be able to use it to advantage and be fully in charge of the situation. And when it comes to washing up, there is only a bowl, lid and blades which take no time at all.

A liquidizers can be bought as an attachment to a food processor, but it is useful to have one as a separate machine, because it is actually easier to deal with small quantities in this. Food for the baby, for instance, is easily puréed in a goblet rather than in a bowl which can leave a ring of ingredients round the edge.

Safety points

The double-bladed knife, the food processor's basic tool, is very sharp. It is important that you remove it from the bowl before you tip out the food inside it, to prevent the blade falling out and giving you a nasty cut.

Above left:
The Magimix 2100 will cover all your basic everyday cooking activities. It comes with shatter-proof bowl and stainless steel blades; it will chop, grate, knead dough, liquidize, purée and slice. Included as accessories are the master and dough blades, slicing/grating disc, and egg whisk. There are other extra tools you can buy.

Above right:
The Magimix 4000 is for the larger family, but one of its accessories is a mini processor for small quantities. The bowl has the capacity to make 1.25 kg/2½ lb dough or a seven egg sponge, and included with it is an extra julienne disc for vegetables, a slicer, coarse grater and citrus press.

Above and below right:
Two classic American designs, the Waring Professional Blender with a heavy-duty motor and a thick glass jar holds 1.2 litres/2 pints and is heat resistant. Full marks for its ability to crush ice. The Kitchen Aid Mixer has a stainless steel bowl, heavy stable base, ten mixing speeds, beater attachment, dough hook and wire whisk

Soups

Soups come in all manner of guises. They can be thin and light, they can be thick and chunky, they can be hot or cold, they can be vegetarian, meaty or fishy, they can be no more than a taster to sharpen your appetite at the beginning of a meal or they can be a hearty meal in themselves. Whatever your taste and whatever the occasion, there is bound to be something here to suit you.

Red pepper soup

Serves 4–6
Preparation: 15 minutes
Cooking: 25–35 minutes
Carbohydrate: 17 g, Protein: 4 g, Fat: 4 g, Fibre: 3 g, Calories: 119 kcal, Sodium: 529 mg (per portion)

What you need:

- 1 tablespoon sunflower oil
- 1 large onion, chopped
- 2 garlic cloves, finely chopped
- 2 tablespoons dry sherry
- 3–4 red peppers, deseeded and chopped
- 1 potato, diced
- 2 tablespoons tomato purée
- 2 large tomatoes, skinned and sliced
- 1 litre/1¾ pints stock
- salt and pepper

To garnish:
- 2–3 tablespoons natural yogurt
- cracked black peppercorns
- sprigs of chervil

1 Heat the oil in a large saucepan and fry the onion for 4–5 minutes, stirring occasionally. Stir in the remaining ingredients and season to taste.

2 Bring to the boil, cover and then simmer for 20–30 minutes. Purée the soup in a blender or food processor, or rub through a sieve. Reheat gently and adjust the seasoning if necessary. Garnish each bowl of red pepper soup with swirls of yogurt, a sprinkling of cracked peppercorns and a few sprigs of chervil. Serve the soup piping hot.

Cook's Tip

For carrot soup, replace the red peppers with 3–4 carrots. Use chicken or vegetable stock in this recipe.

Left: *Red pepper soup*

Split pea and ham soup

Serves 8
Preparation: 10–15 minutes
Cooking: 40–45 minutes
Carbohydrate: 58 g, Protein: 24 g,
Fat: 22 g, Fibre: 6 g, Calories: 507 kcal,
Sodium: 560 mg (per portion)

What you need:

- 25 g/1 oz butter
- 1 onion, chopped
- 1 carrot, diced
- 500 g/1 lb yellow split peas, rinsed
- 250 g/8 oz cooked ham, cut into chunks
- 2 bay leaves
- 1 celery stick
- 1 garlic clove, crushed
- 125 ml/4 fl oz double cream
- salt and pepper

To garnish:

- croûtons (see Cook's Tip)
- double cream

1 Melt the butter in a large saucepan and fry the onion and carrot for 2–3 minutes, stirring occasionally. Then add 2 litres/3½ pints water and the split peas and bring to the boil. Add the ham, bay leaves, celery, garlic and seasoning. Cover and simmer gently for 40–45 minutes.

2 Discard the bay leaves, then purée the soup in a blender or food processor – you will have to do this in batches. Return the puréed soup to the cleaned pan, stir in the double cream and reheat gently, without boiling, stirring constantly. Taste and adjust the seasoning if necessary. Garnish with a few croûtons and a swirl of double cream.

Pumpkin soup

Serves 6
Preparation: 20 minutes
Cooking: 40–50 minutes
Carbohydrate: 27 g, Protein: 14 g,
Fat: 26 g, Fibre: 2 g, Calories: 385 kcal,
Sodium: 498 mg
(per portion)

What you need:

- 50 g/2 oz butter
- 750 g/1½ lb pumpkin, deseeded and cut into chunks
- ½ teaspoon grated nutmeg
- ½ teaspoon dried thyme
- 1.5 litres/2½ pints milk
- 50 g/2 oz rice
- salt and pepper

1 Melt the butter in a large saucepan. Add the pumpkin and cook for 10 minutes, stirring occasionally. Add the nutmeg, thyme and salt and pepper to taste, then add 150 ml/¼ pint water, cover and cook over a high heat until the pumpkin is tender.

2 Purée the pumpkin mixture in a blender or food processor, or rub through a sieve.

3 Return the pumpkin purée to the cleaned pan, then add the milk and rice and cook, covered, for 20–30 minutes until the rice is cooked, stirring occasionally.

Cook's Tip

To make croûtons for 4–6 people, cut the crusts from 2 slices of bread and cut into 1 cm/½ inch cubes. Heat 2 tablespoons butter and 2 tablespoons oil in a frying pan; when it is hot, add the bread and fry for 1–2 minutes, stirring frequently, until the bread is crisp and golden. Drain well.
For garlic croûtons, crush 1–2 garlic cloves with 1 teaspoon salt. Add to the frying pan when the bread is nearly cooked.

Left: *Split pea and ham soup*
Right: *Pumpkin soup*

Variation

Curried pumpkin soup

Cook the pumpkin in 2 tablespoons oil with 1 onion, 1 green pepper and 2 garlic cloves (all chopped), until softened. Add a little chopped fresh ginger, 2 teaspoons chilli powder and 2 teaspoons turmeric and cook for 2–3 minutes, stirring frequently. Add 150 ml/¼ pint water, cook till pumpkin is tender, then purée. Simmer the purée with 400 ml/14 fl oz coconut milk, 900 ml/1½ pints water and the rice.

Soupe au pistou

Serves 8
Preparation: 15 minutes
Cooking: 1 hour 5 minutes
Carbohydrate: 50 g, Protein: 25g,
Fat: 14 g, Fibre: 8 g, Calories: 408 kcal,
Sodium: 460 mg (per portion)

What you need:

- 250 g/8 oz green beans, sliced
- 250 g/8 oz fresh or dried haricot beans
- 1 onion, finely chopped
- 3 courgettes, sliced
- 4 potatoes, diced
- 4 tomatoes, skinned, deseeded and chopped
- 2 litres/3½ pints hot water
- 250 g/8 oz shell pasta
- salt and pepper

For the pistou:
- 3–4 garlic cloves, peeled
- 15–20 fresh basil leaves
- 2 tablespoons olive oil
- 250 g/8 oz grated Parmesan cheese

1 Put all the beans, onion, courgettes, potatoes and most of the chopped tomatoes in a saucepan. Cover with the hot water and season. Bring to the boil, reduce the heat and simmer for 45 minutes.

2 Meanwhile, make the pistou. Place the garlic, basil leaves and remaining tomato in a mortar and crush with a pestle. Add the olive oil, half the Parmesan and salt and pepper and make a smooth paste. After 45 minutes, add the pasta to the soup and continue cooking over a low heat for a further 15–20 minutes.

3 To serve, stir half the pistou into the hot soup. Ladle the soup into individual bowls and top with grated cheese and more pistou.

Right: *Soupe au pistou*

Vichyssoise

Serves 6
Preparation: 15 minutes, plus
3 hours chilling
Cooking: 35 minutes
Carbohydrate: 36 g, Protein: 11 g,
Fat: 34 g, Fibre: 6 g, Calories: 482 kcal,
Sodium: 675 mg (per portion)

What you need:

- 1 kg/2 lb leeks
- 50 g/2 oz butter
- 1 onion, chopped
- 1 litre/1¾ pints chicken or
  vegetable stock
- 750 g/1½ lb potatoes, diced
- pinch of grated nutmeg
- 600 ml/1 pint milk
- 300 ml/½ pint single cream
- 150 ml/¼ pint double cream,
  chilled
- salt and white pepper
- small bunch of fresh chives,
  to garnish

1 Cut off the green tops of the leeks and discard. Slice the white parts thinly. Melt the butter in a large saucepan. Add the leeks and onion, and fry over a medium–low heat for 5 minutes, stirring constantly, until soft.
2 Add the stock and potatoes,

Below: Vichyssoise
Above right: Tomato
and courgette soup

nutmeg and seasoning to taste. Bring to the boil, reduce the heat and simmer, partially covered, for 25 minutes. Add the milk and simmer for a further 5–8 minutes.
3 Purée the soup in a food processor – you will have to do this in batches – then rub through a sieve into a bowl. Add the single cream, then cover and chill in the refrigerator for at least 3 hours.
4 To serve, swirl in the double cream, taste and adjust the seasoning. Garnish with chives.

Tomato and courgette soup

Serves 4
Preparation: 15 minutes, plus
3 hours chilling
Cooking: 15 minutes
Carbohydrate: 11 g, Protein: 4 g,
Fat: 8 g, Fibre: 3 g, Calories: 124 kcal,
Sodium: 533 mg (per portion)

What you need:

- 3 tablespoons olive oil
- 1 garlic clove, crushed
- 1 kg/2 lb ripe tomatoes,

skinned, deseeded and chopped
- 2 tablespoons tomato purée
- 1 tablespoon chopped fresh basil
- 750 ml/1¼ pints chicken stock
- 2 courgettes, coarsely shredded
- salt and pepper

To garnish:
- 4 ice cubes
- 3 tablespoons natural yogurt
- basil leaves

1 Heat the oil in a saucepan, add the garlic, tomatoes and tomato purée and cook over a low heat for 10 minutes. Stir in the basil, stock and seasoning.
2 Bring to the boil, then reduce the heat, cover and simmer for about 5 minutes.
3 Purée the soup in a food processor, then leave to cool. Stir in the courgettes, cover and chill in the refrigerator for at least 3 hours, or overnight.
4 To serve, place an ice cube in each bowl, then pour in the soup and add a swirl of yogurt and a few basil leaves.

That's
entertainment!

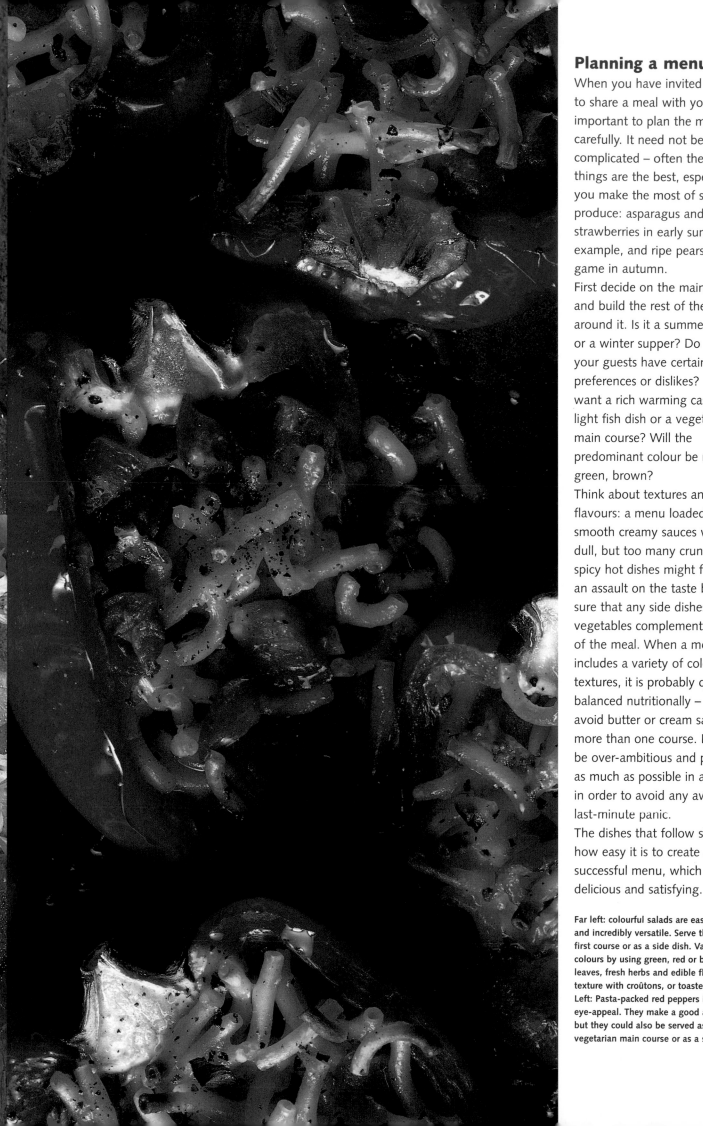

Planning a menu

When you have invited people to share a meal with you, it is important to plan the menu carefully. It need not be complicated – often the simplest things are the best, especially if you make the most of seasonal produce: asparagus and strawberries in early summer, for example, and ripe pears or rich game in autumn.

First decide on the main course and build the rest of the menu around it. Is it a summer lunch or a winter supper? Do any of your guests have certain preferences or dislikes? Do you want a rich warming casserole, a light fish dish or a vegetarian main course? Will the predominant colour be red, green, brown?

Think about textures and flavours: a menu loaded with smooth creamy sauces would be dull, but too many crunchy or spicy hot dishes might feel like an assault on the taste buds. Be sure that any side dishes and vegetables complement the rest of the meal. When a menu includes a variety of colours and textures, it is probably quite well balanced nutritionally – but avoid butter or cream sauces in more than one course. Do not be over-ambitious and prepare as much as possible in advance, in order to avoid any awkward last-minute panic.

The dishes that follow show just how easy it is to create a successful menu, which is both delicious and satisfying.

Far left: colourful salads are easy to prepare and incredibly versatile. Serve them as a first course or as a side dish. Vary the colours by using green, red or bronze salad leaves, fresh herbs and edible flowers. Add texture with croûtons, or toasted nuts.
Left: Pasta-packed red peppers have instant eye-appeal. They make a good appetizer, but they could also be served as a vegetarian main course or as a side dish.

Chocolate crumb tart with exotic fruit

Serves 6
Preparation: 20 minutes, plus chilling

What you need:

- 75 g/3 oz butter
- 1 tablespoon golden syrup
- 175 g/6 oz chocolate digestive biscuits, crushed
- 300 ml/½ pint crème fraîche
- selection of exotic fruits, such as papaya, pineapple, star fruit and pomegranate
- 2 tablespoons redcurrant jelly
- 1 tablespoon lime juice

1 Melt the butter with the golden syrup, add the biscuits and mix well. Press the mixture on to the base and sides of a greased loose-bottomed 20 cm/8 inch round flan tin. Then chill until firm.

2 Carefully remove the crumb base from the tin and place on a serving plate. Fill with the crème fraîche. Prepare the fruit and arrange over the cream.

3 Warm the redcurrant jelly with the lime juice and drizzle over the fruit.

Strawberry crumble flan

Serves 6
Preparation: 20 minutes, plus chilling

What you need:

- 75 g/3 oz butter
- 175 g/6 oz ginger biscuits, crushed
- 250 g/8 oz cream cheese, softened
- 75 g/3 oz caster sugar
- 1 teaspoon grated lemon rind
- 4 tablespoons single cream
- 375 g/12 oz strawberries
- icing sugar, for dusting

1 Melt the butter, add the biscuit crumbs and mix well. Press the mixture on to the base and sides of a loose-bottomed 20 cm/8 inch round flan tin. Chill the biscuit base in the refrigerator until firm.

2 Beat together the cream cheese, sugar, lemon rind and single cream.

3 Carefully remove the chilled ginger biscuit base from the flan tin and place on a serving plate. Fill with the cream cheese mixture, arrange the strawberries over the filling and dust with icing sugar.

French apple flan

Serves 8
Preparation: 30 minutes
Cooking: 40–45 minutes

What you need:

- 250 g/8 oz sweet shortcrust pastry

For the filling:
- 750 g/1½ lb eating apples
- 3 tablespoons lemon juice
- 4 tablespoons warmed, sieved apricot jam
- 175 ml/6 fl oz single cream
- 2 eggs, beaten
- 50 g 2 oz caster sugar

1 Roll out and line a 25 cm/10 inch flan tin. Chill the pastry case for 30 minutes.

2 Make the filling: peel and core the apples, slice thinly into a bowl and toss with lemon juice. Drain and arrange in concentric circles over the pastry case. Brush with apricot jam. Bake in a preheated oven, at 220°C (375°F), Gas Mark 7, for 10 minutes. Then lower the oven to 190°C (375°F), Gas Mark 5.

3 Whisk the single cream, beaten eggs and caster sugar in a bowl. Pour this mixture carefully over the slices of apple. Return the flan to the oven for 30–35 minutes, until the pastry is golden and the filling is cooked.

Left: French apple flan
Above: Chocolate crumb tart with exotic fruit
Right: Strawberry crumble flan
These stunning fruit tarts are easy to vary, depending on what fresh fruits are available. Use fruit singly or in combinations, such as raspberries, blackberries and sliced ripe peaches glazed with redcurrant jelly, or bananas, kiwifruit, pineapple and mango, dusted with coconut

Starters

Starters are just that: they are only the opening paragraph, the introduction to the meal, not the main part of it. As such, they should arouse interest while not providing the complete answer, they should whet the appetite rather than satisfying it. You and your guests should still be hungry and eager for the delights that the meal will have to offer next. Ideally, starters should also be quick and easy to serve, so that you are free to concentrate on the next course. Many of these recipes can be prepared in advance.

Goat's cheese and cherry tomato puff tartlets

Makes 4–6
Preparation: 15 minutes
Cooking:10–15 minutes
Carbohydrate: 13 g, Protein: 6 g, Fat: 14 g, Fibre: 1 g, Calories: 201 kcal, Sodium: 347 mg (per portion)

What you need:

- 250 g/8 oz puff pastry, thawed if frozen
- 2 tablespoons olive oil
- 250 g/8 oz cherry tomatoes, preferably a mixture of red and yellow, halved
- 250 g/8 oz firm goat's cheese, sliced
- 2 teaspoons chopped fresh thyme
- salt and pepper

1 Roll out the pastry on a lightly floured surface and cut into 7 cm/3 inch rounds. Place on a greased baking sheet and brush lightly with olive oil.

2 Arrange half the cherry tomatoes over each pastry round to within 2.5 cm/1 inch of the edge. Place the goat's cheese on top and finally arrange the remaining tomatoes. Season with a little salt and pepper to taste. Sprinkle with the fresh thyme and drizzle 1–2 tablespoons of olive oil over the top.

3 Bake in a preheated oven, 220°C (425°F), Gas Mark 7, for 10–15 minutes, until the pastry is risen, crisp and golden brown. Serve hot, accompanied by a salad of bitter leaves.

Cook's Tip

To make one big tart, cut the pastry into a 23 cm/9 inch round and place on a lightly greased baking sheet. Top as in the main recipe above and bake in the oven for 20–25 minutes. Serve piping hot either as a starter or as a light lunch.

Left: *Goat's cheese and cherry tomato puff tartlets*

French country pâté

Serves 8
Preparation: 30 minutes, plus
cooling and chilling overnight
Cooking: 1½ hours
*Carbohydrate: 4 g, Protein: 33 g,
Fat: 29g, Fiber: 1 g, Calories: 405 kcal,
Sodium: 785 mg (per portion)*

What you need:

- 50 g/2 oz butter, plus extra
  for greasing
- 2 onions, finely chopped
- 4 garlic cloves, crushed
- 500 g/1 lb pig's liver, carefully
  trimmed
- 275 g/9 oz streaky bacon
  rashers, rind removed
- 500 g/1 lb lean pork, minced
  or chopped
- 2 tablespoons chopped fresh
  parsley
- ½ teaspoon dried sage
- ¼ teaspoon ground mace
- ¼ teaspoon ground nutmeg
- 2 egg whites
- 2 tablespoons brandy
- 2 bay leaves
- salt and pepper

1 Melt the butter in a frying pan and sauté the onions and garlic gently for a few minutes until tender and golden. Transfer to a large bowl. Add the pig's liver to the pan and fry until lightly browned. Remove and mince or chop finely.

2 Chop 200 g/7 oz of the streaky bacon and add to the bowl along with the liver, pork, parsley, sage, mace, nutmeg, salt, pepper, egg whites and brandy. Mix well together until all the ingredients are thoroughly combined.

3 Line a lightly greased 500 g/ 1 lb terrine or loaf tin with the remaining bacon rashers so that they hang over the sides. Fill with the pâté mixture and fold the bacon over the top. Put the 2 bay leaves on top and place in a roasting pan of hot water. Cook in a preheated oven at 190°C (375°F), Gas Mark 5 for 1½ hours, or until the juices run clear and the pâté has shrunk slightly from the sides of the tin.

4 Leave the pâté to cool for 30 minutes, then cover with a piece of greaseproof paper or foil and weight lightly. Leave until completely cold and set. If you wish, replace the bay leaves with fresh ones. Cover and refrigerate for about 36 hours. Serve sliced with hot toast or fresh crusty bread.

Chicken liver pâté

Serves 4–6
Preparation: 20 minutes, plus cooling and chilling
Cooking: 10 minutes

Carbohydrate: 1 g, Protein: 16 g, Fat: 57 g, Fibre: 0 g, Calories: 614 kcal, Sodium: 209 mg (per portion)

What you need:

- 375 g/12 oz unsalted butter
- 2 garlic cloves, crushed
- 500 g/1 lb chicken livers,
  trimmed, chopped roughly
- 6–8 tablespoons brandy,
  according to taste
- salt and pepper
- parsley sprigs, to garnish

1 Melt 50 g/2 oz of the butter in a large frying pan over a moderate heat until foaming. Lower the heat, add the garlic and stir for 2–3 minutes until softened but not coloured.

2 Add the chicken livers to the frying pan, increase the heat to moderate again, and toss vigorously for about 5–8 minutes until the livers are browned on the outside but still tinged with pink in the centre.

3 Pour in the brandy and stir well to mix. Let the mixture bubble in the frying pan for about 1–2 minutes, then transfer to a food processor or blender. Cut all but 50 g/2 oz of the remaining butter into pieces and add to the machine. Work the mixture to a smooth purée and add salt and pepper to taste.

4 Turn the mixture into individual ramekins or a large serving bowl and smooth the surface. Melt the remaining butter in a clean pan, then pour over the surface of the pâté. Leave until cold, then cover and chill in the refrigerator overnight. Serve chilled, garnished with sprigs of parsley and accompanied by triangles of hot wholemeal toast.

Left: *French country pâté*
Right: *Chicken liver pâté*

Guacamole

Serves 6
Preparation: 15 minutes, plus
1 hour chilling
Carbohydrate: 2 g, Protein: 2 g,
Fat: 11 g, Fibre: 2 g, Calories: 110 kcal,
Sodium: 138 mg (per portion)

What you need:

- 2 large, ready-to-eat ripe avocados
- 3 tablespoons lemon or lime juice
- 2 garlic cloves, crushed
- 40 g/1½ oz chopped spring onions
- 1–2 tablespoons chopped mild green chillies or jalapeños
- 2 tablespoons chopped fresh coriander
- 125 g/4 oz tomatoes, skinned, deseeded and chopped
- salt and pepper

Below: Guacamole
Above right: *Potato skins with soured cream dip*

1 Cut the avocados in half and remove the stones. Scoop out the flesh and sprinkle with a little of the lemon or lime juice to prevent discoloration.

2 Put the avocado flesh in a mixing bowl with the remaining lemon or lime juice, and mash coarsely. Add the garlic, spring onions, chillies, coriander and some seasoning to taste. Mix in the chopped tomatoes. Cover the bowl and place in the refrigerator for at least 1 hour. Serve the dip with tortilla chips or toast.

Potato skins with soured cream dip

Serves 4–8
Preparation: 20 minutes
Cooking: 1¼ hours
Carbohydrate: 15 g, Protein: 3 g,
Fat: 11 g, Fibre: 1 g, Calories: 169 kcal,
Sodium: 217 mg (per portion)

What you need:

- 4 large baking potatoes, scrubbed and dried
- 150 ml/¼ pint soured cream
- 1 teaspoon snipped fresh chives
- sunflower oil, for frying
- coarse sea salt and pepper
- snipped fresh chives, to garnish

1 Prick the potatoes with a fork. Bake in a preheated oven, 200°C (400°F), Gas Mark 6, for about 1¼ hours until tender.

2 Meanwhile, prepare the dip. In a bowl, mix the soured cream with the chives. Season to taste. Cover the bowl and leave to chill.

3 When the potatoes are cooked, cool for a few minutes, then cut each one into quarters lengthways. Scoop out most of the potato flesh, leaving a thin layer next to the skin. (The scooped-out potato may be reserved and used to top a pie.)

4 Pour the oil into a frying pan to a depth of 7 cm/3 inches. Heat the oil to 180–190°C (350–375°F), or until a cube of bread browns in 30 seconds. Add the potato skins carefully to the hot oil. Fry for about 2 minutes until brown and crisp. Remove and drain on kitchen paper. To serve, arrange the potato skins on a plate with the dip, sprinkled with chives, in the centre.

Wild mushrooms in crispy bread cases

Serves 8
Preparation: 15 minutes
Cooking: 10–15 minutes
Carbohydrate: 10 g, Protein: 3 g, Fat: 12 g, Fibre: 1 g, Calories: 157 kcal, Sodium: 291 mg (per portion)

What you need:

For the bread cases:
- 8 thin slices bread, crusts removed
- 50 g/2 oz butter, melted

For the filling:
- 25 g/1 oz butter
- 1 shallot, chopped
- 175 g/6 oz mushrooms (chestnut, oyster, shiitake), sliced evenly

Variation

Chicken tartlets

Prepare eight bread cases as in the main recipe. For the filling, melt 25 g/1 oz butter, add 1 chopped celery stick and fry for about 3–4 minutes until softened. Then add 2 chopped rindless smoked back bacon rashers and 125 g/4 oz chopped skinless chicken breast and cook for a further 10–12 minutes until the bacon is crispy and the chicken thoroughly cooked. Remove from the heat and stir in 1 tablespoon sherry and allow the mixture to bubble in the pan. Stir in 4 tablespoons double cream and 1 tablespoon chopped parsley or 2 teaspoons chopped coriander. Add seasoning. Cook over a moderate heat for a few minutes until the mixture thickens to a sauce.

- 1 tablespoon Madeira
- 4 tablespoons double cream
- 1 tablespoon chopped fresh parsley
- salt and pepper
- assorted salad leaves, to serve

1 Brush both sides of the bread with the butter. Press firmly into 8 tartlet or bun tins. Bake in a preheated oven, 200°C (400°F), Gas Mark 6, for 10–15 minutes, until the bread cases are crisp and golden brown.

2 Meanwhile, make the filling. Melt the butter in a small saucepan, add the shallot and fry for about 5 minutes until softened. Add the mushrooms and cook for a further 5 minutes until the mushrooms are tender. Stir in the Madeira and allow the mixture to bubble briefly, then stir in the cream and chopped parsley, and season with salt and pepper to taste. Cook over a moderate heat for a few minutes more, until the mixture thickens slightly and forms a sauce.

3 Arrange the assorted salad leaves on 8 small serving plates and place a bread case on each. Fill with the mushroom mixture and serve warm.

Above: *Wild mushrooms in crispy bread cases*

Beefsteak tomato salad

Serves 4
Preparation: 15 minutes, plus
15 minutes standing
Carbohydrate: 3 g, Protein: 1 g,
Fat: 11 g, Fibre: 1 g, Calories: 113 kcal,
Sodium: 525 mg (per portion)

What you need:

- 4 beefsteak tomatoes, sliced
- 5 tablespoons extra virgin olive oil
- 2 spring onions, chopped
- 2 tablespoons chopped fresh oregano or marjoram
- a few leaves of fresh basil, roughly torn
- 50 g/2 oz black olives
- coarse sea salt and pepper

1 Arrange the tomatoes, over-lapping slightly, in concentric circles on a large platter. Drizzle the olive oil carefully over the top of the tomatoes and add salt and pepper to taste.

2 Sprinkle the spring onions over the tomatoes, together with the oregano or marjoram and the basil. Scatter the olives over the top. Leave the salad to stand for about 15 minutes before serving, to allow the flavours to mingle.

Cook's Tip

Black olives are preserved in a number of ways. The most appropriate for salads are those preserved in olive oil. However, olives in brine would be just as good.

Right: *Beefsteak tomato salad*
Centre: *Spinach and goat's cheese salad*
Far right: *Wild rice, orange and walnut salad*

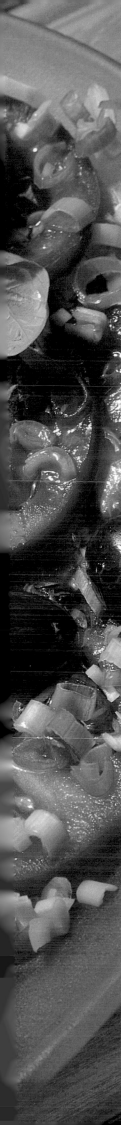

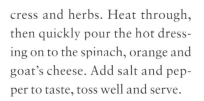

Spinach and goat's cheese salad

Serves 4
Preparation: 15 minutes
Carbohydrate: 9 g, Protein: 10 g,
Fat: 24 g, Fibre: 3 g, Calories: 289 kcal,
Sodium: 472 mg (per portion)

What you need:

- 175 g/6 oz young spinach leaves
- 2 oranges, peeled and segmented
- 175 g/6 oz goat's cheese, diced
- 5 tablespoons olive oil
- 50 g/2 oz hazelnuts, roughly chopped
- 1 garlic clove, crushed
- juice of 1 large orange
- 1 bunch of watercress, leaves stripped from the stalks, very finely chopped
- 2 tablespoons chopped fresh mixed herbs (e.g. parsley, tarragon, mint, dill, basil)
- salt and pepper

1 Combine the spinach leaves, orange segments and goat's cheese in a large salad bowl.
2 Heat the olive oil in a small frying pan, add the hazelnuts and garlic and cook for 1–2 minutes. Stir in the orange juice, water-cress and herbs. Heat through, then quickly pour the hot dressing on to the spinach, orange and goat's cheese. Add salt and pepper to taste, toss well and serve.

Wild rice, orange and walnut salad

Serves 4
Preparation: 25 minutes
Cooking: 30 minutes
Carbohydrate: 26 g, Protein: 5 g,
Fat: 41 g, Fibre: 3 g, Calories: 483 kcal,
Sodium: 205 mg (per portion)

What you need:

- 250 g/8 oz wild rice
- 2 small oranges
- 1 small fennel bulb, trimmed and thinly sliced
- 3 spring onions, finely chopped
- 50 g/2 oz walnut pieces
- 125 ml/4 fl oz vinaigrette made with walnut oil
- salt and pepper
- chopped fennel tops, to garnish

1 Bring a large saucepan of water to the boil. Add the rice, lower the heat and simmer for 30 minutes, or until tender. Drain the rice in a colander, refresh under cold running water, then drain. Transfer the rice to a large salad bowl.
2 Using a small, sharp knife, peel away the skin and all the pith from the oranges. Slice them as thinly as possible and add to the rice with the sliced fennel and spring onions.
3 Spread the walnuts on a baking sheet and toast under a pre-heated hot grill for 1–2 minutes, until they are lightly browned. Add to the salad, with salt and pepper to taste.
4 Pour over the dressing and toss lightly. Sprinkle with chopped fennel tops to garnish.

3

4

5

Minced meat samosas

Makes 12
Preparation: 1 hour
Cooking: 10 minutes
Carbohydrate: 36 g, Protein: 9 g,
Fat: 7 g, Fibre: 2 g, Calories: 234 kcal,
Sodium: 290 mg (per portion)

What you need:

For the dough:
- 500 g/1 lb plain flour
- ½ teaspoon baking powder
- 1 teaspoon salt
- 25 g/1 oz butter, melted
- 4 tablespoons natural yogurt
- about 8 tablespoons tepid water

For the filling:
- 1 tablespoon butter
- 1 small onion, chopped
- ½ teaspoon cumin seeds
- 250 g/8 oz minced beef or lamb
- 1 green chilli, finely chopped
- 1 teaspoon salt
- 125 g/4 oz cooked peas
- pepper
- 1 teaspoon chopped coriander leaves

To assemble:
- 2 tablespoons milk
- oil for deep-frying
- chutney, to serve

1 Make the samosa dough. Sift the flour with the baking powder and salt into a mixing bowl. Make a well in the centre and add the melted butter and yogurt. Draw the flour into the liquid, using a wooden spoon, adding water as necessary to make a smooth dough. Knead until free from cracks and set aside.

2 Make the filling: melt the butter in a saucepan, and fry the onion and cumin seeds over a moderate heat, stirring occasionally, for 5–7 minutes. Add the minced beef or lamb, chilli and salt. Mix thoroughly. Reduce the heat and simmer for 10 minutes.

3 Stir in the peas and continue cooking over a moderate heat for 5 minutes, or until the liquid has evaporated. Remove the pan from the heat and mix in the pepper and coriander. Leave to cool before using to stuff the samosas.

4 Divide the samosa dough into 12 equal portions, and roll out each one to a thin 18 cm/7 inch diameter circle. Cut each circle in half with a sharp knife, and then cover the semi-circles with a damp cloth while you fill them, one at a time.

5 Brush the edges of each semi-circle with a little milk and spoon some filling on to the centre. Fold in the corners, overlapping them to form a cone. Fold over and seal the top to make a triangle. Deep-fry in hot oil, in batches, until crisp and golden. Drain on absorbent kitchen paper and serve hot with chutney.

Cook's Tip

Samosas are a tasty traditional Indian snack. Indian doughs generally require much more kneading than is usual. This helps to break down the gluten in the flour and changes a sticky unmanageable dough into one that can be rolled out smoothly and thinly. Before rolling out the dough in this recipe, shape each of the 12 portions into a small ball between the palms of your hands and flatten slightly to form a disc shape.

Right: *Minced meat samosas*

Squid and green peppers

Serves 2–4
Preparation: 15 minutes
Cooking: 5 minutes
Carbohydrate: 3 g, Protein: 10 g,
Fat: 8 g, Fibre: 1 g, Calories: 118 kcal,
Sodium: 411 mg (per portion)

What you need:

- 250 g/8 oz squid
- 1 green pepper, cored, deseeded and thinly sliced
- oil for deep-frying
- 2 slices fresh root ginger, peeled and shredded
- 1 tablespoon soy sauce
- 1 teaspoon vinegar
- 1 teaspoon sesame oil
- salt and pepper

1 Clean the squid, discarding the head and transparent backbone as well as the ink bag. Wash well under cold running water and pat dry with kitchen paper.
2 Peel off the thin skin of the squid and cut the flesh into small pieces – about the size of a matchbox.

3 Heat the oil in a wok or deep frying pan until it is fairly hot. Deep-fry the prepared squid for about 30 seconds and then remove from the wok or frying pan with a slotted spoon. Carefully pour off the excess oil, leaving about 1 tablespoon of oil in the bottom of the pan. Add the ginger, pepper and squid.
4 Stir-fry for a few seconds and then stir in the salt, soy sauce, vinegar and pepper. Cook for about 1 minute, and then add the sesame oil and serve.

Steamed sea bass

Serves 2
Preparation: 10 minutes, plus soaking
Cooking: 15 minutes
Carbohydrate: 13 g, Protein: 56 g,
Fat: 8 g, Fibre: 1 g, Calories: 358 kcal,
Sodium: 2048 mg (per portion)

What you need:

- 2 Chinese dried mushrooms
- 1 x 500 g/1 lb sea bass, cleaned and scaled
- 2 slices fresh root ginger, peeled
- 2 spring onions
- 50 g/2 oz cooked ham
- 50 g/2 oz bamboo shoots
- 3 tablespoons dry sherry
- 2 tablespoons soy sauce
- 1 teaspoon sugar
- 1 teaspoon salt

1 Put the mushrooms in a bowl. Cover with warm water and leave to soak for 10 minutes. Squeeze the mushrooms dry and then discard the stalks.
2 Slash both sides of the fish diagonally, as deep as the bone, at intervals of 1 cm/½ inch. Dry the sea bass on absorbent kitchen paper and place it on a plate.

Above: *Squid and green peppers*
Right: *Steamed sea bass*
Far right: *Seafood with vegetables*

3 Thinly shred the fresh root ginger, spring onions, cooked ham, bamboo shoots and the mushrooms. Arrange them on top of the sea bass.

4 Mix together the sherry, soy sauce, sugar and salt, and pour over the fish. Place the fish on the plate in the top of a steamer set over simmering water. Cover and steam vigorously for 15 minutes. Serve hot.

Cook's Tip

Slashing both sides of the fish as described in this recipe prevents the skin from bursting during cooking. It also allows the heat to penetrate more quickly and more evenly.

Seafood with vegetables

Serves 3–4
Preparation: 20 minutes
Cooking: 5 minutes
Carbohydrate: 12 g, Protein: 25 g,
Fat: 6 g, Fibre: 2 g, Calories: 207 kcal,
Sodium: 655 mg (per portion)

What you need:

- 4–6 fresh scallops
- 125–175 g/4–6 oz headless uncooked prawns
- 1 egg white
- 1 tablespoon cornflour
- vegetable oil for deep-frying
- 3 celery sticks, sliced
- 1 red pepper, deseeded and sliced
- 1–2 carrots, sliced
- 2 slices fresh root ginger, peeled and shredded
- 2–3 spring onions, chopped
- 2 tablespoons sherry
- 1 tablespoon light soy sauce
- 2 teaspoons chilli bean paste
- 1 teaspoon salt
- 1 teaspoon sesame oil, to finish

1 Cut each scallop into 3 or 4 pieces. Peel the prawns and remove the black vein running along the back. Leave whole if small, or cut into 2 or 3 pieces if large. Put all the scallops and prawns in a bowl together with the egg white and half the cornflour, and mix well.

2 Heat the vegetable oil in a deep wok, and then deep-fry both the scallops and the prawns for 1 minute, stirring all the time to keep the pieces separate. Remove with a slotted spoon and then drain well on absorbent kitchen paper.

3 Pour off all but 2 tablespoons of oil from the wok. Increase the heat to high and add the celery, sliced red pepper, carrots, ginger and spring onions. Stir-fry for about 1 minute. Add the scallops and prawns and then stir in the sherry, soy sauce, chilli bean paste and salt.

4 Mix the remaining cornflour to a smooth paste with just a little water, and then add this mixture to the wok. Stir until thickened and mixed in with the seafood and vegetables. Sprinkle over the sesame oil and serve at once.

Salmon in puff pastry

Serves 6–8
Preparation: 30 minutes
Cooking: 35–40 minutes
Carbohydrate: 32 g, Protein: 43 g,
Fat: 49 g, Fibre: 0 g, Calories: 726 kcal,
Sodium: 628 mg (per portion)

What you need:

- 1 kg/2 lb salmon, skinned and filleted, cut into 2 pieces
- 25 g/1 oz butter
- 2 rashers bacon, chopped
- 125 g/4 oz mushrooms, chopped
- 125 g/4 oz soft cheese with garlic and herbs
- 2 tablespoons milk
- 500 g/1 lb puff pastry, thawed if frozen
- beaten egg, to glaze
- salt and pepper

Below: Salmon in puff pastry

1 Season the salmon fillets on both sides. Melt the butter in a frying pan, add the bacon and fry for about 5 minutes, until crisp. Add the mushrooms and fry for about 2 minutes, until softened, stirring all the time. Stir in the soft cheese and milk with salt and pepper to taste. Cook gently, stirring until well mixed. Remove from the heat and leave to cool.

2 Roll out half the pastry to measure 2.5 cm/1 inch larger all round than the fish. Transfer the pastry to a greased baking sheet and place one fish fillet, skinned side down, in the centre. Spread with the cheese mixture and then cover with the second fillet, skinned side up.

3 Brush the edges of the pastry with a little of the egg. Roll out the remaining pastry and cover the fish. Trim the edges, then pinch them together to seal. Roll out the pastry trimmings and cut them into strips. Brush the top of the pie with beaten egg and arrange the strips in a lattice design over the top. Brush again with beaten egg.

4 Bake in a preheated oven, 200°C (400°F), Gas Mark 6, for 35–40 minutes, until the pastry is crisp and golden. Serve the pie hot with asparagus or courgettes, or cold with a fresh green salad.

Provençal-style salt cod

Serves 4
Preparation: 15 minutes, plus soaking overnight
Cooking: 1¼–1½ hours
Carbohydrate: 27 g, Protein: 77 g,
Fat: 9 g, Fibre: 4 g, Calories: 610 kcal,
Sodium: 721 mg (per portion)

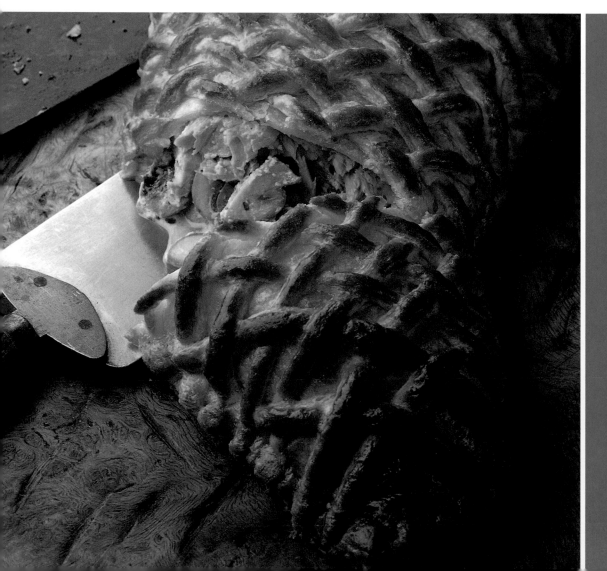

Variation

Bass in puff pastry

For this, you need 1 kg/2 lb bass, skinned and filleted. Season the bass fillets. Trim off any tough stalks from a bunch of watercress, and wash and dry it. Plunge the watercress into a pan of salted, boiling water, cook for 1 minute, then drain and cool quickly under cold running water. Drain again and then dry well, chop finely. Beat 25 g/1 oz butter, 1 garlic clove and 1 tablespoon of lemon juice in a bowl. Season to taste. Beat in the watercress. Continue from step 2 of the salmon recipe, substituting the watercress butter for the cheese mixture. Bake as for the main recipe.

What you need:

- 1 kg/2 lb salt cod
- 2 onions, sliced
- 500 g/1 lb potatoes, peeled and thickly sliced
- 4 large tomatoes, skinned, deseeded and quartered
- 3 garlic cloves, crushed
- 50 g/2 oz capers
- 125 g/4 oz black olives, pitted
- 600 ml/1 pint dry white wine
- 1 tablespoon chopped basil
- 1 bay leaf
- 2 tablespoons olive oil
- pepper
- 1 tablespoon chopped parsley, to garnish

1 Put all of the salt cod in a large bowl and cover it with water. Leave to soak overnight, and then rinse well and drain before using.

2 Cut the cod into large chunks and place them in a large earthenware casserole. Cover the cod with a layer of the sliced onions.

3 Next add a layer of sliced potatoes, to cover the onions, and then add a layer of one of the quartered tomatoes. Continue making these layers, in the same order, until all the onions, potatoes and tomatoes are used up. Sprinkle the garlic over the top with the capers and olives, and then pour over the white wine. Try to pour the white wine over the whole dish so that its flavour is taken into all the ingredients.

4 Sprinkle with the chopped basil and add the bay leaf. Lastly, drizzle the olive oil over the top and add a good grinding of pepper. Bake in a preheated oven, 200°C (400°F), Gas Mark 6, for 1¼–1½ hours, or until tender. Sprinkle with chopped parsley just before serving.

Scalloped fish pie

Serves 4
Preparation: 25 minutes
Cooking: 15 minutes
Carbohydrate: 44 g, Protein: 42 g, Fat: 16 g, Fibre: 4 g, Calories: 481 kcal, Sodium: 480 mg (per portion)

What you need:

- 750 g/1½ lb haddock or cod fillet
- 2 bay leaves
- 6 peppercorns
- 450 ml/¾ pint milk
- 65 g/2½ oz butter
- 1 leek, trimmed, cleaned and sliced
- 40 g/1½ oz plain flour
- 2 tomatoes, skinned and quartered
- 2 tablespoons chopped fresh parsley
- 750 g/1½ lb potatoes, cooked and sliced thinly
- salt and pepper

1 Place the fish in a frying pan together with the bay leaves, peppercorns and the milk. Add just a little salt and pepper, to taste. Gradually bring the contents of the pan to the boil, then cover the pan, lower the heat and simmer gently for about 10 minutes, until the fish is tender and flakes easily when tested with the tip of a knife. Using a slotted spoon, remove the fish from the frying pan leaving the cooking liquid in the pan; remove the skin from the fish and flake the fish flesh. Strain the cooking liquid left in the frying pan into a jug.

2 Melt 40 g/1½ oz of the butter in a large saucepan, add the sliced leek and fry for just about 5 minutes until it is softened and tender. Stir in the plain flour and cook for 1 minute. Gradually add the reserved milk/cooking liquid to the saucepan, stirring continuously until the sauce is both thickened and smooth.

3 Remove the saucepan from the heat and then stir in the fish, tomatoes and parsley. Season with salt and pepper to taste. Melt the remaining butter in a small saucepan. Turn the fish mixture into a greased 1.2 litre/2 pint ovenproof dish. Neatly arrange the potatoes over the top of the fish mixture in overlapping rows and then brush the potatoes generously with the butter.

4 Carefully place the pie in a preheated oven, 200°C (400°F), Gas Mark 6, and bake for about 25 minutes, or until the topping is golden brown. Serve the pie hot with green vegetables such as green beans and mangetout.

Above: *Provençal-style cod*
Below left: *Scalloped fish pie*

Mussels with Thai herbs

Serves 4
Preparation: 20 minutes
Cooking: 20 minutes
Carbohydrate: 6 g, Protein: 28 g,
Fat: 4 g, Fibre: 1 g, Calories: 171 kcal,
Sodium: 2134 mg (per portion)

What you need:

- 2.4 litres/4 pints fresh mussels
- 1.2 litres/2 pints water
- 6 kaffir lime leaves
- rind of 1 lemon
- 2 blades lemon grass
- 1 tablespoon salt
- 3 fresh red chillies, sliced
- 3 spring onions, chopped
- a few coriander leaves, torn

1 Wash the mussels under cold water and then scrape away any barnacles. Remove the beards, and discard any mussels that do not close tightly when tapped sharply against the work surface.
2 Put the water in a pan and bring to the boil. Add the kaffir lime leaves, lemon rind, lemon grass and salt. Add the mussels, cover and bring back to the boil.
3 Cook the mussels, shaking the pan occasionally, until the mussels open. Then drain them, reserving half the cooking liquor. Transfer the mussels to a deep serving dish, discarding any that have not opened.

4 Strain the reserved cooking stock, discarding the lime leaves, lemon rind and lemon grass. Bring to the boil, add the red chillies and spring onions, boil vigorously for 2 minutes. Pour over the mussels and sprinkle with the torn coriander leaves.

Cook's Tip

Thai food takes quite a long time to prepare but the actual cooking is very simple and quick. It is an extremely healthy fast food. This recipe uses two ingredients that help to give Thai food its distinctive flavour. Strongly citrus-flavoured kaffir lime (makrut) leaves are used in many dishes including curries and soups. If you cannot find them, you can substitute bay leaves but the flavour will be different. Lemon grass (takrai) is an aromatic root which looks rather like a small, slim leek. It has a strong lemon fragrance and flavour and is used sliced, crushed or chopped in a wide range of Thai dishes, especially curries, soups and salads.

Right: *Mussels with Thai herbs*

Prawns in coconut sauce

Serves 4
Preparation: 10 minutes
Cooking: 17–20 minutes
Carbohydrate: 25 g, Protein: 68 g,
Fat: 38 g, Fibre: 2 g, Calories: 393
kcal, Sodium: 695 mg (per portion)

What you need:

- 16 large uncooked prawns
- 2 tablespoons oil
- 1 large onion, finely chopped
- 2 stalks lemon grass, chopped
- 2 fresh red chillies, sliced
- 2.5 cm/1 inch piece fresh ginger, shredded
- 1 tablespoon ground cumin
- 1 tablespoon ground coriander
- 2 tablespoons fish sauce
- 250 ml/8 fl oz coconut milk
- 3 tablespoons roasted peanuts, coarsely ground
- 2 tomatoes, skinned and chopped
- 1 teaspoon sugar
- juice of ½ lime
- fresh coriander leaves, chopped

Below: Prawns in coconut sauce
Right: Mexican garlic prawns

1 Remove the prawns from their shells, leaving the tails intact. Remove the dark veins running along the back of the prawns and then slit them right down the underside.
2 Heat the oil in a wok or heavy frying pan. Add the onion and fry until soft and golden. Add the lemon grass, sliced red chillies, ginger, cumin and coriander, and sauté for 2 minutes
3 Add the fish sauce and coconut milk to the wok. Stir well and then add the peanuts and chopped tomatoes. Cook gently over a low heat until the tomato is soft and the flavours of the sauce are well developed.
4 Stir in the prepared prawns and simmer gently for 5 minutes, or until the prawns are pink and tender. Add the sugar and transfer to a serving dish. Serve hot sprinkled with the lime juice and chopped coriander leaves.

Mexican garlic prawns

Serves 4–6
Preparation: 15 minutes, plus 1 hour marinating
Cooking: 5 minutes
Carbohydrate: 1 g, Protein: 61 g,
Fat: 22 g, Fibre: 1 g, Calories: 449 kcal,
Sodium: 941 mg (per portion)

What you need:

- 24 uncooked king-sized prawns
- 6 garlic cloves, crushed
- 2 red chillies, deseeded and chopped
- 3 tablespoons olive oil
- 50 g/2 oz butter
- juice of 2 limes
- 3 tablespoons chopped fresh coriander
- sea salt and whole black peppercorns

To serve:
- lime wedges
- sliced avocado

1 Prepare the prawns: remove the heads and, leaving them in their shells, split them carefully down the middle towards the tail end without separating them. Remove the dark vein running along the back of the prawns.
2 Mix the garlic with sea salt, peppercorns and chillies in a pestle and mortar, to make a thick aromatic paste.
3 Coat the prawns with this mixture and place in a bowl. Cover the bowl and leave in a cool place to marinate for at least 1 hour.

- 1 kg/2 lb mixed seafood, (e.g. scallops, white fish fillets, king prawns)
- oil for deep-frying
- sea salt

For the garnish:
- lemon wedges
- sprigs of parsley

1 Make the batter: sift the flour and salt into a mixing bowl and make a well in the centre. Pour in the olive oil and gradually beat in the tepid water to make a smooth, thick batter. Cover the bowl and put in the refrigerator to rest for 2 hours.

2 Immediately before using, whisk the egg white until it forms stiff peaks, then lightly fold, but do not beat, the egg white into the batter with a metal spoon.

3 Meanwhile, prepare the seafood: wash all the fish and shellfish under cold running water and pat dry. Clean the scallops. Cut the white fish into smallish pieces, and remove any remaining skin and bones. Shell all the prawns, leaving the tails intact and removing the black vein running along the back. Dip them in the prepared batter and shake off any excess batter.

4 Heat the olive oil and butter in a large heavy-based frying pan and add the prawns and garlic paste. Quickly sauté them over medium heat for 2–3 minutes, until they turn pink. Remove from the pan and keep warm. Add the lime juice to the pan and stir into the pan juices. Boil vigorously for a couple of minutes and then pour this liquid over the prawns. Sprinkle with coriander, and serve with lime wedges and sliced avocado.

Smoky chillied prawns

Serves 4
Preparation: 10 minutes plus marinating
Cooking: 6 minutes
Carbohydrate:01 g, Protein: 50 g, Fat: 12 g, Fibre:0 g, Calories: 309 kcal, Sodium: 1032 mg (per portion)

What you need:

- 10 green chillies, deseeded and halved lengthways
- 20 raw king-sized prawns, peeled, with tails left intact
- 5 tablespoons olive oil
- coarsely ground sea salt
- lemon wedges, to serve

1 Wrap one half of each chilli round the middle of each king-sized prawn and thread 5 prawns on to each of 4 metal or soaked bamboo skewers.

2 Place the skewers in a long shallow dish and sprinkle over the oil and the salt. Cover the dish and leave to marinate in a cool place for about 30 minutes.

3 Cook the prawns on an oiled preheated barbecue, or under a preheated grill, for 3 minutes on each side, basting with any remaining marinade. Serve the prawns hot with lemon wedges.

Fried mixed seafood

Serves 4
Preparation: 15 minutes, plus 2 hours chilling
Cooking: 3–6 minutes
Carbohydrate: 29 g, Protein: 98 g, Fat: 14 g, Fibre: 1 g, Calories: 630 kcal, Sodium: 1097 mg (per portion)

What you need:

- 125 g/4 oz plain flour
- pinch of salt
- 2 tablespoons olive oil
- 150 ml/¼ pint tepid water
- 1 egg white

4 Heat the oil for deep-frying to 190°C (375°F). Cook the battered fish, scallops and prawns for 3–6 minutes, until crisp and golden. Lift out and drain on crumpled kitchen paper. Sprinkle with sea salt and pile up on a warm serving dish. Garnish with lemon wedges and parsley and serve immediately.

Above left: Smoky chillied prawns
Below: *Fried mixed seafood*

Crab Creole

Serves 4
Preparation: 15 minutes
Cooking: 30 minutes
Carbohydrate: 18 g, Protein: 37 g,
Fat: 14 g, Fibre: 1 g, Calories: 353 kcal,
Sodium: 1122 mg (per portion)

What you need:

- 4 medium-sized cooked crabs
- 75 g/3 oz breadcrumbs
- 2 red peppers, deseeded and finely chopped
- 1 garlic clove, crushed
- 1 fresh red chilli, deseeded and finely chopped
- pinch of ground mace
- ½ teaspoon ground allspice berries
- 2 tablespoons chopped parsley
- juice of 1 lime
- 2 tablespoons rum (optional)
- 15 g/½ oz butter
- salt and pepper

1 Remove the crab claws and legs and crack them to extract the meat. Open the crabs by pressing with your thumbs on the edge of the section of the shell to which the legs were attached. Pull out the central section.

2 Discard the stomach sac and feathery gills. Scoop out the meat from inside the shell and put in a bowl with the meat from the claws and legs. Remove the meat from the leg sockets with a skewer and mix with the other crab meat. Mash with a fork.

3 Add 50 g/2 oz of the bread-crumbs to the crab meat, together with the peppers, garlic, chilli, mace, allspice and parsley. Add the lime juice and rum (if using), with salt and pepper.

4 Scrub and wash all the empty crab shells and fill with the

crab meat mixture. Sprinkle with the remaining breadcrumbs and dot with butter. Bake in a pre-heated oven, 180°C (350°F), Gas Mark 4, for 30 minutes.

Fried scallop salad

Serves 4
Preparation: 25 minutes
Cooking: about 6 minutes
Carbohydrate: 3 g, Protein: 10 g, Fat: 7 g, Fibre: 1 g, Calories: 114 kcal, Sodium: 276 mg (per portion)

What you need:

- 3 large fresh scallops
- 3 tablespoons light olive oil
- ½ small red pepper, cored, deseeded and cut into matchstick strips
- 150 ml/¼ pint vinaigrette
- 1 tablespoon chopped parsley
- 125 g/4 oz rocket
- ½ small head frisé, leaves roughly torn
- 2 spring onions, finely shredded
- salt and pepper

1 Remove the corals from the scallops and set aside. Trim the white parts of the scallops and cut each one in half horizontally. Using a very sharp knife, lightly score each scallop piece in a small lattice pattern.

2 Heat the oil in a large frying pan. Add the scallops, including the corals. Cook, stirring frequently, for 3–4 minutes or until opaque. Using a slotted spoon, transfer the scallops to a plate.

3 Add the red pepper strips to the pan and cook, stirring, for 1 minute. Pour the dressing into the pan and heat through. Stir in the parsley, then remove the frying pan from the heat. Return the scallops to the pan and add salt and pepper to taste.

4 Arrange a bed of rocket and frisé on individual serving plates. Scatter over the shredded spring onions. Spoon the warm scallop mixture on to the plates and serve at once.

Red snapper in coriander

Serves 4
Preparation: 10 minutes
Cooking: 20 minutes
Carbohydrate: 39 g, Protein: 54 g, Fat: 11 g, Fibre: 2 g, Calories: 462 kcal, Sodium: 1581 mg (per portion)

What you need:

- 1 kg/2 lb red snapper or other white fish fillets
- 4 tablespoons lime or lemon juice
- 2 teaspoons salt
- 4 tablespoons olive oil
- 25 g/1 oz fresh breadcrumbs
- 1 garlic clove, crushed
- 6 tablespoons crushed coriander leaves
- 1 teaspoon grated lime or lemon rind
- salt and pepper
- warmed tortillas, to serve

1 Rinse the fish under cold running water and pat dry with absorbent kitchen paper. Rub with half of the lime or lemon juice and 1 teaspoon of the salt, and place skin side down in a lightly oiled heavy frying pan.

2 Add sufficient cold water to cover the fish and then simmer gently for 5 minutes, turning twice during the cooking time.

3 In another pan, heat half the olive oil, add the breadcrumbs, garlic, remaining salt and 4 tablespoons of the coriander. Cook over a low heat, stirring, until golden brown. Spread over the fish and simmer for 7–10 minutes, until the fish flakes easily.

4 Blend the remaining juice and oil together and pour over the fish. Cook for 2–3 minutes. Mix the remaining coriander with the lime or lemon rind and sprinkle over the fish. Serve with tortillas.

Far left: *Crab creole*
Below left: *Fried scallop salad*
Above: *Red snapper in coriander*

Poultry

Chicken, turkey, duck and other farmyard birds, as well as game birds such as pheasant, are all incredibly versatile. They can be successfully combined with a great variety of other ingredients, including fruit, vegetables, herbs and spices, and cooked in hundreds of different ways. Most poultry is low in fat compared with other meats and, especially if it is cut into pieces and baked, poached or stir-fried, can make a simple, healthy meal in next to no time. Dressed up with a classic, rich or elaborate sauce, poultry lends itself to many splendid dishes from around the world.

Coq au vin

Serves 4
Preparation: 30 minutes
Cooking: 50 minutes
Carbohydrate: 15 g, Protein: 36 g,
Fat: 34 g, Fibre: 3 g, Calories: 576 kcal,
Sodium: 967 mg (per portion)

What you need:

- 1 chicken, cut into 8 pieces
- 3 tablespoons sunflower oil
- 175 g/6 oz smoked bacon, chopped
- 16 small onions, peeled
- 250 g/8 oz button mushrooms
- 3 garlic cloves, crushed
- 3 tablespoons brandy
- 350 ml/12 fl oz red wine
- 2 tablespoons plain flour
- 1 tablespoon butter
- salt and pepper

1 Fry the chicken in the oil in a flameproof casserole dish until golden brown. Remove with a slotted spoon, add the bacon and onions, fry for 5 minutes, then add the mushrooms and garlic.

2 Pour in the brandy and wine and bring to the boil. Return the chicken to the casserole, and add salt and pepper. Cover and simmer for 40 minutes, until the chicken is cooked.

3 Remove the chicken and vegetables and keep hot.

4 Mash the flour into the butter to form a smooth paste. Whisk into the sauce and simmer, stirring, for 2–3 minutes, until thick. Season to taste. Spoon over the chicken and vegetables.

Basque-style chicken

Serves 4
Preparation: 20 minutes
Cooking: 1 hour
Carbohydrate: 15 g, Protein: 38 g,
Fat: 17 g, Fibre: 4 g, Calories: 360 kcal,
Sodium: 1165 mg (per portion)

What you need:

- 175 g/6 oz smoked ham or streaky bacon, diced
- 4 tablespoons olive oil
- 4 large chicken pieces
- 4 onions, sliced
- 3 garlic cloves, crushed
- 2 green peppers, deseeded and diced
- ½ teaspoon dried marjoram
- 425 g/14 oz fresh or canned tomatoes
- 150–300 ml/¼–½ pint chicken stock (see method)
- salt and pepper
- 2 tablespoons chopped fresh parsley, to garnish

1 Fry the diced ham or bacon in the oil in a sauté pan until lightly browned, then remove with a slotted spoon. Add the chicken to the pan and cook until brown all over. Remove the chicken, add the onions and garlic and cook gently until soft and golden. Add the peppers and marjoram, cover and cook gently for 10 minutes.
2 Add the tomatoes, seasoning and stock (300 ml/½ pint if using fresh tomatoes; 150 ml/¼ pint if canned). Return the chicken and ham to the pan, cover and simmer for 40–45 minutes, until the chicken is cooked and tender.
3 Transfer the chicken to a serving dish. Boil the sauce to thicken slightly, pour over the chicken and sprinkle with parsley.

Far left: *Coq au vin*
Left: *Basque-style chicken*

Chicken in tarragon cream

Serves 4
Preparation: 10 minutes
Cooking: 30 minutes
*Carbohydrate: 2 g, Protein: 33 g,
Fat: 35 g, Fibre: 0 g, Calories: 485 kcal,
Sodium: 609 mg (per portion)*

What you need:

- 600 ml/1 pint well-flavoured chicken stock
- 200 ml/7 fl oz dry white wine
- 8 fresh tarragon sprigs
- 4 boneless, skinless chicken breasts
- 250 ml/8 fl oz double cream
- pinch of mustard powder
- salt and pepper

Below: *Stuffed chicken breasts*
Above right: *Chicken in Tarragon cream*

1 Pour the stock and wine into a flameproof casserole, add 2 tarragon sprigs, season, and bring to a simmer.

2 Add the chicken, cover and simmer over a low heat for 20–25 minutes, or until just tender, turning occasionally.

3 Remove the chicken with a slotted spoon and set aside. Pour the cream into the casserole and bring to the boil, stirring constantly, then reduce the heat and simmer, stirring frequently, for about 15 minutes, until the cream sauce is reduced by one-third and is very slightly thickened.

4 Strip the leaves from 2 of the remaining tarragon sprigs and chop finely. Add the chopped tarragon and mustard powder to the casserole, then add the chicken, together with any of the cooking juices that have collected on the plate. Heat through gently for 5 minutes, basting the chicken frequently with the sauce. Adjust the seasoning to taste and serve hot, garnished with the remaining tarragon sprigs.

Stuffed chicken breasts

Serves 4
Preparation: 10 minutes
Cooking: 20 minutes
*Carbohydrate: 5 g, Protein: 39 g,
Fat: 21 g, Fibre: 1 g, Calories: 371 kcal,
Sodium: 1155 mg (per portion)*

What you need:

- 4 boneless, skinless chicken breasts
- 4 small, thin slices Parma ham
- 4 thin slices Bel Paese cheese
- 4 cooked or canned asparagus spears, plus extra to garnish
- flour for dusting
- 50 g/2 oz butter

Variation

Chicken with Champagne

Sauté the chicken in 50 g/ 2 oz butter for 7–10 minutes. Flambé with 4 tablespoons Cognac, then add 200 ml/7 fl oz stock and 2 tarragon sprigs, season and then simmer for 20 minutes, until the chicken is tender, turning often.

Remove the chicken to a warm plate. Add 200 ml/7 fl oz Champagne, 1 tablespoon tomato purée and 125 ml/4 fl oz cream. Bring to the boil, then simmer for about 5 minutes, until thickened. Pour over the chicken and serve at once.

- 1 tablespoon olive oil
- 6 tablespoons Marsala or dry white wine
- 2 tablespoons chicken stock
- salt and pepper

1 Place each chicken breast between 2 sheets of clingfilm or damp greaseproof paper and beat with a rolling pin until thin. Season lightly.

2 Place a slice of ham on top of each beaten chicken breast, then a slice of cheese and, finally, an asparagus spear. Carefully roll up each chicken breast and wind a piece of cotton around it to hold the stuffing in place. Tie securely and dust with flour.

3 Heat 25 g/1 oz of the butter with the oil in a frying pan. Sauté the chicken rolls over a very low heat, turning them frequently, for about 15 minutes or until they are tender, golden brown and cooked through. Remove the cotton, transfer the chicken to warm serving plates and keep warm while you make the sauce.

4 Add the Marsala or wine, stock and remaining butter to the juices in the pan. Bring to the boil and simmer for 3–4 minutes, stirring and scraping the base of the pan with a wooden spoon. Spoon the sauce over the chicken and garnish with asparagus spears.

Chicken with white wine, Gruyère and mushrooms

Serves 4
Preparation: 30 minutes
Cooking: about 35 minutes
Carbohydrate: 10 g, Protein: 42 g, Fat: 41 g, Fibre: 1 g, Calories: 595 kcal, Sodium: 575 mg (per portion)

What you need:

- 4 boneless, skinless chicken breasts
- 50 g/2 oz unsalted butter
- ½ teaspoon dried mixed herbs
- ½ teaspoon dried tarragon
- 250 g/8 oz button mushrooms, sliced thinly
- 25 g/1 oz plain flour
- 300 ml/½ pint milk
- 150 ml/¼ pint dry white wine
- 75 ml/3 fl oz double cream
- 125 g/4 oz Gruyère cheese, grated
- good pinch of grated nutmeg
- salt and pepper

1 Put the chicken in a single layer in an ovenproof dish, dot with half the butter and sprinkle with the herbs, salt and pepper. Cover with foil and place in a preheated oven, 180°C (350°F), Gas Mark 4, for 30 minutes, or until just tender.

2 Meanwhile, melt the remaining butter in a saucepan, add the mushrooms and sauté over a moderate heat, stirring frequently, for about 5 minutes.

3 Sprinkle in the flour and cook, stirring constantly, for 1–2 minutes. Remove the pan from the heat and add the milk, a little at a time, beating vigorously with a balloon whisk or wooden spoon after each addition. Add the wine in the same way.

4 Return the pan to the heat and bring to the boil, stirring all the time. Reduce the heat and simmer, stirring, for about 5 minutes, until thickened.

5 Add the cream, two-thirds of the Gruyère, the nutmeg and salt and pepper to taste, and simmer gently for a further 5 minutes.

6 When the chicken is tender, remove from the oven and increase the oven temperature to maximum. Carefully tip any cooking juices from the chicken into the sauce and stir well to mix. Pour the sauce over the chicken in the dish and sprinkle with the remaining Gruyère.

7 Return the chicken to the oven and bake for 5 minutes, until golden and bubbling.

Above: *Chicken with white wine, Gruyère and mushrooms*

Chicken with 40 garlic cloves

Serves 4
Preparation: 15 minutes
Cooking: 2–2¼ hours
*Carbohydrate: 17 g, Protein: 73 g,
Fat: 23 g, Fibre: 2 g, Calories: 565 kcal,
Sodium: 431 mg (per portion)*

What you need:

- 2 kg/4 lb oven-ready chicken
- 1 bouquet garni
- 4 tablespoons olive oil
- 1 celery stick, chopped
- 40 garlic cloves, separated, but not peeled
- salt and pepper
- a few sprigs each of fresh rosemary, sage and thyme, to garnish

To seal:
- 4 tablespoons plain flour
- 4 teaspoons water

1 Wash and dry the chicken cavity, insert the bouquet garni and some seasoning, then truss the chicken with string.
2 Heat the oil in a large flame-proof casserole into which the chicken just fits. Add the celery and all the garlic, then add the chicken, and cook over a moderate heat until it is lightly coloured on all sides.
3 Cover the casserole with its lid. Make a paste with the flour and water and seal the edge.
4 Place in a preheated oven, 180°C (350°F), Gas Mark 4, for 2–2¼ hours, without opening the oven door.
5 Break the flour and water seal, then lift out the chicken and place on a warmed serving platter. Arrange the garlic cloves around the chicken and garnish with sprigs of fresh herbs.

Chicken in a brick

Serves 4
Preparation: 10 minutes
Cooking: 2 hours
*Carbohydrate: 12 g, Protein: 71 g,
Fat: 16 g, Fibre: 3 g, Calories: 472 kcal,
Sodium: 442 mg (per portion)*

What you need:

- 2 kg/4 lb oven-ready chicken
- 2 onions, quartered
- 2 garlic cloves, quartered
- 4 small carrots, cut into strips
- 1 teaspoon dried tarragon
- 2 teaspoons chopped fresh tarragon
- salt and pepper

1 Soak the chicken brick in cold water for 30 minutes.
2 Wash and dry the chicken cavity, then put half the onion and garlic quarters inside the bird, with some salt and pepper.
3 Put the chicken in the bottom half of the soaked brick, surrounded by the carrots and the remaining onion and garlic. Sprinkle with the dried tarragon and salt and pepper. Cover with the top half of the brick and place in a cold oven. Set the oven to 230°C (450°F), Gas Mark 8, and cook for exactly 2 hours, without opening the oven door.
4 Carefully lift the chicken out of the brick and place on a warmed serving platter. Discard the onion and garlic from the chicken cavity. Drain off most of the juices from the vegetables in the brick, then stir the fresh tarragon into the vegetables. Serve the chicken at once, surrounded by all the vegetables.

Cook's Tip

Chicken bricks must always be soaked in cold water for about 30 minutes before use. They provide a healthy way of cooking, because no extra fat is required. None of the natural juices are lost, so the food retains its flavour, moisture and tenderness.

Left: *Chicken with 40 garlic cloves*
Right: *Chicken in a brick*

Variation

Turkey in a brick with cranberries and orange

Mix 250 g/8 oz fresh or thawed frozen cranberries with the grated rind and juice of 1 orange, 2 tablespoons soft brown sugar and a little thyme. Put them in the bottom half of the soaked chicken brick.

Soften 50 g/2 oz butter with the grated rind of 1 orange and salt and pepper to taste. Lift the skin away from a bone-in turkey breast, weighing about 2 kg/4 lb, and spread the butter over the flesh. Press the skin back into place.

Put the turkey, skin side up, on the cranberries in the brick. Cover and cook as in the main recipe.

Lift the turkey out of the brick and place on a warmed serving platter. Remove the cranberries with a slotted spoon and arrange around the turkey. Garnish with fresh thyme. Serve the juices separately.

Variation

Five-spice chicken with cashew nuts

Heat 1 tablespoon oil and stir-fry 75 g/3 oz shelled unsalted cashews and 4–6 sliced spring onions for 1 minute. Remove and drain on paper towels.

Add 2 tablespoons oil and stir-fry 500 g/1 lb chicken, cut into strips, and 1 crushed garlic clove for 5 minutes.

Mix 1 teaspoon cornflour with 2 tablespoons each of water, sherry and soy sauce, and ½ teaspoon five-spice powder. Pour into the wok and continue stir-frying until the sauce thickens.

Return the nuts and spring onions to the wok and stir-fry for 30 seconds. Taste for seasoning and add more soy sauce if liked.

Stir-fried duck with pineapple

Serves 3–4
Preparation: 10 minutes
Cooking: 10 minutes
Carbohydrate: 9 g, Protein: 35 g, Fat: 13 g, Fibre: 1 g, Calories: 286 kcal, Sodium: 607 mg (per portion)

What you need:

- 2 tablespoons sunflower oil
- 4 duck breast fillets, about 175 g/6 oz each, skin and fat removed, cut into thin strips
- ¼–½ teaspoon chilli powder
- 2 tablespoons soy sauce
- 2 tablespoons sweet sherry
- 1 x 250 g/8 oz can pineapple chunks in natural juice, drained, with juice reserved
- 4–6 spring onions, cut diagonally into 5 cm/2 inch lengths
- salt and pepper

1 Heat a wok or a large, deep frying pan over a moderate heat until hot. Add the oil and heat until hot but not smoking. Add the duck and stir-fry for about 5 minutes, until it changes colour on all sides.

2 Sprinkle in the chilli powder, according to taste, and stir-fry for 1 minute. Add the soy sauce, sherry, pineapple juice and salt and pepper to taste.

3 Stir-fry for about 5 minutes or until the duck is tender, adding the pineapple chunks and spring onions for the last minute or so to heat through.

Duck breasts with spicy mango relish

Serves 6
Preparation: 30 minutes, plus 1 hour chilling, or overnight
Cooking: 25 minutes
Carbohydrate: 15 g, Protein: 24 g, Fat: 8 g, Fibre: 2 g, Calories: 220 kcal, Sodium: 464 mg (per portion)

What you need:

- 6 duck breast fillets, about 175 g/6 oz each
- salt
For the mango relish:
- 3 ripe mangoes
- 1 tablespoon sunflower oil
- 1 small onion, chopped finely
- 2.5 cm/1 inch piece of fresh root ginger, finely chopped

- 1 garlic clove, crushed
- 2 teaspoons dark brown sugar
- ¼ teaspoon chilli powder
- 2 tablespoons chopped fresh coriander

1 First make the mango relish. (It can be made the day before.) Slice each mango on either side of the stone. Cut the flesh in these pieces into a criss-cross pattern, then push the skin inside out and slice off the flesh in neat dice. Cut the remaining mango flesh away from the stones and dice neatly.
2 Heat the oil in a saucepan, add the onion, ginger and garlic and fry gently, stirring frequently, for about 5 minutes, until soft but not coloured.
3 Add the diced mango, sugar, chilli and a pinch of salt. Sauté for a few minutes or until the mango softens slightly. Transfer to a bowl and leave to cool. Add the coriander, cover and chill for at least 1 hour or overnight.
4 Put the duck breasts, skin side down, between 2 sheets of clingfilm or greaseproof paper and flatten them with a rolling pin.
5 Score the duck skin in a criss-cross pattern with a sharp knife and rub all over with salt.
6 Put the duck, skin side up, on a rack in a roasting tin. Place in a preheated oven, 200°C (400°F), Gas Mark 6, for 20–25 minutes, until tender.
7 Slice the breasts on the diagonal, removing the skin if preferred. Serve on warmed plates, with the chilled mango relish.

Jamaican jerked chicken

Serves 6
Preparation: 20 minutes, plus 1–2 hours marinating
Cooking: 20–30 minutes
Carbohydrate: 61 g, Protein: 33 g, Fat: 6 g, Fibre: 2 g, Calories: 411 kcal, Sodium: 244 mg (per portion)

What you need:

- 25 g/1 oz allspice berries
- 5 cm/2 inches cinnamon stick
- 1 teaspoon grated nutmeg
- 1 fresh red chilli, deseeded and finely chopped
- 4 spring onions, thinly sliced
- 1 bay leaf, crumbled
- 1–2 tablespoons dark rum
- 6 chicken pieces
- salt and pepper

For the pineapple chutney:
- 2 fresh pineapples, peeled and chopped
- 2.5 cm/1 inch piece of fresh root ginger, finely chopped
- 1 onion, finely chopped
- 1 fresh red chilli, deseeded and finely chopped
- 125 ml/4 fl oz vinegar
- 250 g/8 oz dark brown sugar

1 Pound the allspice, cinnamon and nutmeg in a mortar, or grind them to a powder in an electric grinder. Add the chilli, spring onions, bay leaf and seasoning and pound to a thick paste.
2 Stir the rum into the paste and mix well. Make 2 or 3 deep cuts in each chicken piece and rub the paste all over the chicken. Leave to marinate in the refrigerator or a cool place for 1–2 hours.
3 For the pineapple chutney, put all the ingredients in a saucepan over moderate heat and stir until the sugar has dissolved. Bring to the boil, then reduce the heat a little and cook vigorously, stirring occasionally, until thick. Pour into sterilized jars and seal. It can be kept for 2–3 weeks in the refrigerator.
4 Roast the jerked chicken at 200°C (400°F), Gas Mark 6, for 20–30 minutes, or cook under a grill. Serve with rice and the pineapple chutney.

Below left: Duck breasts with spicy mango relish
Above: Jamaican jerked chicken

Above:
Chicken biryani

Chicken biryani

Serves 4
Preparation: 30 minutes, plus
30 minutes marinating
Cooking: 50 minutes
Carbohydrate: 103 g, Protein: 40 g,
Fat: 28 g, Fibre: 2 g, Calories: 790 kcal,
Sodium: 422 mg (per portion)

What you need:

- 8 chicken drumsticks
- 50 g/2 oz ghee or butter
- 25 g/1 oz almonds, chopped
- 25 g/1 oz cashew nuts,
  chopped
- 1 large onion, finely chopped
- 4 bay leaves
- biryani spice mixture (see
  Cook's Tip)
- 425 g/14 oz long-grain rice
- ½ teaspoon saffron threads
- salt

For the paste:

- 1 teaspoon garam masala
- 1 small onion, chopped
- 2 garlic cloves, crushed
- 5 cm/2 inch piece of fresh
  root ginger, peeled
- 150 ml/5 fl oz natural
  yogurt
- 1 teaspoon salt

To garnish:

- fresh coriander
- slivers of red chilli

1 Grind all the paste ingredients together with a pestle and mortar until smooth. Rub the paste over the chicken and leave to marinate for 30 minutes.
2 Heat the ghee in a frying pan and fry the almonds and cashews until golden brown. Remove with a slotted spoon and drain on kitchen paper. Set aside for the garnish. Add the onion to the pan and fry until golden. Remove half and reserve for the garnish.
3 Add the bay leaves and biryani spices to the onion in the pan, stir well, then add the chicken. Cook over a moderate heat for 20 minutes. Stir in the rice, then add 900 ml/1½ pints warm water and some salt. Cover and cook for 15–20 minutes, until the rice is tender and all the water absorbed.
4 Steep the saffron in a little hot water for 5 minutes; stir into the rice. Garnish with the fried nuts and onions, coriander and chilli.

Cook's Tip

To make a biryani spice
mixture, mix together 4 whole
cloves, 8 black peppercorns,
4 green cardamom pods,
1 crushed black cardamom,
5 cm/2 inch cinnamon stick
and ½ teaspoon turmeric.

Chicken vindaloo

Serves 6
Preparation: 15 minutes, plus 1
hour marinating
Cooking: 55 minutes
Carbohydrate: 7 g, Protein: 42 g,
Fat: 16 g, Fibre: 2 g, Calories: 338 kcal,
Sodium: 798 mg (per portion)

What you need:

- 2 tablespoons hot curry
  powder
- 4 tablespoons vinegar
- 6 large chicken pieces
- 6 tablespoons mustard oil
- 4 bay leaves
- 1 teaspoon green cardamom
  seeds
- 1 large onion, thinly sliced
- 2 teaspoons turmeric
- 1 teaspoon chilli powder
- 10 garlic cloves, crushed
- 15 g/½ oz fresh root ginger,
  thinly sliced
- 2 tomatoes, skinned and
  quartered
- 2 teaspoons desiccated
  coconut
- salt

1 Put the curry powder, 2 teaspoons of the vinegar and 2 teaspoons salt in a bowl and mix until smooth.
2 Make 2 or 3 deep cuts in each chicken piece and rub the paste over the chicken. Leave to marinate in the refrigerator or a cool place for 1 hour.
3 Heat the oil in a large saucepan and stir in the bay leaves and cardamom seeds. Add the onion and fry until light brown. Stir in the turmeric and chilli, then add the chicken. Cook, stirring occasionally, for 15 minutes. Add the garlic, ginger, tomatoes and 1 teaspoon salt, and cook for about 10 minutes.

4 When the fat starts to separate, add the remaining vinegar and 75 ml/3 fl oz water. Stir well, cover the pan and simmer gently for 20–25 minutes, until the chicken is tender. Sprinkle with coconut and serve.

Cook's Tip

Mustard oil is a pungent yellow oil that is widely used in Indian cooking. It is available from many Asian stores, but if you cannot obtain it, groundnut oil can be substituted.

Chilli chicken with pine nuts

Serves 4
Preparation: 30 minutes
Cooking: 15 minutes
Carbohydrate: 15 g, Protein: 35 g, Fat: 21 g, Fibre: 1 g, Calories: 391 kcal, Sodium: 1101 mg (per portion)

What you need:

- 4 boneless, skinless chicken breasts
- 4 tablespoons sunflower oil
- 1 red pepper, deseeded and cut into thin strips
- 1 green pepper, deseeded and cut into thin strips
- 1 fresh red chilli, deseeded and finely chopped
- 1 fresh green chilli, deseeded and finely chopped
- 50 g/2 oz pine nuts
- 1 garlic clove, finely chopped
- 4 tablespoons dry white wine
- 2 tablespoons lemon juice
- 3 tablespoons oyster sauce
- 2 teaspoons caster sugar
- 1 teaspoon chilli sauce
- 4 tablespoons light soy sauce

- 1 tablespoon cornflour
- salt and pepper
- 2 spring onions, sliced diagonally, to garnish

1 Cut the chicken into 1 x 5 cm/ ½ x 2 inch strips. Sprinkle with salt and pepper. Heat 2 tablespoons of the oil in a wok or large frying pan, add the chicken strips and cook, stirring constantly, for 5 minutes, or until tender. Remove the chicken and reserve.

2 Heat the remaining oil in the wok or frying pan and stir-fry the red and green pepper strips for 2 minutes, until just cooked. Lift out and reserve.

3 Add the chillies, pine nuts and garlic to the pan and stir-fry for 1 minute. Drain off and discard any excess fat, then add the white wine, lemon juice, oyster sauce, caster sugar and chilli

sauce. Cook, stirring frequently, for 1 minute.

4 Blend the soy sauce and cornflour together, then add to the chilli mixture and bring to the boil. Return the cooked chicken and pepper strips to the wok or frying pan, then cover and cook over a medium heat until the chicken has warmed through.

5 Serve at once, sprinkled with the sliced spring onions.

Above: *Chicken vindaloo*
Below: *Chilli chicken with pine nuts*

Turkey, spinach and Brie filo pie

Serves 6–8
Preparation: 25 minutes
Cooking: 25 minutes
Carbohydrate: 26 g, Protein: 25 g,
Fat: 28 g, Fibre: 2 g, Calories: 446 kcal,
Sodium: 332 mg (per portion)

What you need:

- 175 g/6 oz frozen leaf spinach, thawed
- 75 g/3 oz butter
- 1 tablespoon olive oil
- 25 g/1 oz pine nuts
- 375 g/12 oz boneless turkey breast, cut into strips
- 175 g/6 oz Brie cheese, rind removed, cut into chunks
- 4 spring onions, chopped
- 1 teaspoon dried oregano
- grated rind and juice of 1 lemon
- 250 g/8 oz filo pastry, thawed if frozen
- salt and pepper

1 Squeeze the spinach to re-move excess water; chop roughly.
2 Melt 25 g/1 oz of the butter with the oil in a frying pan. Fry the pine nuts for 1–2 minutes, then add the turkey and fry until browned. Lower the heat and fry for 5 minutes, or until cooked. Mix the contents of the pan with the spinach, Brie, spring onions, oregano, lemon rind and juice, and seasoning.
3 Grease a baking sheet and have the filo pastry ready, keep-ing it covered while you work. Melt the remaining butter.
4 Cover the baking sheet with 3 layers of filo pastry, brushing each layer with melted butter. Put the spinach filling on the centre third of the pastry, about 2.5 cm/ 1 inch from the top and bottom

edges. Layer the remaining pastry over the filling, brushing with the butter. Fold in the all sides of the pastry to enclose the filling, then scrunch the pastry on top.

5 Place in a preheated oven, 200°C (400°F), Gas Mark 6, for 25 minutes, until the pastry is golden and crisp.

Chicken pie

Serves 4–6
Preparation: 30 minutes
Cooking: 1¼ hours
Carbohydrate: 40 g, Protein: 16 g, Fat: 47 g, Fibre: 3 g, Calories·637 kcal, Sodium: 850 mg (per portion)

What you need:

- 1 tablespoon plain flour
- 4 skinless chicken pieces, halved
- 25 g/1 oz butter
- 1 tablespoon olive oil
- 2 onions, chopped
- 300 ml/½ pint chicken stock
- 2 tablespoons lemon juice
- 150 ml/¼ pint double cream
- 1 bunch of parsley, chopped
- 250 g/8 oz shortcrust pastry
- beaten egg, or milk, to glaze
- 1 tablespoon sesame seeds
- salt and pepper

1 Put the flour in a polythene bag, season, then add the chicken and toss until coated.

2 Melt the butter and oil in a frying pan, and fry the onions for 5 minutes, until soft. Remove the onions with a slotted spoon.

Left: *Turkey, spinach and Brie filo pie*
Above right: *Chicken pie*

3 Add the chicken to the pan and fry for 10 minutes, until evenly browned. Using a slotted spoon, transfer the chicken to a 1.5 litre/2½ pint pie dish. Sprinkle the onions over the top.

4 Stir any remaining flour into the pan and cook for 1 minute. Gradually add the stock, stirring until the sauce is thick and smooth, scraping the base of the pan to incorporate any sediment. Stir in the lemon juice, then the cream, parsley and seasoning to taste. Bring to the boil, then pour the sauce over the chicken.

5 Roll out the pastry to measure 5 cm/2 inches larger than the pie dish. Cut off a 2.5 cm/1 inch strip all round. Dampen the edges of the dish and attach the pastry strip. Brush the strip with water and cover the pie with the remaining pastry. Press the edge to seal, and make a hole in the centre to allow steam to escape.

6 Brush with milk or beaten egg and sprinkle with sesame seeds. Place in a preheated oven, 200°C (400°F), Gas Mark 6, for 30 minutes, then reduce to 180°C (350°F), Gas Mark 4 and bake for a further 45 minutes. Cover with foil if it becomes too brown. Serve hot.

Roast pheasant flambéed with Calvados

Serves 4
Preparation: 30 minutes
Cooking: 45 minutes
Carbohydrate: 21 g, Protein: 53 g, Fat: 36 g, Fibre: 3 g, Calories:665 kcal, Sodium: 473 mg (per portion)

What you need:

- 2 pheasants, preferably hen birds, plucked and cleaned, ready for the oven
- 1 large onion, quartered
- 50 g/2 oz butter
- 4 tart dessert apples, peeled, cored and thickly sliced
- 25 g/1 oz plain flour
- 300 ml/½ pint dry white wine
- 4 tablespoons Calvados
- 75 ml/3 fl oz double cream
- 2 tablespoons chopped fresh parsley
- salt and pepper

Below:
Roast pheasant flambéed with Calvados

1 Place the prepared pheasants in a roasting tin. Tuck the onion quarters under the birds and sprinkle with a little salt and pepper. Dot with the butter and place in a preheated oven, 190°C (375°F), Gas Mark 5. Roast for about 45 minutes, or until the pheasants are cooked and tender.
2 Add the apples to the tin 15–20 minutes before the end of the cooking time.
3 Have ready a warmed serving dish. Remove the pheasants from the roasting tin and transfer them to the dish. Place the apple slices in a separate dish and keep them hot while making the sauce.
4 Stir the flour into the pan juices and cook over a moderate heat for 1 minute. Stir in the dry white wine and bring to the boil, stirring all the time. Remove from the heat.
5 Heat the Calvados in a small saucepan until it is just warm, carefully set it alight and then, when the flames die down, add it to the sauce. Stir in the cream and chopped parsley and adjust the seasoning to taste, then reheat the sauce gently without boiling.
6 Cut the pheasants in half or carve the meat neatly. Serve the pheasants with the apple slices and a little of the sauce; serve the remaining sauce separately.

Cook's Tip

It is best to use young pheasants for roasting, as older birds can be dry. Adapt the recipe for older pheasants by cooking them in a covered casserole with the wine. Remove them and keep warm while you finish the sauce. Whisk in a little beurre manié (see Cook's Tip, right), then finish the sauce as in Step 5,

Canard à la niçoise

Serves 4
Preparation: 15 minutes
Cooking: 1¾ hours
Carbohydrate: 21 g, Protein: 53 g, Fat: 83 g, Fibre: 7 g, Calories: 1103 kcal, Sodium: 1558 mg (per portion)

What you need:

- 2–2.5 kg/4–4½ lb duck
- 2 tablespoons olive oil
- 1 onion, finely chopped
- 1 kg/2 lb tomatoes, skinned and chopped
- 2 red peppers, deseeded and diced
- 1 celery stick, chopped
- 2 carrots, finely diced
- 4 garlic cloves, crushed
- 400 ml/14 fl oz dry white wine
- 1 bay leaf
- 2 teaspoons thyme
- 200 g/7 oz small black olives
- salt and pepper

1 Season the inside of the duck with salt and pepper. Place the duck in a lightly oiled roasting tin and cook in a preheated oven, 200°C (400°F), Gas Mark 6, for 30 minutes.
2 Meanwhile, heat the remaining oil in a frying pan and add the onion, tomatoes, peppers, celery and carrots. Cook gently until the vegetables are soft, and then stir in the garlic.
3 Add 250 ml/8 fl oz of the wine, the bay leaf and thyme and cook gently for 15–20 minutes. Stir in the olives.
4 Remove the duck from the oven and pour the sauce over the top. Reduce the oven temperature to 180°C (350°F), Gas Mark 4, and continue to roast the duck for about 1¼ hours, or until cooked and tender.

5 Remove the duck and keep it warm. Stir the remaining wine into the sauce in the roasting tin and cook over a high heat for a few minutes, stirring constantly, until reduced and thickened. Carve the duck and serve with the sauce.

Duck with oranges

Serves 6
Preparation: 20 minutes
Cooking: 1½ hours
*Carbohydrate: 11 g, Protein: 56 g,
Fat: 99 g, Fibre: 1 g, Calories: 1247
kcal, Sodium: 1244 mg (per portion)*

What you need:

- 50 g/2 oz butter
- 2 tablespoons olive oil
- 2 kg/4 lb duck, trussed
- 4 garlic cloves, crushed
- 125 g/4 oz streaky bacon, cut into thin strips
- 600 ml/1 pint dry white wine
- 200 ml/7 fl oz chicken stock
- 1 bouquet garni
- juice and pared rind of 2 oranges
- 1 tablespoon flour
- 1 tablespoon wine vinegar
- salt and pepper
- 2 oranges, cut into thin rings, to garnish

1 Heat 25 g/1 oz of the butter with the oil in a deep flameproof casserole and add the duck. Fry over medium heat until it is golden brown all over.
2 Add the garlic and strips of bacon to the casserole and fry for 1–2 minutes. Pour in the wine and stock, bring to the boil and then simmer for a few minutes, until slightly reduced. Add the bouquet garni, salt and pepper and orange juice, and then cover the casserole. Reduce the heat

and simmer gently for 1½ hours, or until the duck is cooked. Baste occasionally during cooking.
3 Using a sharp knife, cut the pared orange rind into fine strips and plunge them into a small saucepan of boiling water. Boil for 5 minutes, then remove and drain. Dry thoroughly on kitchen paper and set aside.
4 Mash the remaining butter with a fork to soften, then mash in the flour until smooth.
5 Remove the cooked duck from the casserole, cut into serving pieces and keep warm. Boil the cooking liquid for about 10 minutes, until reduced and well flavoured. Add the vinegar, strips of orange rind and little pieces of the butter and flour paste, stirring all the time, until the sauce thickens. Carve the duck and serve with the orange sauce, garnished with orange rings.

Cook's Tip

Add the butter and flour paste (beurre manié) at the end of cooking to thicken and enrich sauces and stews.

Above: *Canard à la niçoise*
Below: *Duck with oranges*

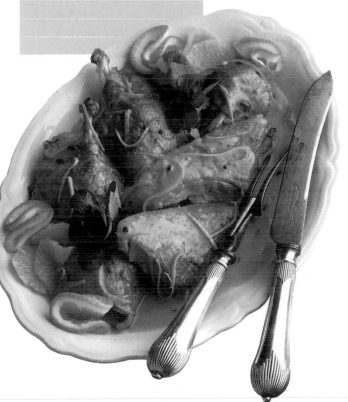

Meat

When it comes to meat dishes, we are spoiled for choice. Choose from lamb, beef, pork, veal or venison, and then choose your favourite method of cooking it. Whether it's leek and ham pie for a family supper, tournedos en croûte for a special celebratory meal, paupiettes de veau for a supper party with friends or gigot au pistou for a grand Sunday lunch, there's something here to suit every taste and every occasion. None of the recipes are difficult and all are absolutely delicious.

Below: *Leg of lamb à l'ail*
Right: *Spiced roast pork*

Leg of lamb à l'ail

Serves 6
Preparation: 25 minutes
Cooking: 2–2½ hours
Carbohydrate:68 g, Protein: 67 g, Fat: 53 g, Fibre: 0.5 g, Calories: 749 kcal, Sodium: 645 mg (per portion)

What you need:

- 125 g/4 oz bacon, chopped
- 3 garlic cloves, crushed
- 2 teaspoons finely chopped fresh basil
- 1 tablespoon finely chopped fresh parsley
- 2 kg/4 lb leg of lamb
- 25 g/1 oz butter
- salt and pepper
- sprigs of fresh rosemary, to garnish

1 In a small bowl mix the bacon, garlic, basil and parsley.
2 Make a cut in the leg of lamb, through to the bone and place the bacon mixture inside. Sew up the joint, enclosing the stuffing.
3 Put the lamb in a roasting pan, spread with the butter and then place in a preheated oven, 180°C (350°F), Gas Mark 4, for 2–2½ hours, depending on how well done you like your lamb.
4 Remove the string from the lamb and serve garnished with the sprigs of rosemary.

Spiced roast pork

Serves 6
Preparation: 10 minutes
Cooking: 2 hours

Carbohydrate: 3.5 g, Protein: 66 g,
Fat: 53 g, Fibre: 0 g, Calories: 810 kcal,
Sodium: 450 mg (per portion)

What you need:

- 2 kg/4 lb loin of pork joint
- ½ teaspoon ground cloves
- ½ teaspoon ground allspice
- 1 teaspoon ground ginger
- 2 garlic cloves, crushed
- 1 bay leaf, crumbled
- 175 ml/6 fl oz dark rum
- 600 ml/1 pint meat stock
- 75 g/3 oz soft brown sugar
- juice of 1 lime
- 2 teaspoons arrowroot
- salt and pepper

1 Using a very sharp knife, cut through the fat on the pork loin making a diamond pattern. Mix together the cloves, allspice, ginger, garlic, crumbled bay leaf and salt and pepper, in a small bowl. Rub this over the scored pork fat.

2 Place the pork in a roasting pan. Pour 125 ml/4 fl oz of the rum and 125 ml/4 fl oz of the meat stock over the pork. Place the pork in a preheated oven, 180°C (350°F), Gas Mark 4, and roast for 1¾–2 hours.

3 After 1 hour, mix the remaining rum with the sugar and lime juice, blend well and use to baste the pork, adding more stock and a little water if necessary to moisten the meat.

4 When the meat is cooked, transfer it to a serving plate and keep warm. Discard most of the fat and add the remaining basting sauce and stock. Stir well to scrape up any meat residues and place the pan over a medium heat and bring to the boil, stirring constantly. Mix the arrowroot with 1 tablespoon of water and stir into the gravy until thickened. Serve with the roast pork.

2 Put one-third of the mixture into a casserole dish. Cover with a layer of potatoes. Repeat the layering twice more, and pour over the stock. Dot with butter.
3 Cover and place in a pre-heated oven, 180°C (350°F), Gas Mark 4, for 1½ hours. Remove the lid and bake for a further 15 minutes to brown the top.

Pork and potato bake

Serves 4–6
Preparation: 30 minutes
Cooking: 1¾ hours
Carbohydrate: 20 g, Protein: 22 g,
Fat: 15 g, Fibre: 2 g, Calories: 295 kcal,
Sodium: 549 mg (per portion)

What you need:

- 1 tablespoon vegetable oil
- 50 g/2 oz rindless streaky bacon, chopped
- 1 large onion, chopped
- 125 g/4 oz mushrooms, quartered
- 1 teaspoon chopped fresh sage, or ½ teaspoon dried
- 1 teaspoon chopped fresh thyme, or ½ teaspoon dried
- 500 g/1 lb lean pork, cubed and tossed in 2 tablespoons seasoned flour
- 500 g/1 lb potatoes, sliced
- 300 ml/½ pint chicken stock
- 25 g/1 oz butter
- salt and pepper

1 Heat the oil in a frying pan over a low heat, add the bacon and fry for 3 minutes. Add the onion and cook until soft. Add the mushrooms, herbs and seasoning and cook for 1 minute. Using a slotted spoon, remove the bacon and mushrooms from the pan and set aside. Brown the pork in the pan, then mix with the bacon and mushrooms.

Sconed lamb

Serves 4–6
Preparation: 40 minutes
Cooking: 25 minutes
Carbohydrate: 36 g, Protein: 26 g,
Fat: 27 g, Fibre: 2 g, Calories: 502 kcal,
Sodium: 663 mg (per portion)

What you need:

- 1 tablespoon olive oil
- 50 g/2 oz rindless smoked streaky bacon, chopped
- 1 onion, chopped
- 500 g/1 lb minced lamb
- 1 teaspoon dried oregano
- 2 tablespoons chopped fresh parsley
- 150 ml/¼ pint red wine
- 1 x 400 g/13 oz can of chopped tomatoes
- salt and pepper

For the topping:
- 250 g/8 oz self-raising flour
- 50 g/2 oz chilled butter, diced
- 75 g/3 oz mature Cheddar cheese, grated
- 2 teaspoons wholegrain mustard
- 125 ml/4 fl oz milk

1 Heat the olive oil in a frying pan, add the chopped bacon and onion and fry for 5 minutes, until softened. Add the lamb and fry, stirring, until evenly browned.

Above left: *Pork and potato bake*
Right: *Sconed lamb*
Far right: *Leek and ham pie with cheese crust*

2 Stir in the herbs, wine and tomatoes, with salt and pepper to taste. Bring to the boil, then lower the heat and simmer, uncovered, for about 25 minutes, until the lamb is cooked and the sauce thickened.

3 For the scone topping, place the flour in a bowl with a little salt and pepper. Rub in the butter until the mixture resembles fine breadcrumbs. Stir in 50 g/2 oz of the cheese, then add the mustard and enough of the milk to mix to a soft dough.

4 Knead the dough briefly on a lightly floured surface, then roll out to a thickness of 1 cm/½ inch. Stamp into 5 cm/2 inch rounds, re-roll the trimmings and stamp out more rounds.

5 Transfer the meat mixture to a large ovenproof dish. Arrange the scones over the top, brush with milk and sprinkle with the remaining cheese. Place in a preheated oven, 200°C (400°F), Gas Mark 6, for 25 minutes, until golden brown. Serve hot.

Leek and ham pie with cheese crust

Serves 4
Preparation: 25 minutes
Cooking: 25–30 minutes
Carbohydrate: 61 g, Protein: 23 g, Fat: 34 g, Fibre:4 g, Calories: 628 kcal, Sodium: 1427 mg (per portion)

What you need:

- 50 g/2 oz butter
- 3 leeks, sliced
- 40 g/1½ oz plain flour
- 300 ml/½ pint milk
- 150 ml/¼ pint vegetable stock
- 175 g/6 oz cooked ham, cut into chunks
- salt and pepper

For the cheese crust:

- 250 g/8 oz self-raising flour
- 50 g/2 oz chilled butter, diced
- 75 g/3 oz mature Cheddar cheese, grated
- 6–8 tablespoons milk, plus extra to glaze

1 Melt the butter in a saucepan, add the leeks and fry gently until softened. Stir in the flour and cook for just 1 minute. Gradually add the milk and vegetable stock, stirring continuously until the sauce is thickened and smooth. Simmer for a further 5 minutes, then remove from the heat and stir in the ham cut into chunks, with salt and pepper to taste.

2 For the cheese crust, place the flour in a bowl with a little salt and pepper, rub in the butter until the mixture resembles fine bread-crumbs. Stir in the cheese, then add enough of the milk to form a soft dough.

3 Transfer the leek mixture to a large ovenproof dish. On a lightly floured surface, press out the dough to a round, which should be the same size as the dish holding the leek mixture. Score into the dough wedges with a sharp knife, then place on top of the pie. Brush with milk.

4 Place the pie in a preheated oven, 200°C (400°F), Gas Mark 6, for 25–30 minutes, until golden brown. Serve hot with a green vegetable or a fresh green salad.

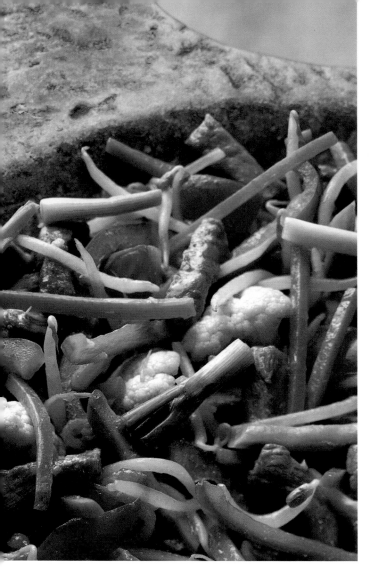

Pork chop suey

Serves 3–4
Preparation: 15 minutes
Cooking: 8–10 minutes
*Carbohydrate: 15 g, Protein: 17 g,
Fat: 7 g, Fibre: 3 g, Calories: 194 kcal,
Sodium: 1412 mg (per portion)*

What you need:

- 2 tablespoons soy sauce
- 1 tablespoon dry sherry
- 2 teaspoons cornflour
- 250 g/8 oz pork fillet, sliced thinly and cut into strips
- 2 spring onions
- 125 g/4 oz fresh bean sprouts
- 1 tablespoon oil
- 1 slice fresh root ginger, peeled and finely chopped
- 1 small green pepper, deseeded and cut into strips
- a few small cauliflower or broccoli florets
- 2–3 tomatoes, cut into pieces
- 2 carrots, cut into matchsticks
- 50 g/2 oz green beans, trimmed
- 2 teaspoons salt
- 1 tablespoon sugar
- 3 tablespoons stock or water

1 Mix together the soy sauce, sherry and cornflour and then add the pork strips. Stir well to coat the pork completely in the soy sauce/cornflour mixture.

2 Cut the spring onions into 2.5 cm/1 inch lengths. Wash the bean sprouts in a basin of cold water and discard any husks that float to the surface.

3 Heat half the oil in a wok or large, heavy frying pan. Stir-fry the pork for 1 minute and then remove with a slotted spoon and set aside.

4 Add the remaining oil to the wok, heat, then add the cut spring onions and the ginger, followed by the rest of the vegetables and the salt and sugar. Stir-fry all of the vegetables for just 1–2 minutes, until they have heated through and have picked up the other flavours from the wok, and then return the pork strips to the wok. Add the stock or water and stir-fry until all the vegetables are tender but still crisp to the bite. Serve with rice.

Ginger beef with peppers

Serves 3–4
Preparation: 10 minutes, plus 30 minutes marinating
Cooking: 5 minutes
*Carbohydrate: 4 g, Protein: 28 g,
Fat: 15 g, Fibre: 1 g, Calories: 258 kcal,
Sodium: 702 mg (per portion)*

What you need:

- 500 g/1 lb lean fillet steak, thinly sliced
- 2 teaspoons soy sauce
- 2 teaspoons sesame oil
- 2.5 cm/1 inch piece fresh root ginger, peeled and sliced
- 2 teaspoons vinegar
- 1 tablespoon water
- 1 teaspoon salt
- 1 teaspoon cornflour
- 1 garlic clove, crushed
- pinch of five-spice powder
- 1 red pepper, deseeded and cut into chunks
- 1 green pepper, deseeded and cut into chunks

To garnish:
- sliced spring onions
- slivers of fresh red chilli

1 Put the steak in a bowl and add the soy sauce, 1 teaspoon of the sesame oil, the ginger, vinegar, water, salt and cornflour. Stir well to mix until the steak slices are thoroughly coated in the mixture. Cover the bowl and leave in the refrigerator to marinate for at least 20 minutes.

2 Heat the remaining sesame oil in a wok or large, heavy frying pan and then add the garlic and the five-spice powder. Stir-fry for 30 seconds and then quickly add the marinated steaks. Stir-fry over a high heat until the meat is browned on the outside yet still pink and tender on the inside. Remove and set aside.

3 Add both the red and green peppers to the wok or frying pan and stir-fry them briskly, over a high heat for 2–3 minutes, tossing them continuously to coat in the oil.

4 Return the strips of steak and any remaining marinade to the pan. Stir-fry for 1 minute, until the meat is heated through.

Transfer to a serving dish and serve garnished with the spring onions and chilli.

Beef pasanda

Serves 4
Preparation: 15 minutes, plus marinating overnight
Cooking: 1¾ hours
Carbohydrate:11 g, Protein: 33 g, Fat: 13 g, Fibre: 1 g, Calories: 280 kcal, Sodium: 662 mg (per portion)

What you need:

- 500 g/1 lb braising or stewing steak, finely sliced
- 1 teaspoon salt
- 300 ml/½ pint natural yogurt
- 2 tablespoons ghee or butter
- 1 large onion, sliced
- 3 garlic cloves, sliced
- 1½ teaspoons ground ginger
- 2 teaspoons ground coriander
- 2 teaspoons chilli powder
- ½ teaspoon ground cumin
- 1½ teaspoons turmeric
- 1 teaspoon garam masala

1 Place the finely sliced beef between 2 sheets of greaseproof paper and beat with a rolling pin or mallet until thin. Rub the beef with the salt, and then cut into serving pieces. Place in a bowl, add the yogurt, cover and leave overnight in the refrigerator.

2 Melt the ghee or butter in a heavy pan and fry the onion and garlic gently for 4–5 minutes, until soft. Add the ground ginger, ground coriander, chilli powder, ground cumin, turmeric and garam masala and fry for 3 minutes, stirring constantly.

3 Add the beef, together with its marinade, to the saucepan and stir. Cover the pan and simmer for 1½ hours, or until the meat is tender. Serve hot with rice.

Below: Beef pasanda

Navarin of lamb printanier

Serves 4–6

Preparation: 40 minutes

Cooking: 1¾ hours

Carbohydrate: 37 g, Protein: 54 g, Fat: 61 g, Fibre: 7 g, Calories: 905 kcal, Sodium: 1047 mg (per portion)

What you need:

- 1 kg/2 lb boned shoulder of lamb, or lamb fillet, trimmed of excess fat and cut into 5 cm/2 inch cubes
- 50 g/2 oz flour, seasoned with salt and pepper
- 2 tablespoons sunflower oil
- 50 g/2 oz butter
- 250 g/8 oz baby carrots, scrubbed
- 250 g/8 oz baby turnips, peeled
- 250 g/8 oz small onions, peeled
- 1 garlic clove, crushed
- 450 ml/¾ pint chicken stock
- 2 teaspoons tomato purée
- small sprig of rosemary
- 125 g/4 oz frozen peas
- salt and pepper

1 Toss the meat in the seasoned flour, shake off and reserve any excess flour. Heat the sunflower oil in a flameproof casserole dish or heavy saucepan large enough to hold all the lamb, vegetables and stock. Add and fry the meat briskly on all sides, then with a slotted spoon remove from the pan and reserve.

2 Add the butter, baby carrots, baby turnips, small onions and crushed garlic to the pan and fry gently until lightly browned all over. Then sprinkle in the reserved seasoned flour and cook gently, stirring all the time, for about 1 minute.

3 Gradually stir in the chicken stock, tomato purée and rosemary. Bring the pan to the boil, stirring constantly, until the sauce has thickened and is really smooth, then return the meat to the pan.

4 Cover the pan, reduce the heat and simmer, stirring just occasionally, for about 1 hour. Add the frozen peas and continue cooking for another 30 minutes, or until the meat is tender. Serve the navarin of lamb immediately with a fresh green vegetable or a mixed salad.

Boeuf à la bourguignonne

Serves 4–6
Preparation: 30 minutes, plus
4 hours marinating
Cooking: 2½ hours
*Carbohydrate: 13 g, Protein: 63 g,
Fat: 54 g, Fibre: 3 g, Calories: 862 kcal,
Sodium: 1166 mg (per portion)*

What you need:

- 1 kg/2 lb chuck steak or top rump, cut into chunks
- a few sprigs of fresh parsley
- a few sprigs of fresh thyme
- 1 bay leaf, crushed
- 2 tablespoons brandy
- 400 ml/14 fl oz red Burgundy wine
- 2 tablespoons olive oil
- 50 g/2 oz butter
- 150 g/5 oz lean bacon, roughly chopped
- 24 small onions, peeled
- 500 g/1 lb button mushrooms, halved
- 25 g/1 oz plain flour
- 300 ml/½ pint beef stock
- 1 garlic clove, crushed
- 1 bouquet garni
- salt and pepper

1 Put the beef into a large bowl together with the parsley, thyme and the bay leaf. Add the brandy, red Burgundy wine and oil, stir once or twice, then cover the bowl and leave to marinate for at least 4 hours.

2 Melt the butter in a flameproof casserole, add the chopped bacon and fry over a moderate heat until golden brown all over. Remove the bacon from the pan with a slotted spoon and set aside. Add the onions to the pan and fry until golden on all sides. Remove and set aside. Add the button mushrooms and fry, stirring, for 1 minute. Remove and set aside. Add the mushrooms and fry, stirring, for 1 minute. Remove and set aside.

3 Remove the beef from the marinade, strain and reserve. Add the beef to the casserole and fry briskly until browned on all sides. Sprinkle in the plain flour and cook, stirring, for 1 minute. Gradually stir in the strained marinade, then add the beef stock, garlic, bouquet garni and the seasoning, to taste. Cover and simmer gently for 2 hours.

4 Skim off any fat from the surface and add the bacon, onions and mushrooms to the casserole. Then cover and simmer for 30 minutes, or until tender. Discard the bouquet garni and serve.

Left: *Navarin of lamb printanier*
Below: *Boeuf à la bourguignonne*

Above: *Mexican chilli shell bake*
Below right: *Parmesan meatballs*

Mexican chilli shell bake

Serves 4
Preparation: 45 minutes
Cooking: 20 minutes
Carbohydrate: 45 g, Protein: 40 g,
Fat: 32 g, Fibre: 6 g, Calories: 609 kcal,
Sodium: 781 mg (per portion)

What you need:

- 1 tablespoon olive oil
- 2 garlic cloves, crushed
- 1 onion, chopped finely
- 1 green chilli, deseeded and chopped
- 250 g/8 oz lean minced beef
- 2 teaspoons mild chilli powder
- 3 tablespoons tomato purée
- 250 g/8 oz dried wholemeal pasta shells
- 150 g/5 oz mozzarella cheese, grated
- 75 g/3 oz Cheddar cheese, grated
- 2 eggs, beaten
- salt and pepper

1 Heat the oil in a heavy saucepan. Add the crushed garlic and chopped onion and fry for 5 minutes, stirring occasionally, until softened.

2 Add the chopped green chilli and minced beef and then fry for 5 minutes, stirring constantly. Stir in the chilli powder, tomato purée and salt and pepper to taste. Simmer quite vigorously,

partially covered, for 25 minutes, until the sauce is really quite dry and thick.

3 Meanwhile, bring at least 1.8 litres/3 pints water to the boil in a large saucepan. Add a dash of oil and a generous pinch of salt. Cook the pasta in the pan for 8–12 minutes, until tender. Drain the pasta and transfer it to a large ovenproof dish. Pour the sauce over the pasta and mix.

4 Mix the two cheeses with the beaten eggs and pour over the beef, chilli and tomato purée mixture. Place the chilli bake in a preheated oven, 190°C (375°F), Gas Mark 5, for 20 minutes.

Parmesan meatballs

Serves 4
Preparation: 20 minutes
Cooking: 20 minutes
Carbohydrate:8 g, Protein: 33 g,
Fat: 25 g, Fibre: 1 g, Calories: 385 kcal,
Sodium: 352 mg (per portion)

What you need:

- 1 onion, grated
- 50 g/2 oz Parmesan cheese, grated
- 500 g/1 lb lean minced lamb
- 1 tablespoon tomato purée
- 1 teaspoon chilli sauce
- 1 tablespoon mixed dried herbs
- 4 tablespoons olive oil
- salt and pepper

For the sauce:

- 1 onion, finely chopped
- 2 garlic cloves, crushed
- 1 tablespoon olive oil
- 1 x 400 g/13 oz can of chopped tomatoes
- 2 tablespoons tomato purée
- 2 tablespoons chopped fresh oregano
- oregano leaves, to garnish

1 In a large bowl combine the onion, Parmesan, minced lamb, tomato purée, chilli sauce and herbs with seasoning to taste, and mix thoroughly.

2 Then using dampened hands, divide and shape the mixture into 30 small balls. Heat the olive oil in a large frying pan and fry the meatballs in 2 batches, fry for 10 minutes each batch. Transfer the meatballs to a baking dish and keep hot.

3 For the sauce, fry the finely chopped onion and the crushed garlic together in the olive oil for 3–5 minutes, until softened. Stir in the chopped tomatoes, tomato purée and the oregano and simmer for 8 minutes.

4 Taste the sauce and adjust the seasoning if necessary, then toss the sauce thoroughly with some freshly cooked spaghetti. Serve the coated spaghetti with the hot meatballs and garnish the whole dish with oregano.

Lamb and pasta bake

Serves 4
Preparation: 20 minutes
Cooking: 45 minutes
Carbohydrate: 75 g, Protein: 34 g,
Fat: 16 g, Fibre: 9 g, Calories: 559 kcal,
Sodium: 992 mg (per portion)

Variation

Coriander and chive meatballs

Replace the dried herbs in the recipe above with a bunch of chopped coriander and a bunch of snipped chives. Add 125 g/4 oz of finely chopped mushrooms to the meatball mixture. Continue as in main recipe.

What you need:

- 1 onion, sliced thinly in rings
- 1 tablespoon vegetable oil
- 250 g/8 oz cooked lean lamb, cubed
- 1 x 400 g/13 oz can of chopped tomatoes
- 4 tablespoons tomato purée
- 2 tablespoons mixed dried herbs
- 1 x 400 g/13 oz can of red kidney beans, drained
- 1 teaspoon cornflour
- 1 tablespoon water
- 175 g/6 oz dried macaroni, cooked
- 75 g/3 oz Cheddar cheese, grated
- 75 g/3 oz fresh wholemeal breadcrumbs
- salt and pepper

1 Fry the onion rings in the oil for 3 minutes, or until softened. Mix the softened onions with the lamb, tomatoes, tomato purée, herbs and kidney beans.

2 Mix the cornflour with the water to form a smooth paste. Stir into the meat mixture, with the cooked pasta. Season to taste.

3 Spoon the lamb mixture into a large ovenproof dish. Mix the cheese with the breadcrumbs and sprinkle over the lamb mixture. Place in a preheated oven, 200°C (400°F), Gas Mark 6, for about 45 minutes. You might need to cover the dish with foil after 30 minutes if the topping starts to over-brown.

Above: *Lamb and pasta bake*

Cook's Tip

Fresh herbs rather than dried herbs can add a lot of flavour and freshness to your dish. Thyme, sage and mint are all herbs that go particularly well with lamb. If you want to replace dried herbs with fresh herbs, use half the quantity given in the recipe.

Right: *Marinated veal with watercress sauce*

Marinated veal with watercress sauce

Serves 4
Preparation: 30 minutes, plus
1–2 hours marinating
Cooking: 10–12 minutes
Carbohydrate: 26 g, Protein: 59 g,
Fat: 24 g, Fibre: 6 g, Calories: 546 kcal,
Sodium: 678 mg (per portion)

What you need:

- 4 veal loin chops, about
  200–250 g/7–8 oz each
- finely grated rind and juice of
  2 oranges
- 1–2 garlic cloves, crushed
- 3 tablespoons olive oil

For the watercress sauce:
- 150 ml/¼ pint vegetable or
  meat stock
- 1 bunch watercress, leaves
  stripped from the stalks
- 50 ml/2 fl oz double cream
- salt and pepper

For the beetroot crisps:
- 4 small whole raw beetroots,
  about 275–300 g/9–10 oz
  each, peeled
- vegetable oil for deep-frying

1 Place the veal chops in a single layer in a shallow dish. Mix the orange rind and juice with the garlic and olive oil, pour over the chops, turn to coat, then cover the dish and leave to marinate for 1–2 hours.

2 For the watercress sauce, place the stock in a saucepan, bring to the boil, add the watercress leaves and then simmer for 1–2 minutes. Tip the contents of the pan into a blender or food processor and then blend until just smooth.

3 To make the beetroot crisps, dice the beetroot into wafer-thin slices, pat dry on kitchen paper and leave for 30 minutes. Heat

the oil in a deep-fat fryer or a deep pan to 190°C (375°F), or until a cube of bread browns in 30 seconds. Fry the beetroot slices in batches for just about 20–30 seconds each batch, until crisp and curly. Drain well on absorbent kitchen paper to take in some of the oil.

4 Remove the veal chops from the marinade and place under a preheated hot grill for 5–6 minutes on each side, basting often with the remaining marinade.

5 To serve, bring the watercress purée to the boil in a small pan, stir in the cream and simmer for about 2 minutes. Season to taste. Serve the sauce with the veal chops and the beetroot crisps.

Venison cutlets with red juniper berries

Serves 4
Preparation: 20 minutes
Cooking: 6–8 minutes
Carbohydrate:12g, Protein: 43 g,
Fat: 10 g, Fibre: 0 g, Calories: 357 kcal,
Sodium: 114 mg (per portion)

What you need:

- 4 dessert pears
- 2 tablespoons lemon juice
- 300 ml/½ pint red wine
- 6 juniper berries, crushed
- pared rind of 1 lemon, cut
  into fine julienne strips
- 1 stick of cinnamon
- 3 tablespoons redcurrant jelly
- 8 venison cutlets
- oil or melted butter, for
  brushing
- bunch of watercress, to garnish

1 Peel the pears, then halve them lengthways and remove the cores with a melon baller. Brush the flesh with the lemon juice to prevent discoloration.

2 Place the red wine, juniper berries, lemon rind and cinnamon stick in a pan. Bring to the boil, add the pears, cover and simmer for 10 minutes.

3 Using a slotted spoon, transfer the pears to a bowl and then set aside. Stir the redcurrant jelly into the liquid remaining in the saucepan. Boil the mixture until

juice, parsley and plenty of pepper, and mix well. (The easiest way to do this is in a blender or a food processor. If you have a pulse button on your processor then use it, to make sure all the ingredients are evenly incorporated; otherwise turn your blender or food processor on and off while mixing to achieve the same result.) Mould the anchovy butter into a fat sausage shape and roll it in aluminium foil. Place in the refrigerator for at least 30 minutes, until chilled and firm.

2 Heat the butter and olive oil in a heavy frying pan. Season the steaks on both sides with salt and pepper, then fry until they are done to your liking; turning once, 2–3 minutes on each side for rare steaks, 6–8 minutes (over a slightly lower heat) for medium to well-done.

4 Serve each steak topped with a slice of the anchovy butter sprinkled with chopped parsley. Allow the butter to melt from the heat of the steak as you serve it.

reduced by half, pour all the reduced liquid over the pears and leave to cool.

4 Brush the venison cutlets with a little oil or butter and place under a hot grill for 2–3 minutes on each side. To serve, place 2 cutlets on each plate and add a portion of pears. Garnish with the watercress and serve the remaining pears separately.

Fillet steaks with anchovy butter

Serves 4
Preparation: 5 minutes, plus
30 minutes chilling
Cooking: 5–10 minutes
Carbohydrate: 0 g, Protein: 33 g,
Fat: 34 g, Fibre: 0 g, Calories: 437 kcal,
Sodium: 530 mg (per portion)

What you need:

- 2 tablespoons butter
- 1 tablespoon olive oil
- 4 fillet steaks, about 150 g/
  5 oz each
- salt and pepper

- 2 tablespoons finely chopped parsley, to garnish

For the anchovy butter:

- 50 g/2 oz unsalted butter
- 4 canned anchovies, drained and chopped
- squeeze of lemon juice
- 2 tablespoons finely chopped parsley

1 First make the anchovy butter: mix the butter with the anchovies until well blended. Add the lemon

Barbecues

As soon as the good weather comes round again, it's out with the charcoal, on with the oven gloves, matches at the ready, and it's barbecue time again! Barbecues have become enormously popular in recent times, with the result that outdoor eating has become a much more sophisticated affair than it used to be. Barbecues are the perfect way of entertaining family and friends. Relaxed and informal, they do much to heighten the exhilaration of summer. There's nothing quite like the smell of charcoal-cooked food wafting in the balmy night air to make any occasion seem like a special one.

Grilled sardines in chilli oil

Serves 4
Preparation: 15 minutes, plus 8–12 hours infusing
Cooking: 6–8 minutes
Carbohydrate: 0 g, Protein: 35 g, Fat: 23 g, Fibre: 0 g, Calories: 347 kcal, Sodium: 697 mg (per portion)

What you need:

- 125 ml/4 fl oz olive oil
- 2 tablespoons chopped dried red chillies
- 12 small sardines, cleaned and scaled
- coarse sea salt

1 Place the oil and chillies in a small saucepan and heat very gently for 10 minutes. Remove the pan from the heat, then cover and leave to cool and infuse for about 8–12 hours.

2 Strain the oil through a sieve lined with muslin or a clean towel, then pour into a sterilized jar or bottle.

3 Brush the prepared sardines with just a little of the chilli oil, then sprinkle with coarse sea salt and cook the fish on an oiled barbecue grill over hot coals for about 6–8 minutes, or until the sardines are just cooked, turning once. Serve the hot sardines immediately, with lemon wedges, hot crusty bread and a mixed salad, if liked.

Left: *Grilled sardines in chilli oil*
Right: *Monkfish with rosemary*

Monkfish with rosemary

Serves 4
Preparation: 30 minutes, plus
1 hour marinating
Cooking: 25–30 minutes
*Carbohydrate: 5 g, Protein: 28 g, Fat:
10 g, Fibre: 1 g, Calories: 219 kcal,
Sodium: 338 mg (per portion)*

What you need:

- 500 g/1 lb ripe tomatoes, skinned
- 1 tablespoon balsamic vinegar
- 2 monkfish fillets, about 375 g/12 oz each, skinned
- 4 garlic cloves, cut into thin slivers
- 2 long rosemary sprigs
- 5 tablespoons olive oil
- 1 tablespoon lemon juice
- salt and pepper

1 Put the tomatoes in a liquidizer or food processor and purée until smooth. Strain through a sieve into a bowl, season with the vinegar, salt and pepper, then cover and set aside.
2 Slice each fillet lengthways, almost but not quite all the way through, making a pocket. Lay the garlic down the pocket lengths. Top with a rosemary sprig and season to taste. Reform both fillets and tie with string at 1.5 cm/³⁄₄ inch intervals.
3 Mix the oil and lemon juice in a large shallow dish. Add the fillets, spoon the marinade over the top and cover. Leave for 1 hour, turning occasionally.
4 Drain the fish and cook on an oiled barbecue grill over fairly hot coals for 20 minutes, basting frequently, until just cooked.
5 Remove the string. Slice the fish thinly. Serve with the tomato sauce, warmed through.

3 Put the drumsticks on the grid over hot charcoal on the barbecue. Cook, turning frequently, for about 20 minutes until the chicken is charred on the outside and no longer pink on the inside.

4 Meanwhile, pour the marinade into a small saucepan, add the stock and bring to the boil over a moderate heat, stirring. Simmer, stirring occasionally, until the sauce has reduced and thickened slightly.

5 Serve the chicken drumsticks hot, with the barbecue sauce. A rice pilaf and a mixed pepper salad are ideal accompaniments.

Turkey, tomato and tarragon burgers

Serves 4
Preparation: 20 minutes
Cooking: 20–25 minutes
Carbohydrate: 26 g, Protein: 38 g,
Fat: 26 g, Fibre: 1 g, Calories: 484 kcal,
Sodium: 1128 mg (per portion)

What you need:

- 8 sun-dried tomato halves in oil, drained and chopped
- 500 g/1 lb minced turkey
- 1 tablespoon chopped fresh tarragon
- ½ red onion, finely chopped
- ¼ teaspoon paprika
- ¼ teaspoon salt

Above: Barbecued chicken drumsticks
Below right: *Turkey, tomato and tarragon burgers*

Barbecued chicken drumsticks

Serves 8
Preparation: 15 minutes, plus 4 hours marinating or overnight
Cooking: about 20 minutes
Carbohydrate: 6 g, Protein: 18 g,
Fat: 4 g, Fibre: 0 g, Calories: 131 kcal,
Sodium: 458 mg (per portion)

What you need:

- 16 chicken drumsticks
- 300 ml/½ pint chicken stock

For the marinade:

- 4 tablespoons tomato ketchup
- 2 tablespoons Worcestershire sauce
- 2 tablespoons wine vinegar
- 2 tablespoons soft brown sugar
- 2 teaspoons chilli powder
- 1 teaspoon celery salt

1 Score the drumsticks deeply with a sharp pointed knife, cutting down as far as the bone.

2 Whisk together all the marinade ingredients in a shallow dish. Add the drumsticks and turn to coat, then cover and leave in the refrigerator for at least 4 hours or preferably overnight, turning the drumsticks in the marinade from time to time.

Variation

Chicken tikka

Replace the chicken portions with 4 large skinned and boned chicken breasts, cut into cubes, and proceed as in the main recipe. After marinating, thread the cubes of chicken on to kebab skewers, then place the skewers on the grid over hot charcoal on the barbecue (or under the grill) and cook turning the skewers often, for about 10–15 minutes until the chicken juices run clear.

- 4 slices of smoked pancetta or rindless streaky bacon, cut in half
- 4 ciabatta rolls
- shredded radicchio and cos lettuce

1 Place the sun-dried tomatoes, turkey and tarragon in a liquidizer or food processor and purée until smooth. Spoon the mixture into a bowl and stir in the onion. Season with the paprika and salt. Mix well, divide into 4 and shape into burgers. Stretch 2 strips of pancetta over each burger and secure with cocktail sticks soaked in water for 30 minutes.

2 Cook on an oiled barbecue grill over hot coals for 20–25 minutes turning frequently. Serve at once in the ciabatta rolls with shredded lettuce.

Tandoori chicken

Serves 4
Preparation: 20 minutes, plus 4 hours marinating or overnight
Cooking: 40 minutes
Carbohydrate: 4 g, Protein: 29 g, Fat: 8 g, Fibre: 0 g, Calories: 186 kcal, Sodium: 116 mg (per portion)

What you need:

- 1 fresh hot red chilli, deseeded and chopped roughly
- 2 garlic cloves, chopped roughly
- 2.5 cm/1 inch piece of fresh root ginger, chopped roughly
- 2 tablespoons lemon juice
- 1 tablespoon coriander seeds
- 1 tablespoon cumin seeds
- 2 teaspoons garam masala
- 6 tablespoons natural yogurt
- a pinch of mild paprika
- a pinch of turmeric
- 4 skinned chicken portions

To garnish:

- lemon wedges
- coriander sprigs

1 Put the chilli, garlic, ginger and lemon juice in an electric spice mill with the whole spices and the garam masala and work to a paste.

2 Transfer the spice paste to a dish in which the chicken portions will fit in a single layer. Add the yogurt, paprika, turmeric and ½ teaspoon of salt, and stir well to mix. Set aside.

3 Score the flesh of the chicken deeply with a sharp pointed knife, cutting right down as far as the bone. Put the chicken in a single layer in the dish, then spoon the marinade over the chicken and brush it into the cuts in the flesh. Cover and marinate in the refrigerator for at least 4 hours, but preferably overnight.

4 Place the chicken on the grid over hot charcoal on the barbecue. Cook, turning often, for about 30 minutes or until the juices run clear when pierced with a skewer or fork. Serve hot, garnished with lemon wedges and coriander sprigs, and accompanied by a salad of lettuce, white cabbage and raw onion slices, a sauce made of yogurt and chopped mint, and plain or garlic naan bread.

Above: *Tandoori chicken*

Cook's Tip

Lamb would make a great substitute for chicken. Lamb cutlets are the best for barbecuing. Before cooking the meat should be marinated, preferably overnight, then grilled to your liking.

Above: *Pork kebabs with prunes and chestnuts*
Below right: *Beef and pineapple kebabs*

Pork kebabs with prunes and chestnuts

Serves 4
Preparation: 15–25 minutes, plus
12 hours marinating
Cooking: 10–12 minutes
*Carbohydrate: 56 g, Protein: 29 g,
Fat:19 g, Fibre: 8 g, Calories: 514 kcal,
Sodium: 309 mg (per portion)*

What you need:

- 500 g/1 lb pork fillet, trimmed
- 24 pitted prunes
- 4 tablespoons Cognac
- 4 tablespoons olive oil
- 2 sprigs of rosemary, leaves stripped from the stalks, then chopped
- 24 chestnuts, roasted, dried or vacuum-packed
- salt and pepper

1 Cut the pork into 1.5 cm/ ¾ inch pieces. Place in a bowl with the prunes, mix the Cognac, oil and rosemary in a jug and pour over the meat. Toss to coat, then cover and leave to marinate overnight in the refrigerator. If using dried chestnuts, soak them in cold water overnight, then drain and treat as fresh.
2 Place the chestnuts in a small pan, cover with cold water, bring to the boil, lower the heat and simmer for 15–20 minutes, until just tender. Drain, rinse well in cold water and drain again.
3 Using a slotted spoon, re-move the meat and prunes from the marinade. Thread on to skewers, alternating with the chestnuts (if the chestnuts are too soft to skewer, stuff one into each prune). Pour the marinade into a small jug and set aside.
4 Cook the skewers on an oiled barbecue grill over hot coals for about 10–12 minutes, turning frequently and basting with the marinade. Season and serve.

Beef and pineapple kebabs

Serves 4
Preparation: 20 minutes, plus
1 hour marinating
Cooking: 10 minutes
*Carbohydrate: 26 g, Protein: 29 g,
Fat:17 g, Fibre: 2 g, Calories: 367 kcal,
Sodium: 277 mg (per portion)*

What you need:

- 500 g/1 lb rump steak
- 3 tomatoes
- 2 onions

- 1 green pepper
- 12 pineapple cubes, fresh or canned
- rice, to serve

For the marinade:
- 1 tablespoon molasses or treacle
- 4 tablespoons pineapple juice
- 2 tablespoons vinegar
- 1 tablespoon oil
- salt and pepper

1 First make the marinade: put the molasses or treacle, pineapple juice, vinegar and oil in a bowl and mix together well. Add a little salt and some pepper.

2 Cut the steak into 2.5 cm/1 inch cubes and add to the marinade. Cover and leave in a cool place for at least 1 hour. Remove the steak, pour the marinade into a small jug and set aside for basting the kebabs.

3 Cut the tomatoes into quarters. Peel the onions and then cut them into small chunks. Remove the core and seeds from the green pepper, and then cut the pepper into squares.

4 Thread the steak, tomatoes, onions, pepper and pineapple chunks alternately on to 4 long or 8 short skewers. Brush with the reserved marinade. Cook under a hot grill for 10 minutes, turning frequently and basting with the marinade. Serve with plain rice with the remaining marinade on top.

Chicken and sweet pepper kebabs

Serves 4
Preparation: 15 minutes, plus 30–60 minutes marinating
Cooking: 20 minutes
Carbohydrate: 8 g, Protein: 39 g, Fat: 12 g, Fibre: 1 g, Calories: 288 kcal, Sodium: 669 mg (per portion)

Variation

Japanese chicken kebabs

Crush a 5 cm/2 inch piece of root ginger to a paste with 4 garlic cloves and 8 black peppercorns.

Place 150 ml/¼ pint Japanese soy sauce (shoyu), 150 ml/¼ pint rice wine (sake), 2 tablespoons soft brown sugar and 1 tablespoon oil in a large shallow dish. Add the ginger and garlic paste and then whisk to combine.

Cut 500 g/1 lb skinned chicken breast fillets diagonally into thick strips. Add to the marinade, cover and marinate at room temperature for at least 30 minutes. Meanwhile, soak 16–18 bamboo skewers in warm water.

Drain the skewers, then thread the chicken strips on to them, and place under a preheated hot grill for 8–10 minutes until the chicken is tender. Turn the skewers and baste the chicken with the marinade frequently during cooking. Serve hot, garnished with spring onion tassels.

What you need:

- 150 ml/¼ pint natural yogurt
- 2 tablespoons extra-virgin olive oil
- 2 garlic cloves, crushed
- 2 tablespoons chopped fresh coriander
- 2 teaspoons ground cumin
- 8 skinned and boned chicken thighs, cut into large chunks
- 1 onion, cut into chunks
- 1 red pepper, cored, deseeded and cut into chunks
- salt and pepper

1 Mix the yogurt, oil, garlic, coriander and cumin together in a large shallow dish with salt and pepper to taste. Add the cubes of chicken and stir well to mix. Cover and leave to marinate at room temperature for at least 30–60 minutes.

2 Thread the chicken cubes on to kebab skewers, alternating with the onion and pepper.

3 Put the kebabs on the rack of the grill pan. Place under a preheated hot grill and cook, turning frequently, for 20 minutes or until the chicken is tender when pierced with a skewer or fork. Serve hot, on a bed of saffron rice with a raita of yogurt, cucumber and chopped fresh coriander.

Above: *Chicken and sweet pepper kebabs*

Baby aubergines with herbed Greek yogurt

Serves 4
Preparation: 20 minutes
Cooking: 6 minutes
Carbohydrate: 7 g, Protein: 6 g,
Fat: 12 g, Fibre: 5 g, Calories: 153 kcal,
Sodium: 1038 mg (per portion)

What you need:

- 12 baby aubergines
- 3 tablespoons olive oil
- salt and pepper

For the herbed Greek yogurt:
- 2 tablespoons chopped fresh parsley
- 2 tablespoons chopped fresh dill
- 2 tablespoons chopped mint
- 1 small red onion, finely chopped
- 2 garlic cloves, crushed
- 75 g/3 oz Kalamata olives, pitted and sliced
- 2 teaspoons fennel seeds, crushed
- 1 tablespoon capers, chopped

Cook's Tip

Mini vegetables are perfect for cooking whole on the barbecue as they are usually sweet and tender, so cook speedily. Little aubergines are usually available in ethnic markets.

Left: Baby aubergines with herbed Greek yogurt
Right: Black bean kebabs

- 15 g/½ oz gherkins, finely chopped
- finely grated rind and juice of 1 lime
- 150 ml/¼ pint strained Greek yogurt
- salt and pepper

1 First make the herbed Greek yogurt, mix all the ingredients together in a bowl and set aside.
2 Slice all the baby aubergines in half lengthways, leaving them attached to their stalks.
3 Using a small brush, coat the aubergines with olive oil. Cook on an oiled barbecue grill over moderately hot coals for about 2–3 minutes on each side.
4 To serve, place the aubergines on a serving dish or plate and spoon over the herbed yogurt.

Black bean kebabs

Serves 4
Preparation: 1 hour 20 minutes, plus soaking overnight
Cooking: 1 hour
Carbohydrate: 18 g, Protein: 10 g,
Fat: 6 g, Fibre: 2 g, Calories: 163 kcal,
Sodium: 28 mg (per portion)

What you need:

- 125 g/4 oz dried black beans
- 3 tablespoons olive oil
- 1 onion, very finely chopped
- 1 garlic clove, crushed
- 1 red chilli, deseeded and finely chopped
- ½ teaspoon ground cumin
- ½ teaspoon ground coriander
- 1 tablespoon chopped fresh coriander
- 2 medium courgettes
- 24 mixed red and yellow cherry tomatoes

1 Place the beans in a large bowl and cover with cold water. Soak overnight, then tip them into a colander and rinse well under cold running water. Transfer the beans to a large saucepan and cover with fresh water. Bring to the boil and boil vigorously for about 10 minutes, then lower the heat and simmer for 40–50 minutes, or until the beans are tender. Drain well and set aside.

2 Heat 2 tablespoons of the olive oil in a frying pan, add the onion, garlic and chilli and cook gently for 5–10 minutes, until the onion is softened but not coloured. Stir in the cumin and ground coriander and cook for about 1–2 minutes more.

3 Turn the onion and spice mixture into a bowl, add the drained beans and fresh coriander and mash well. Divide the mixture into 24 and then roll into balls.

4 Using a potato peeler, cut the courgettes lengthways into thin strips. Brush with the remaining olive oil. Thread the bean balls on to metal skewers, alternating with the cherry tomatoes and weaving the courgette strips in between them.

5 Cook the black bean kebabs on a well-oiled barbecue grill over moderately hot coals for about 4 minutes on each side. Serve with rice.

Stuffed mini peppers

Serves 4
Preparation: 15 minutes
Cooking: 10–15 minutes
Carbohydrate: 7 g, Protein: 9 g, Fat: 11 g, Fibre: 2 g, Calories: 160 kcal, Sodium: 391 mg (per portion)

What you need:

- 8 mini peppers
- tomato sauce, preferably homemade
- Greek yogurt, to serve

For the stuffing:
- 125 g/4 oz soft fresh goat's cheese
- 50 g/2 oz ricotta
- 1½ tablespoons chopped fresh mint
- 1 red or green chilli, deseeded and finely chopped (optional)
- salt and pepper

1 First make the stuffing, combine the goat's cheese, ricotta and mint in a large bowl. Stir in the chilli, if using, and season with salt and pepper to taste.

2 Make a small slit in the side of each pepper, carefully scrape out the seeds and core with a teaspoon, keeping the pepper shells intact. Half fill each pepper with stuffing – do not be tempted to fill them completely, or they may burst during cooking.

3 Cook the filled peppers on an oiled barbecue grill over moderately hot coals for about 10–15 minutes, turning the peppers occasionally, until softened.

4 Place 2 of the filled peppers on each plate and serve with a tomato sauce and Greek yogurt.

Grilled sweet potatoes

Serves 4
Preparation: 15 minutes
Cooking: 10 minutes
Carbohydrate: 27 g, Protein: 2 g, Fat: 7 g, Fibre: 3 g, Calories: 172 kcal, Sodium: 50 mg (per portion)

What you need:

- 500 g/1 lb sweet potatoes, scrubbed
- 4 tablespoons olive oil

1 To prepare the sweet potatoes, cut each potato into 5 mm/¼ inch slices.

2 Brush with the oil and place on an oiled barbecue grill over moderately hot coals. Grill for about 5 minutes on each side until tender. Serve with aïoli.

Left: *Stuffed mini peppers*
Above: *Grilled sweet potatoes*

Above: *Baked bananas with cinnamon and rum mascarpone cream*
Below right: *Rum-flambéed pineapple parcels*

Variation

Baked bananas with chocolate ricotta cream

Mix 250 g/8 oz ricotta and 1–2 tablespoons of maple syrup in a large bowl. Stir in 15 g/½ oz hazelnuts and beat in 50 g/2 oz melted chocolate. Prepare the baked bananas as in the main recipe. Serve with the ricotta cream and a few more hazelnuts sprinkled over the top

Baked bananas with cinnamon and rum mascarpone cream

Serves 4
Preparation: 5 minutes
Cooking: 10–12 minutes
Carbohydrate: 49 g, Protein: 6 g, Fat: 5 g, Fibre: 2 g, Calories: 258 kcal, Sodium: 21 mg (per portion)

What you need:

- 1–2 tablespoons caster sugar
- ½ teaspoon ground cinnamon
- 1–2 tablespoons rum
- 250 g/8 oz mascarpone
- 8 small bananas

1 Mix the sugar, cinnamon and rum together in a large bowl. Stir in the mascarpone, mix well and then set aside.
2 Place the whole unpeeled bananas on a barbecue grill over hot coals. Cook for about 10–12 minutes, turning as the skins darken, until they are black all over and the flesh is very tender.
3 To serve, carefully split the bananas open and spread the flesh with the cinnamon and rum mascarpone cream.

Rum-flambéed pineapple parcels

Serves 4
Preparation: 15 minutes
Cooking: 10–15 minutes
Carbohydrate: 45 g, Protein: 4 g, Fat: 21 g, Fibre: 3 g, Calories: 396 kcal, Sodium: 107 mg (per portion)

What you need:

- 1 ripe pineapple, peeled
- 50 g/2 oz butter
- 75 g/3 oz light muscovado sugar
- 4 tablespoons dark rum (optional)
- 50 g/2 oz pecan nuts, roasted and coarsely chopped
- crème fraîche or fromage blanc, to serve

1 Cut the pineapple into 8 even slices, then carefully remove the cores with a small pastry cutter to make rings.
2 Using doubled aluminium foil, cut out 4 aluminium foil squares, each large enough to hold 2 pineapple rings.
3 Melt the butter in a small saucepan, stir in the sugar and cook gently until the sugar has dissolved completely. Divide the mixture evenly between the parcels, then bring the edges of the foil together and press lightly to seal.
4 Cook on a barbecue grill over moderately hot coals for about 10–15 minutes.
5 When the pineapple is cooked, gently open each parcel, spoon 1 tablespoon of rum into each and carefully ignite with a match. Scatter over the chopped pecans and serve the parcels at once with either crème fraîche or fromage blanc.

The Great
Outdoors

Planning a Barbecue

A simple barbecue of sausages, steaks or burgers can make an easy informal supper, but with a little planning you can include some unusual dishes .

● A marinade of flavoured oil, wine and herbs can transform a piece of chicken or pork, and also keeps the meat tender and moist.

● Vegetables such as mushrooms, peppers, aubergine and courgettes do not need long cooking – thread on to skewers and marinate in seasoned oil for ½-1 hour before barbecuing for 10–15 minutes.

● Corn on the cob in its husk cooks perfectly on the barbecue: peel back the husks and remove silky threads, brush the corn with melted butter, then replace husks. Barbecue for ¾–1 hour.

● Pitta bread is ideal for filling with salad and barbecued meat. Sprinkle the bread with water and place on the barbecue for 5–10 minutes, turning once.

● Besides food and drink, you will also need some heavy-duty foil; tongs; large paper napkins; and enough charcoal to keep the barbecue going.

Countdown to barbecue time

● The day before – prepare the desserts. As an alternative to barbecued fruit, serve a simple fruit salad or ice cream. Marinate your meat or fish and leave in the refrigerator.

● Earlier in the day – chill the wine, beer and soft drinks. Marinate the vegetables. Prepare salads and dressings – but only toss them together at the very last minute.

● 2 hours ahead – nominate a chef to take charge. Light coals.

● 1 hour ahead – start cooking the baked potatoes in coals.

Figs and blackberries on toast

Serves 4
Preparation: 5-10 mins
Cooking: 8-10 mins

What you need:

- 12 ripe figs
- 125 g/4 oz blackberries
- pared rind and juice of 2 oranges
- 2 tablespoons crème de cassis (blackcurrant liqueur)
- 1 tablespoon caster sugar
- ½ teaspoon cinnamon
- 25 g/1 oz butter, melted
- 4 slices white bread

1 Cut the figs into quarters, slicing almost but not all the way through to the base. Cut 4 squares of double-thickness foil and place 3 figs and a quarter of the blackberries on each.

2 Cut the orange rind into thin strips, mix with orange juice and crème de cassis and divide between the fig parcels. Bring up the edges of the foil and then press to seal.

3 Mix the sugar, cinnamon and melted butter in a bowl and brush over one side of each of the four slices of bread.

4 Cook the fig parcels on a barbecue grill over moderately hot coals for 8-10 minutes. After 5-6 minutes, place the bread on the grill, buttered side up, and toast until golden.

5 Serve the cinnamon toast on individual plates, topped with the figs and blackberries.

Grilled fruit skewers

Serves 4
Preparation: 20 minutes
Cooking: 4-6 mins

What you need:

- 1 kg/2 lb assorted exotic fruits
- 75 g/3 oz butter
- 2 tablespoons muscovado sugar
- 1 tablespoon rum

1 If using wooden skewers, soak them in cold water for 30 minutes. Prepare the fruit according to type and cut it into evenly sized pieces. Thread on to 8 skewers.

2 Melt the butter and sugar in a small pan over a low heat, then stir in the rum.

3 Brush the fruit skewers with some of the rum butter. Cook on a barbecue grill over moderately hot coals for 2–3 minutes on each side, brushing them with more rum and butter as they cook. Serve at once.

Two delicious fruity puddings that can be prepared in advance, and then cooked on the barbecue for a few minutes.
Above: Figs and blackberries on toast.
Right: Grilled fruit skewers

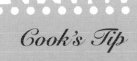

Cook's Tip

Use strawberries, mango, cherries papaya, oranges or pears

Picnics

The great steak sandwich

Serves 4
Preparation: 35 minutes
Cooking:
4–6 minutes (very rare)
6–8 minutes (rare)
8–10 minutes (medium rare)
10–12 minutes (medium)
Carbohydrate: 36 g, Protein: 48 g,
Fat: 22 g, Fibre:3 g, Calories: 513 kcal,
Sodium: 906 mg (per portion)

What you need:

- 6 tablespoons olive oil
- 2 teaspoons mustard seeds
- 2 large red onions, thinly sliced
- 2 garlic cloves, crushed
- 15 g/½ oz fresh flat leaf parsley, chopped
- 1 tablespoon balsamic vinegar
- 2 rump or sirloin steaks, about 250 g/8 oz each
- 8 slices of olive bread or crusty bread
- 75 g/3 oz fontina cheese, thinly sliced
- 2 ripe beefsteak tomatoes, sliced
- 125 g/4 oz rocket
- sea salt flakes and crushed black peppercorns

1 Heat 4 tablespoons of the oil in a frying pan, add the mustard seeds, cover and let them pop for 30 seconds over a moderate heat – do not burn. Add the onions and garlic, cover and cook over a very low heat for 30 minutes until very soft but not coloured.

2 Purée the softened onion mixture in a liquidizer or food processor, then spoon into a bowl. Stir in the parsley and vinegar, with salt and pepper to taste. Cover and set aside.

3 Brush the steaks with a little of the remaining oil and season with crushed black peppercorns. Cook on an oiled barbecue grill over hot coals for 2–3 minutes on each side for very rare, up to 5–6 minutes each side for medium (see cooking times, left).

4 Toast the bread slices on both sides until lightly golden. Spread with the onion purée. Slice the steaks thinly and divide between 4 of the bread slices. Top with the fontina, tomato and rocket. Season with the sea salt flakes and black pepper, top with the remaining bread slices and then serve immediately.

Picnics conjure up an idyllic picture of long, hazy days spent basking in the sunshine, or perhaps cooling off in the shade of a tree while nibbling delicate morsels of delicious food and sipping long cool drinks. The three most important essentials for the perfect picnic are good weather, good food and a corkscrew. It is not, unfortunately, within our power to dictate the weather, but all the other ingredients are up to us. With the help of these delicious recipes, the food should be no problem. As for the corkscrew — you're on your own!

Below: *The great steak sandwich*

Above: *Club sandwich*
Right: *Leafy salad with cheese and sun-dried tomatoes*
Far right: *Smoked chicken and citrus salad*

Club sandwich

Serves 2
Preparation: about 20 minutes
Carbohydrate: 54 g, Protein: 50 g,
Fat: 62 g, Fibre: 3 g, Calories: 960 kcal,
Sodium: 2297 mg (per portion)

What you need:

- 6 rindless streaky bacon rashers
- 6 slices white bread
- 6 tablespoons mayonnaise
- 8 small lettuce leaves
- 2 large slices of cooked turkey
- 2 tomatoes, sliced thinly
- salt and pepper

1 Cook the bacon in a heavy-based frying pan or under a pre-heated hot grill for 5–7 minutes, turning once, until crisp on both sides. Remove and drain on kitchen paper.
2 Toast the bread slices lightly

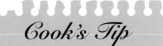

Cook's Tip

This famous American sandwich always has three layers of white bread, but you can use granary or wholemeal if you prefer. Turkey is traditional, but chicken makes a good substitute.

on both sides, then cut off and discard the crusts.
3 Arrange the toasted bread slices on a large board or work surface and spread one side of each slice with mayonnaise.
4 Arrange 2 of the lettuce leaves on each of 2 slices of toast and sprinkle with salt and pepper.
5 Arrange 1 slice of turkey on top of the lettuce on each sandwich, then top with another slice of toast, with the mayonnaise side up. Arrange the remaining lettuce on top and add the tomato, then bacon, cutting the rashers to fit wherever necessary.

6 Cover with the remaining 2 slices of bread, mayonnaise side down. Leave the sandwiches whole, or cut into 4 triangles and serve. Ice-cold beer is the traditional accompaniment.

Leafy salad with cheese and sun-dried tomatoes

Serves 4
Preparation: 20 minutes
Carbohydrate: 3 g, Protein: 11 g,
Fat: 31 g, Fibre: 1 g, Calories: 335 kcal,
Sodium: 559 mg (per portion)

What you need:

- 1 small cos lettuce, separated into leaves
- about 50 g/2 oz rocket
- ½ head radicchio, separated into leaves
- 125 g/4 oz cheese (e.g. Gruyère, Emmental or hard goat's cheese)
- 5 tablespoons olive oil
- 1 garlic clove, chopped
- 4 spring onions, chopped
- 6 sun-dried tomatoes preserved in oil, drained and sliced
- 2 tablespoons balsamic vinegar
- salt and pepper
- 2 tablespoons pine nuts, toasted (optional)

1 Tear the salad leaves into bite-sized pieces and place in a shallow serving bowl. Using a cheese slicer or vegetable peeler, shave the cheese into wafer-thin slices and scatter over the salad.

2 Heat the oil in a frying pan. Add the garlic and cook over a medium-high heat for 1 minute. Do not let the garlic brown. Stir in the spring onions and sun-dried tomatoes; cook for about 1–2 minutes to heat through, then remove from the heat.

3 Stir the balsamic vinegar into the pan and season to taste. Spoon over the salad and serve, sprinkled with pine nuts, if liked.

Cook's Tip

Take dressings separately in a sealed container, such as a jam jar. Then you can dress and toss your salad once you have set up your picnic and just before serving.

Smoked chicken and citrus salad

Serves 4
Preparation: 30 minutes
Carbohydrate: 11 g, Protein: 29 g, Fat: 5 g, Fibre: 3 g, Calories: 196 kcal, Sodium: 112 mg (per portion)

What you need:

- 375 g/12 oz smoked chicken, off the bone
- 1 pink grapefruit
- 2 small oranges
- ½ cucumber, thinly sliced
- 1 small fennel bulb, trimmed and thinly sliced (optional)
- 1 round lettuce, separated into leaves
- about 50 g/2 oz frisé
- about 50 g/2 oz lambs' lettuce or watercress
- pink peppercorns (optional)
- 150 ml/¼ pint yogurt dressing
- salt and pepper

1 Skin the smoked chicken, cut the flesh into even bite-sized pieces and place in a large bowl.

2 Using a small sharp knife, peel the grapefruit and oranges, taking care to remove all the white pith. Working over a small bowl to catch the juices, segment and roughly chop the flesh, removing and discarding any pips. Pour the juice into a small jug and set aside. Add the citrus fruit to the chicken with the cucumber and fennel, if liked, and toss lightly.

3 Neatly arrange the chicken mixture and the salad leaves on individual plates.

4 Stir the reserved citrus juices and the pink peppercorns, if liked, into the yogurt dressing, and pour over the salad. Serve with crusty bread.

Vegetarian

If you think that a meal isn't a proper meal without meat or fish, think again. You don't have to be a vegetarian to enjoy vegetarian food, as the dishes in this chapter will prove to even the most committed meat-eaters. Both delicious and nutritious, these recipes make full use of the flavour and colour of the ingredients to create interesting and unusual combinations. Most of us could do with cutting down on meat, and this chapter should succeed in convincing you that you should try.

Below: *Garlic bread cassoulet*
Right: *Spicy aubergines*

Garlic bread cassoulet

Serves 6
Preparation: 40 minutes
Cooking: 1½ hours
Carbohydrate: 32 g, Protein: 11 g, Fat: 12 g, Fibre: 6 g, Calories: 283 kcal, Sodium: 677 mg (per portion)

What you need:

- 6 tablespoons olive oil
- 250 g/8 oz shallots
- 2 garlic cloves, chopped
- 2 carrots, diced
- 2 celery sticks, sliced
- 1 red pepper, diced
- 150 ml/¼ pint red wine
- 1 x 400 g/14 oz can beans
- 4 tablespoons tomato purée
- 175 g/6 oz mushrooms, sliced
- 3 tablespoons fresh mixed herbs
- salt and pepper

For the crust:
- ½ French stick, sliced thinly
- 2 tablespoons olive oil
- 1 garlic clove, crushed
- 2 tablespoons chopped fresh thyme
- 25 g/1 oz Parmesan cheese

1 Heat half the oil in a pan and fry the shallots and garlic for about 10 minutes.

2 Heat the remaining oil and fry the carrots, celery and pepper for 5 minutes. Add the wine and boil for 3 minutes. Add the beans, tomato purée, shallots, mushrooms and herbs. Season and spoon into a gratin dish.

3 Layer bread on top. Mix oil, garlic and thyme, brush over the bread, sprinkle with Parmesan. Cover. and place in a preheated oven, 190°C (375°F), Gas Mark 5, for 30 minutes. Uncover and bake for 20 minutes until golden.

Spicy aubergines

Serves 4–6
Preparation: 20 minutes
Cooking: 30 minutes
Carbohydrate: 8 g, Protein: 3 g, Fat: 9 g, Fibre: 4 g, Calories: 111 kcal, Sodium: 500 mg (per portion)

What you need:

- 4–6 aubergines, halved
- 1 bay leaf
- 1 large onion, finely chopped
- 2 garlic cloves, chopped
- 2 tablespoons ghee or butter
- 2 teaspoons coriander seeds
- 1 teaspoon cumin seeds
- 2–4 dried red chillies, chopped
- 1 teaspoon salt

1 Put the aubergines in a tin, cut sides up. Add the bay leaf, 150 ml/¼ pint water, cover. Place in a preheated oven, 160°C (325°F), Gas Mark 3, for 25 minutes.

2 Fry the onion and garlic in the ghee or butter for 5 minutes. Add the coriander, cumin, chillies and salt and fry for 3 minutes.

3 Pat the aubergines dry with kitchen paper. Scrape out the flesh, mash and add to the spice mixture. Fry for 2–3 minutes.

4 Put the skins under a medium hot grill for 5 minutes until dried out, and then fill with the fried mixture and serve.

Pepper and tomato pancakes

Serves 4
Preparation: 10 minutes
Cooking: 30–40 minutes
Carbohydrate: 50 g, Protein: 15 g,
Fat: 32 g, Fibre: 10 g, Calories: 540
kcal, Sodium: 378 mg (per portion)

What you need:

- 125 g/4 oz wholemeal flour
- 1 large egg, beaten
- 1 egg yolk
- 150 ml/¼ pint milk
- 150 ml/¼ pint water
- 2 tablespoons melted butter
- extra butter, for frying

For the filling:
- 750 g/1½ lb red peppers
- 2 tablespoons olive oil
- 1 onion, chopped
- 1.5 kg/3 lb tomatoes, skinned, deseeded and chopped
- 2 tablespoons chopped fresh parsley
- salt and pepper

To serve:
- 300 ml/½ pint soured cream or Greek yogurt
- paprika

1 First make the filling: place the peppers under a hot grill, turning frequently, until the skins blacken and blister. Peel off the skins under cold running water. Remove the seeds and cut the peppers into small pieces.

2 Heat the oil in a large pan and fry the onion until soft. Add the peppers and tomatoes and cook, uncovered, for 30 minutes, until the mixture is thick and dry. Stir frequently towards the end of cooking to prevent burning. Add the parsley and season to taste.

3 Make the pancakes: put all the ingredients and ½ teaspoon

of salt into a blender or food processor and then blend until smooth. Heat 1 teaspoon of butter in a small frying pan; when it sizzles, pour off the excess butter, so that the pan is just glistening. Keeping the pan over a high heat, give the batter a stir, then put 2 tablespoons into the pan, tipping it so the batter covers the base of the pan. Cook for 30 seconds, or until the top is set and the underside is tinged golden. Flip over and cook the other side. Place the cooked pancake on a warmed plate. Make 12 more pancakes, piling them up on top of each other, interleaved with grease-proof paper. Keep warm.

4 To serve, put a spoonful of the filling on each pancake and roll up neatly. Spoon the cream or yogurt over the pancakes, and sprinkle with paprika. Serve at once, with salad.

Spanakopita

Serves 6
Preparation: 30 minutes
Cooking: 45–50 minutes
Carbohydrate: 33 g, Protein: 20 g,
Fat: 51 g, Fibre: 5 g, Calories: 662
kcal, Sodium: 1372 mg (per portion)

What you need:

- 1 kg/2 lb fresh spinach
- 2 tablespoons olive oil
- 1 onion, chopped
- 1 teaspoon dried oregano
- 250 g/8 oz feta cheese, crumbled
- 4 eggs, beaten
- grated nutmeg
- 375 g/12 oz filo pastry, thawed if frozen
- 50 g/2 oz butter, melted
- salt and pepper

1 Wash the spinach in several

changes of water, then place in a large pan with only the water that clings to the leaves. Cover and cook for 8 minutes, shaking occasionally, until tender. Drain well, pressing out as much water as possible, then chop finely.

2 Heat the oil and fry the onion for 4–5 minutes, until soft. Add the spinach, oregano, feta and eggs, with the nutmeg. Season to taste and mix well.

3 Butter a shallow ovenproof dish, about 25 cm x 18 cm/10 x 7 inches. Layer the filo pastry in the dish, brushing each layer with melted butter. Continue until you have 3 sheets of filo left.

4 Fill the pie with the spinach mixture. Fold over the pastry edges, covering the filling. Cover with the remaining filo sheets, tucking them in to fit the top and brush with more melted butter.

4 Place in a preheated oven, 190°C (375°F), Gas Mark 5, for 45–50 minutes until the pastry is crisp and golden.

Vegetable fritters

Serves 6
Preparation: 15 minutes
Cooking: 1¾ hours
Carbohydrate: 34 g, Protein: 6 g, Fat: 4 g, Fibre: 2 g, Calories: 191 kcal, Sodium: 145 g (per portion)

What you need:

- 3 small courgettes, peeled
- oil for deep-frying
- 1 fennel bulb, sliced thinly
- 1 aubergine, sliced thinly

For the batter:
- 250 g/8 oz plain flour
- pinch of salt
- 1 tablespoon vegetable oil
- 15 g/½ oz yeast creamed with 2 tablespoons warm water
- 250–300 ml/8–10 fl oz warm water
- 1 egg white, lightly beaten

1 First make the batter: sift the flour and salt into a bowl and make a well in the centre. Pour the oil and the creamed mixture into the well, and gradually stir in the flour. Add the warm water and mix. Fold in the egg white and leave for 2 hours.

2 Heat the oil in a heavy pan or deep-fat fryer. Dip the sliced vegetables into the prepared batter and fry in batches until crisp and golden, turning as necessary. Drain on kitchen paper. Keep warm while cooking the rest of the vegetables. Serve at once, with garlic mayonnaise (aïoli).

Left: *Spanakopita*
Above: *Vegetable fritters*

Onion tart tatin

Serves 4–6
Preparation: 30 minutes
Cooking: 20–25 minutes
*Carbohydrate: 37 g, Protein: 9 g,
Fat: 26 g, Fibre: 7 g, Calories: 402 kcal,
Sodium: 410 mg (per portion)*

What you need:

- 175 g/6 oz self-raising
  wholemeal flour
- 75 g/3 oz chilled butter,
  diced
- 2 tablespoons chopped fresh
  parsley

- 2 teaspoons chopped fresh
  thyme
- 2–3 tablespoons lemon juice

For the topping:

- 500 g/1 lb shallots
- 25 g/1 oz butter
- 2 tablespoons olive oil
- 2 teaspoons muscovado sugar
- salt and pepper

1 Place the flour in a bowl and
rub in the butter until the mixture resembles breadcrumbs. Stir
in the parsley, thyme and lemon
juice and mix to a firm dough.
Knead briefly, then wrap and
chill while preparing the topping.

2 Boil the shallots in a pan of
water for 10 minutes, then drain.
Heat the butter and oil and fry
the shallots stirring, for 10 minutes, until they start to brown.
Sprinkle over the sugar, season to
taste and cook for 5 minutes
more, until the shallots are well
coloured. Remove from the heat.
3 Roll out the dough on a
lightly floured surface to form
a round a little larger than the
pan. Support the dough over the
rolling pin and place it over
the shallots, tucking the pastry
edges down the side of the pan.
Place in a preheated oven, 200°C

Variation

Garden vegetable tart

Bake a pastry case as in the main recipe. Prepare a selection of vegetables – such as asparagus, mangetout, baking carrots, sliced leeks, broad beans – and cook until tender. Cut 125 g/4 oz cherry tomatoes in half. Neatly arrange all the vegetables in the pastry case.

To make the filling, put 125 g/4 oz soft cheese with garlic and herbs in a blender or food processor with 150 ml/¼ pint milk and 2 eggs. Blend until the mixture is completely smooth, adding salt and pepper to taste.

Pour over the vegetables in the pastry case. Sprinkle with freshly grated Parmesan cheese, and bake in a preheated oven, at 180°C (350°F), Gas Mark 4, for about 20–25 minutes.

mix to a firm dough. Roll out the dough on a lightly floured surface and line a 20 cm/8 inch flan tin. Chill for 30 minutes.

2 Fill the pastry case with crumpled foil and place in a preheated oven, 200°C (400°F), Gas Mark 6, for 15 minutes, then remove the foil and return the flan case to the oven for 10 minutes more. Reduce the oven temperature to 180°C (350°F), Gas Mark 4.

3 Cook the asparagus spears in a wide frying pan in boiling water for about 7–10 minutes, until tender. Drain well and refresh under cold running water, then drain again thoroughly.

4 Beat 1 egg with the cream. Season with salt and pepper to taste. Arrange the asparagus neatly in the flan case. Break each of the 4 remaining eggs in turn into a saucer, then slide them carefully into the flan case. Pour over the cream mixture and sprinkle with grated Parmesan.

5 Return the tart to the oven for about 15–20 minutes, until the eggs have just set. Serve the tart warm with salad and bread.

(400°F), Gas Mark 6, for 20–25 minutes, until the pastry is crisp.

4 Leave to cool in the pan for 5 minutes, then place a plate over the pan and invert the tart on to it. Serve warm or cold.

Asparagus, Parmesan and egg tart

Serves 4
Preparation: 35 minutes
Cooking: 40–45 minutes
Carbohydrate: 36 g, Protein: 19 g, Fat: 34 g, Fibre: 2 g, Calories: 513 kcal, Sodium: 541 mg (per portion)

What you need:

- 175 g/6 oz plain flour
- 75 g/3 oz chilled butter, diced

For the filling:

- 175 g/6 oz thin asparagus spears, trimmed
- 5 eggs
- 150 ml/¼ pint single cream
- 25 g/1 oz grated Parmesan
- salt and pepper

1 Place the flour in a bowl and rub in the butter until the mixture resembles fine breadcrumbs. Add 2 tablespoons of water and

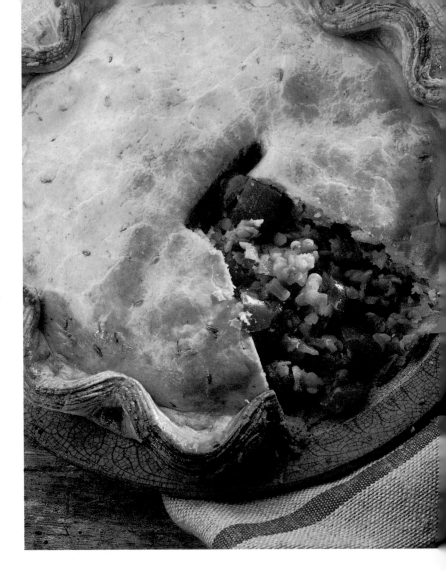

Right: *Spiced lentil pie*

Spiced lentil pie

Serves 6
Preparation: 40 minutes
Cooking: 35–40 minutes
Carbohydrate: 65 g, Protein: 14 g,
Fat: 30 g, Fibre:4 g, Calories: 557 kcal,
Sodium: 596 mg (per portion)

What you need:

- 375 g/12 oz plain flour
- 175 g/6 oz chilled butter, diced
- 2 teaspoons cumin seeds
- 2 teaspoons ground coriander
- 3 tablespoons lemon juice

For the filling:

- 1 onion, chopped
- 2 cloves garlic, crushed
- 2 tablespoons sunflower oil
- 2 sticks celery, chopped
- 1 red pepper, deseeded and chopped
- 125 g/4 oz red lentils
- 3 ripe tomatoes, skinned and chopped
- ¾ teaspoon chilli powder
- 450 ml/¾ pint vegetable stock
- 3 tablespoons chopped fresh coriander
- 2 tablespoons lemon juice
- salt and pepper
- beaten egg, to glaze

1 Place the flour in a bowl and rub in the butter until the mixture resembles breadcrumbs. Stir in the spices and salt, then add the lemon juice and 1–2 tablespoons water and mix to a firm dough. Wrap and leave to rest at room temperature.

2 Fry the onion and garlic in the oil for 5 minutes until soft. Add the celery and pepper and cook for 2 minutes. Stir in the lentils, tomatoes, chilli powder and stock and simmer stirring occasionally, for 25–30 minutes, until the stock has been absorbed. Add the coriander, lemon juice and salt and pepper. Leave to cool.

3 Roll out just over half the pastry and line a 23 cm/9 inch pie dish. Add the filling and brush the pastry edges with water.

4 Roll out the remaining pastry and cover the pie. Pinch the edges together to seal. Brush the top with beaten egg and place in a preheated oven, 200°C (400°F), Gas Mark 6, for 35–40 minutes, until golden. Cover with foil if it starts to over-brown. Serve hot.

Cook's Tip

For an even quicker bean pie, replace the lentils with a small (300 ml/10 oz) can of red kidney beans or black-eyed beans and leave out the stock.

Spiced cauliflower crumble pie

Serves 4
Preparation: 25 minutes
Cooking: 25 minutes
Carbohydrate: 42 g, Protein: 17 g,
Fat: 20 g, Fibre: 9 g, Calories: 395 kcal,
Sodium: 625 mg (per portion)

What you need:

- 1 onion, chopped
- 1 garlic clove, chopped
- 1 teaspoon chopped fresh root ginger
- 1 teaspoon cumin seeds
- 1 teaspoon mustard seeds
- 2 tablespoons oil
- 375 g/12 oz cauliflower, cut into small florets
- 1 tablespoon curry paste
- 1 x 400 g/14 oz can of chopped tomatoes
- 1 x 400 g/14 oz can of chickpeas, drained

- salt and pepper

For the crumble:

- 2 garlic cloves, chopped
- 3 tablespoons olive oil
- 50 g/2 oz fresh brown breadcrumbs
- 25 g/1 oz flaked almonds, toasted
- 2 tablespoons chopped fresh coriander

1 Fry the onion, garlic, ginger, cumin and mustard seeds in the oil for 5 minutes, until the onion is soft. Add the cauliflower and coat in the spices.

2 Add the curry paste and tomatoes and season to taste. Bring to the boil, then cover the pan and cook gently for 10–12 minutes or until the cauliflower is tender. Stir in the chickpeas and heat through.

3 For the crumble, fry the garlic in the oil for 2 minutes. Add the breadcrumbs, almonds, coriander, salt and pepper and mix. Turn the vegetable mixture into an ovenproof dish and sprinkle the crumble over the top.

4 Place in a preheated oven, 200°C (400°F), Gas Mark 6, for 25 minutes, until the topping is crisp and golden. Serve the pie piping hot.

Chestnut, celery and mushroom pie

Serves 6
Preparation: 30 minutes
Cooking: 40–45 minutes

Carbohydrate: 57 g, Protein: 11 g, Fat: 16 g, Fibre: 3 g, Calories: 405 kcal, Sodium: 802 mg (per portion)

What you need:

- 375 g/12 oz plain flour
- 1 teaspoon salt
- 75 g/3 oz butter
- beaten egg, to glaze

For the filling:

- 1 onion, chopped
- 1 carrot, chopped
- 2 tablespoons olive oil
- 3 celery sticks, chopped
- 1 garlic clove, chopped
- 400 g/14 oz canned or vacuum-packed cooked chestnuts, drained and chopped
- 250 g/8 oz mushrooms, chopped
- 150 ml/¼ pint vegetable stock
- 50 g/2 oz ground almonds
- 1 tablespoon chopped fresh herbs
- 2 eggs, beaten
- salt and pepper

1 Make the filling. Fry the onion and carrot in the oil for 5 minutes, until soft. Add the celery and garlic and cook for 2–3 minutes, stirring occasionally. Mix in the chestnuts, mushrooms, stock, almonds, herbs and seasoning. Bring to the boil, stirring, until heated through. Leave to cool, stir in the eggs and leave to cool again.

2 For the pastry, mix the flour and salt together. Melt the butter with 175 ml/6 fl oz water. Add to the flour and mix to a soft dough. Wrap and leave to rest at room temperature for 15 minutes.

3 Roll out two-thirds of the pastry on a floured surface and line a greased 900 g/2 lb loaf tin. Spread the filling over the pastry and dampen the pastry edges.

4 Roll out the remaining pastry and cover the pie, pinching the edges to seal. Make a hole in the centre. Roll out the pastry trimmings and cut into leaves to decorate. Fix in place, then brush the top of the pie with egg.

5 Place in a preheated oven, 200°C (400°F), Gas Mark 6, for 40–50 minutes, until crisp and golden. Leave to cool in the tin for 10 minutes, remove the pie from the tin and serve hot.

Above: *Chestnut, celery and mushroom pie*
Below left: *Spiced cauliflower crumble pie*

Right: *Vegetable bolognese*
Below: *Deep-fried Camembert with fettuccine*
Far right: *Saffron barley with sun-dried tomatoes*

Deep-fried Camembert with fettuccine

Serves 4
Preparation: 10 minutes, plus 30 minutes chilling
Cooking: 12 minutes
Carbohydrate: 30 g, Protein: 34 g, Fat: 38 g, Fibre: 3 g, Calories: 585 kcal, Sodium: 1150 mg (per portion)

What you need:

- 8 Camembert wedges, chilled
- 2 eggs, beaten
- 125 g/4 oz fresh wholemeal breadcrumbs
- 1 teaspoon paprika
- 300 g/10 oz fresh fettuccine
- oil for deep-frying
- 1 tablespoon olive oil
- 1 tablespoon raspberry vinegar
- salt and pepper
- fresh raspberries, with leaves, to garnish

1 Dip the Camembert in egg and then coat in breadcrumbs. Sprinkle with paprika and chill for 30 minutes.
2 Cook the pasta in boiling salted water for 4–6 minutes, until the pasta is just tender.
3 Heat the oil to 180–190°C (350–375°F), or until a cube of bread browns in 30 seconds. Fry the Camembert for 1 minute, turning. Drain and keep hot.
4 Drain the pasta and return to the pan. Add the oil, vinegar and seasoning. Toss, twirl into 4 nests and arrange on plates. Add 2 Camembert wedges to each plate and serve with raspberries.

Vegetable bolognese

Serves 4
Preparation: 15 minutes
Cooking: 12 minutes
Carbohydrate: 66 g, Protein: 12 g, Fat: 4 g, Fibre: 6 g, Calories: 334 kcal, Sodium: 470 mg (per portion)

What you need:

- 300 g/10 oz dried spaghetti
- 1 onion, chopped
- 250 g/8 oz carrots, diced
- 1 tablespoon olive oil
- 1 leek, sliced
- 2 celery sticks, sliced
- 400 g/14 oz canned plum tomatoes, drained and roughly chopped
- 1 tablespoon tomato purée
- 1 teaspoon cayenne pepper
- 125 g/4 oz mushrooms, sliced
- salt and pepper
- basil leaves, to garnish

1 Cook the pasta in boiling salted water for 8–12 minutes, until just tender.
2 Fry the onion and carrot in the oil for 3–5 minutes. Add the leek, celery, tomatoes, tomato purée, cayenne, mushrooms, seasoning and cook for 10 minutes.
3 Drain the pasta, twist into 4 nests and put on plates. Spoon sauce into each nest. Season, garnish with basil and serve.

Saffron barley with sun-dried tomatoes

Serves 4
Preparation: 15–20 minutes
Cooking: about 30 minutes
Carbohydrate: 54 g, Protein: 8 g,
Fat: 29 g, Fibre: 0 g, Calories: 494 kcal,
Sodium: 850 mg (per portion)

What you need:

- 250 g/8 oz pearl barley
- 750 ml/1¼ pints chicken or vegetable stock
- ¼ teaspoon saffron threads
- 1 shallot, finely chopped
- 6 tablespoons olive oil
- 1 garlic clove, crushed
- 375 g/12 oz oyster mushrooms, halved if large
- 8–12 sun-dried tomatoes preserved in oil, drained and chopped
- a few basil leaves, shredded
- 2 tablespoons wine vinegar
- salt and pepper

1 Put the pearl barley in a pan with the stock. Crumble in the saffron. Bring to the boil, cover, then simmer for 20–25 minutes, until the liquid has absorbed. Leave to cool in a bowl.

2 Fry the shallot in 3 tablespoons oil for 3 minutes, until soft. Add the garlic and mushrooms and cook for 3 minutes, until tender. Remove from the heat and stir in the tomatoes and basil. Pile the mixture on top of the barley.

3 Add the remaining oil and the vinegar to the pan, season and spoon over the barley and serve.

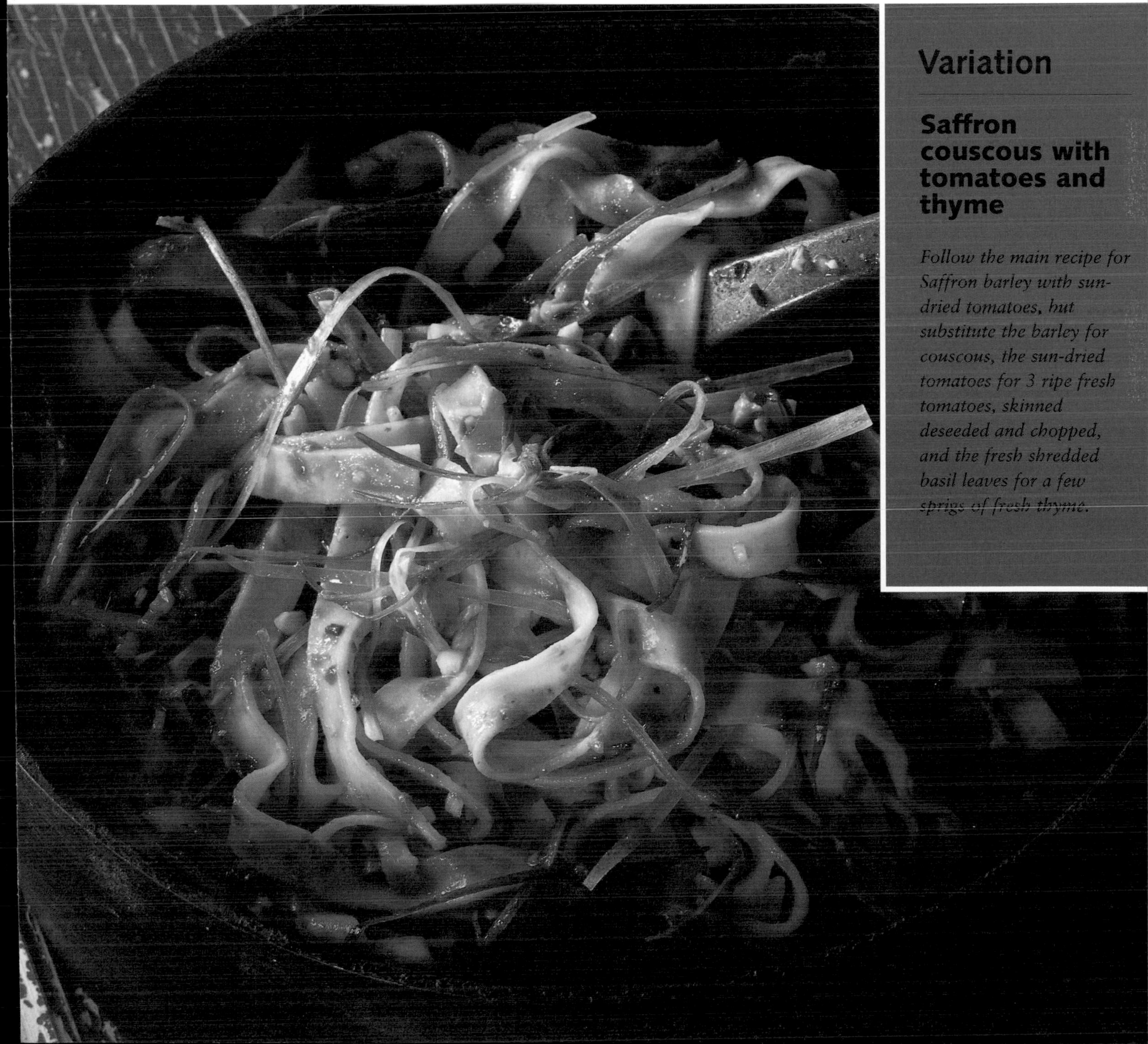

Variation

Saffron couscous with tomatoes and thyme

Follow the main recipe for Saffron barley with sun-dried tomatoes, but substitute the barley for couscous, the sun-dried tomatoes for 3 ripe fresh tomatoes, skinned deseeded and chopped, and the fresh shredded basil leaves for a few sprigs of fresh thyme.

Above: *Tomato, spinach and ricotta casserole*
Above right: *Carrot and almond loaf with tomato sauce*
Right: *Courgette tian*

Tomato, spinach and ricotta casserole

Serves 4
Preparation: 15 minutes
Cooking: 30 minutes
Carbohydrate: 11 g, Protein: 18 g,
Fat: 20 g, Fibre: 5 g, Calories: 292 kcal,
Sodium: 691 mg (per portion)

What you need:

- 750 g/1½ lb spinach, shredded
- 25 g/1 oz butter
- 1 onion, chopped
- 1 garlic clove, crushed
- 2 beefsteak tomatoes, skinned and sliced
- 375 g/12 oz ricotta cheese
- 2 tablespoons grated Parmesan cheese
- salt and pepper

1 Put the spinach in a large saucepan with 1 tablespoon of water and a little salt. Cook for 2–3 minutes until soft, then drain the spinach well.

2 Melt the remaining butter in a saucepan, add the onion and garlic and cook until soft, then mix with the spinach.

3 Layer half the sliced tomatoes and half the ricotta cheese in an oiled casserole dish then repeat the layers seasoning each layer with salt and pepper, sprinkle the Parmesan over the top.

4 Cover and place in a preheated oven, 180°C (350°F), Gas Mark 4, for 30 minutes. Remove the lid and cook for a further 10 minutes to brown the top.

Courgette tian

Serves 4–6
Preparation: 25 minutes
Cooking: 20–30 minutes
Carbohydrate: 23 g, Protein: 16 g,
Fat: 21 g, Fibre: 3 g, Calories: 341 kcal,
Sodium: 494 mg

What you need:

- 750 g/1½ lb courgettes, roughly chopped
- 1 onion, chopped
- 2 garlic cloves, crushed
- 5 tablespoons olive oil
- 75 g/3 oz long-grain rice
- 2 eggs
- salt and pepper
- 50 g/2 oz grated Gruyère cheese
- 3–4 tablespoons fresh breadcrumbs
- 2 tablespoons grated Parmesan cheese

1 Gently fry the courgettes, onion and garlic in 3 tablespoons of the olive oil in a large frying pan for 8–10 minutes, until soft and slightly golden.

2 Meanwhile, cook the rice in a large saucepan of boiling salted water until tender, but not sticky. Drain well.

3 Beat the eggs with salt and pepper in a large bowl, and then stir in the cooked courgette mixture, grated Gruyère cheese and drained rice. Transfer to an oiled shallow ovenproof dish.

4 Sprinkle with the breadcrumbs and Parmesan and drizzle the remaining olive oil over the top. Place in a preheated oven at 180°C (350°F), Gas Mark 4, for 20–30 minutes, until crisp and golden brown. Serve hot, warm or cold.

Cook's Tip

Tian is a wide, shallow baking dish from Provence, and also refers to the food cooked in it.

Variation

Courgettes Neapolitan

Fry the courgettes separately in a little butter, then fry 500 g/1 lb tomatoes (skinned, deseeded and chopped) with the onion and garlic. Replace the rice with macaroni. Place the courgettes in a shallow baking dish and cover with 125 g/4 oz grated or sliced mozzarella, then the macaroni, the tomato mixture and the remaining mozzarella. Sprinkle over the breadcrumbs, Parmesan cheese and olive oil, and bake as in the main recipe.

Carrot and almond loaf with tomato sauce

Serves 6–8
Preparation: 30 minutes
Cooking: 45 minutes
*Carbohydrate: 28 g, Protein: 12 g,
Fat: 23 g, Fibre: 6 g, Calories: 354 kcal,
Sodium: 511 g (per portion)*

What you need:

- 50 g/2 oz butter
- 1 onion, thinly sliced
- 2 garlic cloves, chopped
- 300 g/10 oz fresh wholemeal breadcrumbs
- 250 g/8 oz carrots, grated
- 125 g/4 oz flaked almonds, toasted
- 2 eggs beaten
- 4 tablespoons lemon juice
- 1 tablespoon chopped fresh parsley
- 1 teaspoon grated nutmeg
- salt and pepper

1 Melt the butter in a large frying pan over a low heat and gently sauté the onion and garlic for about 5 minutes, or until the onion is just translucent.

2 Mix the breadcrumbs, carrots and almonds together in a large bowl, add the onion and garlic and stir well. Add the beaten eggs, lemon juice, parsley and nutmeg, season with salt and pepper to taste and mix well. Add a little water if the mixture seems dry.

3 Spoon the mixture into a greased 500 g/ 1 lb loaf tin and bake in a preheated oven, 200°C (400°F), Gas Mark 6, for about 45 minutes or until the loaf is browned and a sharp knife inserted in to the centre comes out clean. Serve the loaf in slices with a fresh tomato sauce.

Salads

A salad is much, much more than a tomato and a limp piece of lettuce with a dollop of salad cream. It can be a well-chosen combination of salad vegetables, fruits and pulses, it can be combined with fish or meat, it can feature rice or pasta, it can be simple or more elaborate, it can be a main course or a side dish, and it can be served either warm or cold. Whatever you choose, it should always surprise both palate and eye with contrasting textures, flavours, shapes and colours. Refreshing and nutritious, salads deserve pride of place in every imaginative cook's repertoire.

Courgette salad with lemon and thyme

Serves 4–6
Preparation: 20 minutes, plus
2 minutes cooking
*Carbohydrate: 5 g, Protein: 3 g,
Fat: 12 g, Fibre: 2 g, Calories: 136 kcal,
Sodium: 469 mg (per portion)*

What you need:

- 500 g/1 lb small courgettes
- about 16 black olives

For the dressing:
- 5 tablespoons extra-virgin olive oil
- pared rind of 1 lemon, cut into thin strips
- 125 g/4 fl oz lemon juice
- 1 garlic clove, crushed
- 1 tablespoon roughly chopped fresh thyme
- 1 teaspoon clear honey
- salt and pepper

1 First make the dressing. Place all the ingredients in a screw-top jar, close the lid tightly and shake to combine.
2 Cut the courgettes in half crossways. Using a sharp knife, cut both ends off each piece of courgette to a point, 'sharpening' it just as you would do a pencil.
3 Bring a pan of water to the boil, add the courgettes and cook for 2 minutes. Drain, blot the excess moisture with kitchen paper and transfer to a bowl. Add the olives.
4 Pour the dressing over the courgettes, toss lightly and leave until cold before serving.

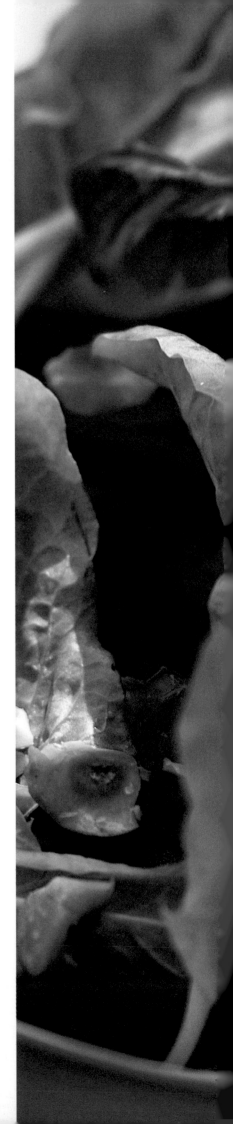

Raw beetroot and pink grapefruit salad

Serves 4–6
Preparation: 20 minutes
Carbohydrate: 20 g, Protein: 8 g,
Fat: 15 g, Fibre: 7 g, Calories: 238
kcal, Sodium: 412 mg (Per portion)

What you need:

- 750 g/1½ lb raw young beetroot
- 2 pink grapefruit
- 50 g/2 oz peeled hazelnuts, roasted and coarsely chopped
- 1 tablespoon raspberry vinegar
- 3 tablespoons hazelnut oil
- 1 garlic clove, crushed
- 1 radicchio, leaves separated
- 250 g/8 oz young spinach leaves
- salt and pepper

1 Peel the beetroot and cut it into fine julienne strips or grate it finely. Place in a salad bowl.

2 Cut a thin slice off the bottom of the grapefruit and place them, cut side down, on a chopping board. Cut off the rind in strips, working from the top down. Take care to remove all the white pith. Holding the grapefruit over the salad bowl to catch any juice, cut out the segments with a sharp knife. Add the segments to the bowl, stir in the hazelnuts and toss lightly.

3 Whisk the raspberry vinegar, hazelnut oil and garlic in a small bowl; pour over the beetroot mixture, add salt and pepper to taste and toss well. Arrange the radicchio and spinach on each plate and spoon over the beetroot, hazelnut and grapefruit.

Far left: *Courgette salad with lemon and thyme*
Left: *Raw beetroot and pink grapefruit salad*

Caesar salad

Serves 4–6
Preparation: 20 minutes
Cooking: about 12 minutes
Carbohydrate: 30 g, Protein: 17 g,
Fat: 40 g, Fibre: 1 g, Calories: 540 kcal,
Sodium: 1379 mg (per portion)

What you need:

- 1 cos lettuce, separated into leaves
- 1 x 50 g/2 oz can of anchovies in olive oil, drained
- 1 small rustic white loaf (uncut)
- 75 g/3 oz butter, melted
- 3 tablespoons freshly grated Parmesan cheese

For the dressing:

- 5 tablespoons mayonnaise
- 4–5 tablespoons water
- 1–2 garlic cloves
- 3 tablespoons finely grated Parmesan cheese
- coarse sea salt and pepper

1 First make the dressing. Put the mayonnaise in a small bowl and stir in enough of the measured water to make a thin, pourable sauce. Crush the garlic to a paste with a little coarse sea salt and add to the mayonnaise with the Parmesan. Stir well. Thin the dressing with a little more water, if necessary, so that the sauce remains pourable. Add pepper to taste and set aside.

2 Tear the lettuce leaves into large pieces and place in a large, shallow salad bowl. Snip the anchovies into small pieces and scatter over the lettuce.

3 To make the croûtons, cut the bread into 3 cm/1¼ inch slices. Cut off the crusts and discard. Dip a pastry brush into the melted butter and lightly butter the slices of bread on all sides. Cut the bread into 3 cm/1¼ inch cubes. Brush a large baking sheet with a little of the butter. Arrange the bread cubes on it in a single layer, brushing the cut sides with any remaining butter. Bake in a preheated oven, 200°C (400°F), Gas Mark 6, for 12 minutes, or until crisp and a deep golden colour. Watch the croûtons carefully towards the end of the cooking time as they tend to colour quickly.

4 To serve, tip the hot croûtons into the salad and quickly drizzle the dressing over the top. Sprinkle the grated Parmesan over and serve at once.

Below: *Caesar salad*

Variation

Chicory and Parmesan salad

Mix together 5 tablespoons mayonnaise, 1 tablespoon chopped parsley, 1 crushed garlic clove and 2 tablespoons grated Parmesan. Stir in water to make a thin, pourable sauce. Season and set aside.

For the croûtons, cut 3 slices of bread, crusts removed, into cubes. Heat 2 tablespoons of olive oil and 25 g/1 oz butter until sizzling. Add the cubes and fry, stirring, for 3–4 minute, until golden. Drain and add salt to taste.

Arrange chicory leaves on each plate. Drizzle the dressing over and pile the croûtons on top. Shave some Parmesan over the top and serve.

Radicchio and orange salad with dates and Brie

Serves 4
Preparation: 15 minutes
Carbohydrate: 25 g, Protein: 11 g,
Fat: 18 g, Fibre: 3 g, Calories: 304 kcal,
Sodium: 519 mg (per portion)

What you need:

- 2 small oranges
- 1 head of radicchio, roughly torn
- 1 bunch of watercress or handful of rocket
- 250 g/8 oz fresh dates, stoned and chopped
- 175 g/6 oz Brie, rind removed, diced
- 6 tablespoons vinaigrette
- salt and pepper

1 With a zester, carefully remove small strips of rind from 1 of the oranges, then set aside. Using a small, sharp knife, peel the rind and pith from both oranges and slice them thinly.
2 Arrange all the salad ingredients in a large serving bowl or on individual plates and scatter the reserved orange rind over the top. Season with salt and pepper. Drizzle the dressing over the salad just before serving it.

Frisé, bacon and hazelnut salad

Serves 4–6
Preparation: 20 minutes
Carbohydrate: 1 g, Protein: 7 g,
Fat: 17 g, Fibre: 0 g, Calories: 178 kcal,
Sodium: 695 mg (per portion)

What you need:

- 1 large head of frisé
- 5 rashers of rindless smoked streaky bacon
- salt and pepper
- 6 tablespoons vinaigrette, made with hazelnut oil

1 Tear the frisé into large pieces and place in a large salad bowl.
2 Grill the bacon on a rack under a preheated hot grill for about 3–4 minutes, or until crisp, turning once or twice. Drain the bacon on kitchen paper, then use scissors to snip into small pieces. Add to the salad and season with salt and pepper to taste.
3 Pour the dressing over the salad, toss lightly and serve at once with crusty bread.

Above: *Radicchio and orange salad with dates and Brie*
Below left: *Frisé, bacon and hazelnut salad*

Cook's Tip

Dates make a delicious addition to the combination of salad leaves, citrus fruit and Brie. They are also highly nutritious and are full of potassium, calcium and iron, as well as being high in fibre and low in sodium.

Chinese duck salad

Serves 4–6
Preparation: 30 minutes
Cooking: 30 minutes
Carbohydrate: 106 g, Protein: 41 g,
Fat: 15 g, Fibre: 3 g, Calories: 725 kcal,
Sodium: 1328 mg (per portion)

What you need:

- oil, see method
- 250 g/8 oz dried vermicelli
- 250 g/8 oz duck breast
- 6 tablespoons hoisin sauce
- 3 spring onions, sliced
- 2.5 cm/1 inch piece of fresh root ginger, grated
- ½ head Chinese leaf salad, shredded
- 2 tomatoes, sliced
- 1 carrot, grated
- 125 g/4 oz broccoli florets, cooked
- 125 g/4 oz baby sweetcorn, cooked and halved

1 Bring at least 1.75 litres/3 pints of water to the boil in a large pan. Add a dash of oil and a generous pinch of salt. Add the pasta, remove from the heat, cover and leave to stand for 6 minutes.

2 Meanwhile, brush the duck breast generously with the hoisin

sauce. Grill under a high heat for 20 minutes, turning once.

3 Drain the pasta and rinse under cold running water, drain again. Transfer to a salad bowl, add a little oil and toss, separating any sticky strands. Add the remaining ingredients and mix.

4 Remove the duck from the grill, cool for 5 minutes and slice thinly. Add to the salad and toss.

Warm chorizo salad

Serves 4
Preparation: 20 minutes
Cooking: 3 minutes
Carbohydrate: 6 g, Protein: 15 g,
Fat: 43 g, Fibre: 1 g, Calories: 465 kcal,
Sodium: 1514 mg (per portion)

What you need:

- about 250 g/8 oz bitter salad leaves
- small handful of sage leaves
- 5 tablespoons olive oil
- 300 g/10 oz chorizo sausage, skinned and thinly sliced
- 1 small red onion, thinly sliced
- 1 garlic clove, chopped
- 2 tablespoons red wine vinegar
- salt and pepper

1 Arrange the salad leaves on each plate, or tear into pieces and arrange in a large bowl. Add the sage leaves.

2 Heat the oil in a frying pan until fairly hot. Add the sliced chorizo and fry over a high heat for 1 minute. Add the onion and garlic and fry for 1–2 minutes, or until the chorizo is browned. Remove from the heat.

3 Stir the vinegar into the pan and season to taste. Quickly spoon the mixture over the salad and toss lightly. Serve at once.

Warm chicken liver salad with honey and mustard dressing

Serves 4
Preparation: 10 minutes
Cooking: 5–8 minutes
Carbohydrate: 4 g, Protein: 13 g,
Fat: 16 g, Fibre: 1 g, Calories: 208 kcal,
Sodium: 496 mg (per portion)

What you need:

- 25 g/1 oz butter
- 250 g/8 oz chicken livers, trimmed, cut into bite-sized pieces
- 250 g/8 oz mixed salad leaves (radicchio, frisé, oak leaf lettuce and rocket)
- salt and pepper

For the dressing:
- 3 tablespoons extra-virgin olive oil
- 1 tablespoon raspberry vinegar
- 2 teaspoons clear honey
- 1 teaspoon coarse-grained mustard
- salt and pepper

1 First make the dressing. Put all the ingredients in a large salad bowl. Whisk with a fork until evenly combined and thickened, then adjust the seasoning to taste. Set aside.

2 Melt the butter in a large frying pan over a moderate heat until foaming. Add the chicken livers and toss vigorously for about 5–8 minutes until the livers are browned on the outside, but still tinged with pink in the centre. Season to taste.

3 Quickly toss the salad leaves in the dressing, then arrange on individual plates. Spoon the chicken livers and cooking juices over the top. Serve immediately with crisp bread.

Warm lentil salad

Serves 4
Preparation: 10 minutes, plus
3–4 hours soaking
Cooking: 45 minutes
*Carbohydrate: 53 g, Protein: 32 g,
Fat: 27 g, Fibre: 11 g, Calories: 571
kcal, Sodium: 990 mg (per portion)*

What you need:

- 375 g/12 oz green lentils, soaked in water for 3–4 hours
- 2 carrots
- 1 onion, peeled
- 1 clove
- 1 bay leaf
- pinch of dried thyme
- 1 garlic clove, peeled
- 1 leek, thinly sliced
- 125 g/4 oz celery, chopped
- 200 g/7 oz smoked streaky bacon, diced
- 1 tablespoon oil
- 1 tablespoon snipped chives

For the vinaigrette:
- 200 ml/7 fl oz walnut oil
- 6 tablespoons sherry vinegar
- 1 tablespoon Dijon mustard
- salt and pepper

1 Put the lentils in a large pan. Peel a carrot and add to the lentils together with the onion studded with the clove, the bay leaf, thyme and garlic. Cover with cold water and bring to the boil, simmer for 30–35 minutes. Discard the vegetables, bay leaf and garlic, then drain the lentils.

2 Slice the remaining carrot thinly and blanch in a pan of lightly salted boiling water with the leek and celery. Drain well.

3 Whisk the vinaigrette ingredients together and fry the bacon until crisp. Stir the vegetables and bacon into the lentils and toss in the vinaigrette. Sprinkle with chives and serve warm.

Right: *Three-bean pasta twist salad*
Below: *Pasta and avocado salad with tomato dressing*

Three-bean pasta twist salad

Serves 4
Preparation: 20 minutes
Cooking: 12 minutes
Carbohydrate: 93 g, Protein: 27 g,
Fat: 8 g, Fibre: 8 g, Calories: 536 kcal,
Sodium: 260 mg (per portion)

What you need:

- oil, see method
- 300 g/10 oz dried tricolore pasta twists
- 2 spring onions, chopped diagonally
- 1 red pepper, cored, deseeded and chopped
- 125 g/4 oz drained, canned red kidney beans
- 125 g/4 oz drained, canned pinto beans
- 125 g/4 oz drained, canned borlotti beans
- 200 ml/7 fl oz crème fraîche
- 4 tablespoons milk
- 3 tablespoons chopped fresh dill
- salt and pepper

1 Bring at least 1.75 litres/3 pints of water to the boil in a large saucepan. Add a dash of oil and a generous pinch of salt. Cook the pasta for 8–12 minutes, until just tender. Drain well, rinse under cold running water, drain again then transfer to a large salad bowl.
2 Add the spring onions, red pepper and beans to the pasta. Mix well. Beat the crème fraîche and milk together in a bowl; fold into the salad and season to taste.
3 Fold in the chopped fresh dill and serve at once.

Pasta and avocado salad with tomato dressing

Serves 4
Preparation: 10 minutes, plus 30 minutes standing
Cooking: 10–12 minutes
Carbohydrate: 68 g, Protein: 13 g,
Fat: 26 g, Fibre: 6 g, Calories: 540 kcal,
Sodium: 215 mg (per portion)

What you need:

- 175 g/6 oz small pasta shells
- 500 g/1 lb ripe tomatoes, skinned, deseeded and finely diced
- 6 tablespoons vinaigrette
- 2 ripe avocados
- salt and pepper

1 Bring a large pan of water to the boil, add the pasta and cook until just tender to the bite. Drain and rinse under cold running water. Drain again and transfer to a large salad bowl.
2 Mix the diced tomatoes and vinaigrette together. Leave to stand for at least 30 minutes, then add to the pasta and toss thoroughly. Season to taste.
3 Just before serving, halve and stone the avocados. Peel and slice them, then arrange on the pasta.

Lumacone and smoked mackerel salad

Serves 4
Preparation: 20 minutes
Cooking: 12 minutes
Carbohydrate: 62 g, Protein: 20 g,
Fat: 23 g, Fibre: 4 g, Calories: 522 kcal,
Sodium: 618 mg (per portion)

What you need:

- 300 g/10 oz dried lumacone
- 2 fillets peppered smoked mackerel, skinned and broken into bite-sized pieces

- 2 oranges, segmented
- ½ cucumber, chopped
- sprigs of fresh dill, to garnish

For the dressing:

- 1–2 tablespoons wholegrain mustard
- 3 tablespoons orange juice
- 1 teaspoon lemon juice
- 3 tablespoons olive oil
- salt and pepper

1 Bring at least 1.75 litres/ 3 pints of water to the boil in a pan. Add a little oil and a pinch of salt and cook the pasta for about 8–12 minutes.

2 Drain and rinse under cold running water. Drain again, transfer to a bowl and add the mackerel. Mix lightly.

3 Make the dressing. Put the mustard, orange juice, lemon juice and oil in a screw-top jar. Close tightly and shake well. Season, shake again and pour over the salad.

4 Fold in the orange segments and cucumber. Garnish with dill.

Chinese noodle and prawn salad

Serves 4–6
Preparation: 15 minutes
Cooking: about 6 minutes
Carbohydrate: 39 g, Protein: 18 g, Fat: 16 g, Fibre: 3 g, Calories: 363 kcal, Sodium: 1296 mg (per portion)

What you need:

- 175 g/6 oz Chinese egg noodles
- 6 spring onions
- 1 small bunch of radishes, trimmed
- 175 g/6 oz sugar snap peas, topped and tailed
- 175 g/6 oz cooked, peeled prawns
- 1 quantity sweet and sour dressing (see Cook's Tip)
- salt and pepper

1 Bring a large pan of water to the boil, add the egg noodles, cover the pan and then remove from the heat. Leave the noodles to stand for 5 minutes, or until they are just tender. Drain in a colander and cool under cold running water. Drain again thoroughly and transfer to a bowl.

2 Cut the spring onions into short lengths and shred finely. Leave the radishes whole or cut them into slices, as preferred. Add the spring onions and the radishes to the noodles.

3 Bring a pan of water to the boil, add the snap peas and blanch for 1 minute. Drain in a colander, refresh under cold running water, drain again. Add to the salad with the prawns and season to taste.

4 Just before serving, add the dressing to the salad and toss.

Left: *Lumacone and smoked mackerel salad*
Below: *Chinese noodle and prawn salad*

Cook's Tip

For the sweet and sour dressing, cut a spring onion into shreds and place in a screw-top jar with 2 plums, diced. Add 5 tablespoons oil, 2 tablespoons sherry vinegar, 2 teaspoons soy sauce, 2 teaspoons tomato purée, ½ crushed garlic clove, ¼ teaspoon light brown sugar, ,salt and pepper and shake until combined. Makes about 350 ml/12 fl oz.

Curried chicken salad

Serves 4
Preparation: 20 minutes
Carbohydrate: 68 g, Protein: 13 g,
Fat: 26 g, Fibre: 6 g, Calories: 540 kcal,
Sodium: 215 mg (per portion)

What you need:

- 1 small, whole, cooked
  chicken, about 1.25 kg/2½ lb
- 175 g/6 oz seedless grapes,
  halved
- about 250 g/8 oz mixed salad
  leaves (e.g. cos, red oak leaf,
  lambs' lettuce, rocket, frisé)
- salt and pepper
- sprigs of fresh coriander, to
  garnish

For the dressing:

- 6 tablespoons mayonnaise
- 1 tablespoon medium-hot
  curry paste
- 1–2 tablespoons mango
  chutney

1 Skin the chicken and remove
all the meat from the carcass.
Shred the meat into bite-sized
pieces and place in a bowl with
the grapes. Season to taste.
2 Tear the salad leaves into
bite-sized pieces and arrange to
form a bed on a serving platter or
on individual plates.
3 Mix all the dressing ingredients together, adding just enough
cold water to give a thick pouring
consistency.
4 Toss the chicken in the dressing, until combined. Pile on to
the salad with the coriander.

Smoked chicken, orange and avocado salad

Serves 4–6
Preparation: 30 minutes
Carbohydrate: 12 g, Protein: 36 g,
Fat: 56 g, Fibre: 5 g, Calories: 690 kcal,
Sodium: 351 mg (per portion)

What you need:

- 1 kg/2 lb smoked chicken
- 3 large oranges
- 50 g/2 oz shelled hazelnuts
- 2 tablespoons lemon juice
- 2 teaspoons coarse-grained
  mustard
- 1 teaspoon clear honey
- 100 ml/3½ fl oz hazelnut oil
- 2 large, ripe avocados
- salt and pepper

1 Remove meat from the bones
and cut into neat, thin slices.
2 Holding the fruit over a bowl,
peel and segment 2 oranges, taking care to remove all the pith.
3 Spread the nuts on a baking
tray and toast under a preheated
grill for 5 minutes until browned.
Turn into a clean tea towel and
rub off the skins. Chop the nuts.
4 Halve the remaining orange,
squeeze the juice and strain into a
bowl. Add the lemon juice, mustard, honey, seasoning and mix.
Gradually add the oil, beating
after each addition until the dressing emulsifies and thickens.
5 Halve, stone and peel the avocados. Slice the avocado flesh
lengthways into thin slices.
6 Arrange the chicken and avocado on a platter. Arrange the
orange segments in the centre.
7 Mix the dressing, then drizzle
over the salad. Sprinkle with the
hazelnuts and serve immediately.

Variation

Chicken and grape salad

*Cover a chicken with water
with 1 onion, studded with
3 cloves, 1 carrot and 1
celery stick, chopped, 1
bunch of tarragon, 1 bay
leaf, a few peppercorns and
salt. Bring to the boil, cover
and simmer until tender.
Remove skin, cut the meat
into pieces. Reduce the
stock by half and
reserve. Whip 75 ml/3 fl oz
double cream until thick
and fold into 150 ml/¼ pint
mayonnaise. Add the stock,
zest and juice of 1 lemon, 1
tablespoon tarragon, season
to taste and mix.*

*Combine the meat with
125 g/4 oz grapes. Spoon
over the dressing and mix.
Cover and chill for 2 hours,
returning to room
temperature before serving.*

Cook's Tip

For the spicy peanut
dressing, heat 25 g/1 oz
chopped creamed coconut
with 4 tablespoons milk for
2 minutes, stirring, until it
forms a paste. Purée the
mixture with ½ chopped
onion, 1 crushed garlic clove,
4 tablespoons smooth
peanut butter, 1 teaspoon
soft brown sugar,
2 teaspoons soy sauce,
½ teaspoon chilli powder and
salt and pepper, until
smooth. Cover and set aside.
Makes about 175 ml/6 fl oz.

Gado gado with chicken

Serves 4
Preparation: 30 minutes
Carbohydrate: 15 g, Protein: 27 g,
Fat: 17 g, Fibre: 6 g, Calories: 313 kcal,
Sodium: 506 mg (Per portion)

What you need:

- 250 g/8 oz carrots, cut into matchsticks
- 175 g/6 oz celery, cut into matchsticks
- 175 g/6 oz leek, cut into matchsticks
- 125 g/4 oz mangetout
- ½ cucumber, peeled and cut in half lengthways
- about 175 g/6 oz pak choi
- 2 cooked chicken breasts, skinned and shredded
- 1 quantity spicy peanut dressing (see Cook's Tip)
- salt and pepper
- chopped fresh coriander, to garnish (optional)

1 Bring a large saucepan of water to the boil, add the carrot, celery and leek matchsticks and blanch for 2 minutes. Drain, refresh under cold running water, then drain again. Tip into a large mixing bowl.

2 Cut the mangetout in half diagonally. Scoop out the seeds from the cucumber and cut the flesh into neat slices.

3 Add the mangetout, cucumber slices and the bean sprouts to the bowl. Season with salt and pepper to taste, then toss all the vegetables together.

4 Arrange the pak choi leaves on a large serving platter, with the shredded chicken and the tossed vegetables. Spoon the dressing over and garnish with a sprinkling of freshly chopped coriander, if liked.

Above left: *Curried chicken salad*
Top: *Smoked chicken, orange and avocado salad*
Above: *Gado Gado with chicken*

Below: *Salade niçoise*
Right: *Monkfish salad with coriander and mint*

Salade niçoise

Serves 4
Preparation: 20 minutes
*Carbohydrate: 13 g, Protein: 31 g,
Fat: 30 g, Fibre: 5 g, Calories: 444 kcal,
Sodium: 1127 mg (per portion)*

What you need:

- 1 garlic clove, peeled and bruised
- 1 lettuce
- 125 g/4 oz celery hearts, thinly sliced
- 125 g/4 oz cucumber, peeled and thinly sliced
- 250 g/8 oz small French beans, topped and tailed

- 250 g/8 oz canned artichoke hearts, thinly sliced
- 500 g/1 lb tomatoes, skinned, deseeded and quartered
- 1 large green pepper, deseeded and sliced
- 1 onion, sliced
- 4 hard-boiled eggs, halved
- 50 g/2 oz black olives
- 8 canned anchovy fillets, drained
- 1 x 250 g/8 oz can tuna in oil, drained

For the dressing:
- 7 tablespoons olive oil
- 4 basil leaves, finely chopped
- salt and pepper

1 Gently rub around the inside of a large salad bowl with the bruised garlic clove. Line the bowl with lettuce leaves. Chop the rest of the lettuce leaves roughly and then arrange in the base of the salad bowl.

2 In a mixing bowl, combine the celery and cucumber with the French beans and artichoke hearts. Arrange the mixture on top of the lettuce leaves in the salad bowl.

3 Arrange the quartered tomatoes, the sliced pepper and onion, eggs, black olives and anchovies on top of the vegetables in the bowl. Cut the tuna into chunks and place in the bowl.

4 Make the dressing: mix together the oil and basil and season with salt and pepper to taste. Pour the dressing over the salad and transfer to individual serving plates.

Monkfish salad with coriander and mint

Serves 4
Preparation: 15 minutes
Cooking: about 10 minutes
Carbohydrate: 4 g, Protein: 22 g, Fat: 10 g, Fibre: 1 g, Calories: 191 kcal, Sodium: 227 mg (per portion)

What you need:

- 500 g/1 lb monkfish, filleted

Variation

Californian potato salad

Boil 750 g/1½ lb new potatoes until tender. Drain. Grill 125 g/4 oz rindless, streaky bacon until crisp, then chop. Mix the bacon with the potatoes and add 125 g/4 oz raisins.

For the dressing, mix 4 tablespoons yogurt with 1 teaspoon honey and 50 g/ 2 oz blue cheese, grated. Season to taste. Add to the potato mixture and toss to coat. Serve warm or cold.

- 1 x 425 g/14 fl oz can of pimientos, drained
- 5 tablespoons olive oil
- 1 tablespoon coriander seeds, crushed
- 1 onion, sliced
- 2 garlic cloves, chopped
- 3 tablespoons capers, rinsed and drained
- pared rind of ½ lemon, cut into thin matchsticks
- a few sprigs of coriander, roughly torn
- a few sprigs of mint, leaves stripped from the stems and roughly torn
- 1 tablespoon balsamic vinegar or lemon juice
- salt and pepper

1 Cut the monkfish fillet into thin slices and set aside.

2 Tip the canned pimientos into a colander and rinse thoroughly under cold running water, drain well and cut the pimientos into thin strips.

3 Heat the olive oil in a large frying pan. Add the crushed coriander seeds and cook over a moderate heat for a few seconds. Add the sliced onion and then cook gently for about 5 minutes, stirring frequently, until the

onion has softened but not browned. Add the garlic and cook for about 1 minute more.

4 Increase the heat to moderately high. Add the monkfish slices to the frying pan and cook, stirring gently, for about 3–4 minutes, or until the fish is firm and opaque. Lower the heat and stir in the pimiento strips, capers and strips of lemon rind. Remove the pan from the heat and leave to cool for a few minutes.

5 Add the coriander and mint to the pan with the balsamic vinegar or lemon juice. Season to taste with salt and pepper and toss lightly. Serve the monkfish salad warm or leave to cool.

Potato salad with salmon and prawns

Serves 4
Preparation: 20 minutes
Cooking: 15–20 minutes

Carbohydrate: 33 g, Protein: 23 g, Fat: 19 g, Fibre: 3 g, Calories: 388 kcal, Sodium: 1265 mg (per portion)

What you need:

- 625 g/1¼ lb waxy potatoes, scrubbed

- 50 g/2 oz smoked salmon, cut into thin strips
- 250 g/8 oz cooked peeled prawns
- 125 g/4 oz seedless white grapes, halved
- 50 g/2 oz pecan nuts
- 1 tablespoon snipped chives
- 1 tablespoon chopped fresh dill, to garnish

For the dressing:

- 1 tablespoon mayonnaise
- 4 tablespoons soured cream
- 1 tablespoon lemon juice
- salt and pepper

1 Cook the potatoes in a saucepan of lightly salted boiling water for about 15–20 minutes until the potatoes are just tender. Drain well. When cool, slice the potatoes into a large salad bowl.

2 Add the smoked salmon, cooked prawns, grapes, pecans and snipped chives. Mix the salad lightly, using two forks.

3 For the dressing, mix the mayonnaise, soured cream and lemon juice together in a small bowl. Season to taste and whisk until thoroughly combined. Pour the dressing over the salad. Toss lightly to coat, sprinkle with dill and serve at once.

Above: *Potato salad with salmon and prawns*

Pasta and rice

Pasta and rice are staple ingredients in every cook's storecupboard. Their place is a well-deserved one, because there is so much you can do with them. They are perfect for every occasion, whether it's a quick family meal, such as Spaghetti bolognese, or a grand dinner party dish like Linguine alla marinara – guaranteed to impress even your smartest friends. Add other grains to your store, such as couscous and bulgar wheat, and you'll be ready for any culinary experience.

Right: *Lasagne*

Cook's Tip

A lot of traditional Italian recipes for lasagne add a pinch of ground nutmeg to the white sauce. To get the authentic flavour just like mamma used to make, add nutmeg and leave out the cloves.

One way of getting rid of any lumps, if you do not achieve a smooth white sauce first time, is to rub it through a fine sieve.

Lasagne

Serves 4
Preparation: 1 hour
Cooking: 1 hour
Carbohydrate: 38 g, Protein: 56 g,
Fat: 60 g, Fibre: 3 g, Calories: 902 kcal
Sodium: 1060 mg (per portion)

What you need:

- 9 dried 'no-presoak' lasagne sheets
- 50 g/2 oz Parmesan cheese, grated
- salt and pepper

For the meat sauce:
- 2 tablespoons olive oil
- 2 onions, chopped finely
- 3 garlic cloves, crushed
- 1 tablespoon dried oregano
- 1 tablespoon dried basil
- 3 tablespoons tomato purée
- 500 g/1 lb lean minced beef
- 1 x 400 g/13 oz can of plum tomatoes

For the cheese sauce:
- 600 ml/1 pint skimmed milk
- 4 cloves
- 1 onion, halved
- 25 g/1 oz butter
- 25 g/1 oz plain flour
- 250 g/8 oz Cheddar cheese, grated

1 Make the meat sauce: heat the oil in a large saucepan and fry the onions for 3–5 minutes until

Variations

Chicken lasagne

Replace the minced beef with the same quantity of lean minced chicken. When making the cheese sauce, subsitute half the milk with natural yogurt and continue as in the main recipe.

Lasagne verde

Replace the plain lasagne with the same quantity of lasagne verde (spinach-flavoured lasagne). Substitute the tomato purée with the same quantity of ready-made pesto or 3 tablespoons freshly chopped basil. Continue as in the main recipe.

softened. Add the garlic and fry for 1 minute more, then stir in the herbs, tomato purée and beef. Fry the mixture, stirring constantly, for 5 minutes. Add the tomatoes to the filling with salt and pepper to taste. Stir well. Cover the pan and simmer the meat sauce for 45 minutes, stirring occasionally.

2 Meanwhile, infuse the milk for the cheese sauce. Stick the cloves in the onion halves and put them in a small saucepan. Add the milk and bring to just below boiling point. Remove the pan from the heat and set aside for 15 minutes. Remove the onion halves and cloves.

3 Melt the butter in a saucepan. Stir in the flour and cook for 1 minute. Add the skimmed milk gradually, whisking or beating the sauce over moderate heat until thickened. Then add the Cheddar cheese, stir well until melted, and stir in salt and pepper to taste. Set aside.

4 Grease both the base and the sides of an oval or rectangular 1.75 litre/3 pint ovenproof dish. Spoon one-third of the meat mixture over the base. Spread over a quarter of the cheese sauce and cover with 3 sheets of lasagne. Some manufacterers of dried 'no-presoak' lasagne suggest that you dip the sheets in hot water just before arranging them in the dish. Follow the instructions on the packet.

5 Repeat the layering process twice more, finishing with a layer of pasta. Cover with the remaining cheese sauce. Sprinkle over the Parmesan. Bake the lasagne in a preheated oven, 190°C (375°F), Gas Mark 5, for 1 hour. Serve with a fresh green salad and crusty bread to mop up all the juices.

Chilli tagliatelle

Serves 4
Preparation: 10 minutes
Cooking: 4–6 minutes
Carbohydrate: 23 g, Protein: 7 g,
Fat: 18 g, Fibre: 2 g, Calories: 278 kcal,
Sodium: 253 mg (per portion)

What you need:

- 4 tablespoons olive oil
- salt
- 375 g/12 oz fresh tagliatelle verde
- 2 garlic cloves, crushed
- 2 fresh red chillies, deseeded and chopped
- 50 g/2 oz button mushrooms, sliced
- 4 tablespoons balsamic vinegar
- 2 tablespoons orange juice
- 3 tablespoons red pesto
- 1 bunch of spring onions, shredded
- 25 g/1 oz toasted hazelnuts, chopped

1 Bring plenty of water to the boil in a saucepan. Add a dash of oil and a pinch of salt. Add the tagliatelle and cook for about 4–6 minutes or until al dente.
2 Meanwhile, heat the remaining oil in a large pan. Add the garlic, chillies and mushrooms and gently fry for 2 minutes. Reduce the heat and stir in the remaining ingredients.
3 Drain the pasta well and add it to the garlic and chilli mixture, tossing well. Serve at once.

Spaghetti alla bolognese

Serves 4
Preparation: 10 minutes
Cooking: 2½–3 hours
Carbohydrate: 41 g, Protein: 40 g,
Fat: 46 g, Fibre: 3 g, Calories: 747 kcal,
Sodium: 879 mg (per portion)

What you need:

- 500 g/1 lb spaghetti
- 1 teaspoon olive oil
- 50 g/2 oz grated Parmesan cheese

For the bolognese sauce:
- 4 tablespoons olive oil
- 1 onion, finely chopped
- 3 garlic cloves, crushed
- 4 rashers rindless bacon, chopped
- 1 carrot, diced
- 1 celery stick, diced
- 500 g/1 lb minced lean beef
- 150 ml/¼ pint red wine
- 125 ml/4 fl oz milk
- grated nutmeg
- 1 x 425 g/14 oz can of chopped tomatoes
- 1 tablespoon sugar
- 1 teaspoon chopped fresh oregano
- salt and pepper

1 Make the sauce: heat the oil in a pan and sauté the onion, garlic, bacon, carrot and celery until softened and golden. Add the beef and then cook, stirring occasionally, until browned.
2 Add the red wine and bring to the boil. Reduce the heat slightly and cook over a medium heat until most of the wine has evaporated. Season to taste.
3 Add the milk and a little grated nutmeg and stir well. Continue cooking until the milk is absorbed by the meat mixture. Add the tomatoes, sugar and oregano. Reduce to a bare simmer and cook, uncovered, for 2–2½ hours until reduced and coloured.

Cook's Tip

Deseeding the chillies gives them a milder flavour. Cut the chilli in half lengthways with a small, sharp knife, then scrape out the seeds and cut away the fleshy white 'ribs' Always wash your hands afterwards and never let any part of the chilli go near your eyes.

Right: *Chilli tagliatelle*
Far right: *Pasta with chicken, cream and mushroom sauce*

4 Bring a saucepan of salted water to the boil. Add the spaghetti and oil and cook until al dente. Drain and season with pepper. Serve with the Bolognese sauce, sprinkled with the Parmesan cheese.

Pasta with chicken, cream and mushroom sauce

Serves 4
Preparation: 30 minutes
Cooking: 30 minutes
Carbohydrate: 79 g, Protein: 37 g, Fat: 35 g, Fibre: 5 g, Calories: 763 kcal, Sodium: 394 mg (per portion)

What you need:

- 3 part-boned chicken breasts
- 1 small onion, quartered
- 1 carrot, chopped roughly
- 1 bouquet garni
- a few black peppercorns
- 300 ml/½ pint water
- 2 tablespoons dry sherry (optional)

- 50 g/2 oz butter
- 250 g/8 oz button mushrooms, sliced thinly
- 2 garlic cloves, crushed
- 1 teaspoon chopped fresh rosemary
- 1 tablespoon extra-virgin olive oil
- 375 g/12 oz dried pasta (e.g. farfalle, penne or fusilli)
- 1½ tablespoons plain flour
- 150 ml/¼ pint double cream
- salt and pepper
- fresh rosemary, to garnish

1 Put the chicken in a saucepan with the onion, carrot, bouquet garni and peppercorns. Pour in the water and sherry, if using.

2 Bring to the boil, then lower the heat, cover and poach the chicken for 20 minutes until just tender when pierced.

3 Meanwhile, melt the butter in a separate saucepan, add the mushrooms, garlic, rosemary and salt and pepper to taste, and sauté over a moderate heat, stirring frequently, for just about

5 minutes until the juices run. Remove from the heat. With a slotted spoon, transfer the mushrooms from the buttery liquid to a bowl.

4 Bring a large saucepan of water to the boil, swirl in the oil and add ½ teaspoon salt. Add the pasta and boil, uncovered, over a moderate heat for 10 minutes, or according to packet instructions.

5 Meanwhile, lift the chicken out of the poaching liquid, then strain the liquid into a jug. Cut the chicken into strips, discarding the skin and bones.

6 Return the mushroom cooking liquid to the heat, sprinkle in the flour and then cook for 1–2 minutes, stirring. Add the chicken poaching liquid, a little at a time, beating vigorously after each addition.

7 Bring to the boil, stirring. Lower the heat and add the chicken, mushrooms, cream and seasoning. Stir well, then simmer over a moderate heat, stirring frequently, for 5 minutes until the liquid has thickened.

8 Drain the pasta and turn into a serving bowl. Pour in the sauce and toss to mix well. Serve garnished with the rosemary and with a mixed salad.

Above: *Spaghetti alla bolognese*

Cook's Tip

Use white button mushrooms for this sauce – dark ones will spoil its appearance.

Above: *Chow mein*
Below right: *Stir-fried noodles*

Chow mein

Serves 3–4
Preparation: 20 minutes
Cooking: about 10 minutes
Carbohydrate: 50 g, Protein: 29 g,
Fat: 16 g, Fibre: 3 g, Calories: 449 kcal,
Sodium: 962 mg (per portion)

What you need:

- 2 tablespoons vegetable oil
- 4 spring onions, or 1 onion, sliced thinly
- 2.5 cm/1 inch piece of fresh root ginger, crushed
- 1 garlic clove, crushed
- 250 g/8 oz skinned chicken breast, cut diagonally in strips
- 250 g/8 oz packet Chinese egg noodles
- 125 g/4 oz mangetout, topped and tailed, cut crossways if large
- 125 g/4 oz boiled ham, cut into thin strips
- 2–3 tablespoons soy sauce, to taste
- 2 tablespoons rice wine or dry sherry
- 2 teaspoons sesame oil
- 1 teaspoon sugar
- salt and pepper

1 Heat a wok or a large, deep frying pan over a moderate heat until hot. Add the oil and heat until hot but not smoking. Add the spring onions or onion, ginger and garlic and stir-fry over a gentle heat for 1–2 minutes until softened but not coloured.

2 Add the strips of chicken breast and stir-fry over a moderate heat for 3–4 minutes until they all change colour on all sides.

3 Meanwhile, put the noodles in a large bowl and cover with boiling water. Leave to stand.

4 Add the mangetout to the chicken in the wok and stir-fry for 2–3 minutes until the chicken is tender when pierced.

5 Drain the noodles, add to the wok with the ham, and toss over a high heat until hot. Add the soy sauce, rice wine or sherry, sesame oil, sugar and season to taste. Toss everything around until all the ingredients are hot and glistening. Serve immediately.

Farfalle alla napoletana

Serves 4
Preparation: 15 minutes
Cooking: 21 minutes
Carbohydrate: 83 g, Protein: 14 g,
Fat: 6 g, Fibre: 6 g, Calories: 446 kcal,
Sodium: 306 mg (per portion)

What you need:

- 2 tablespoons olive oil
- 1 onion, chopped
- 2 garlic cloves, crushed
- 2 carrots, chopped finely,

Variations

Bacon and sweet-corn farfalle

Make the sauce as for the main recipe. Five minutes before the end of cooking time, add 125 g/4 oz grilled rindless bacon rashers, crumbled, with 125 g/4 oz sliced mushrooms and 50 g/2 oz sweetcorn niblets. Serve as in the main recipe.

Coriander and sun-dried tomato farfalle

Make the sauce as for the main recipe, omitting the carrots and basil. Substitute 8 sliced, sun-dried tomatoes and 4 tablespoons chopped coriander leaves scattered over the sauce to garnish.

3 Meanwhile, bring at least 1.75 litres/3 pints of water to the boil in a large saucepan. Add a dash of olive oil and a generous pinch of salt. Add the pasta, bring back to the boil and cook for 8–12 minutes, until the pasta is al dente.

4 Drain the pasta in a colander, tip on to a large serving platter, and season well with pepper. Drizzle with a little more olive oil if you wish. Pour the tomato sauce over the pasta. Roughly shred the basil leaves and then scatter them on top of the tomato sauce to garnish.

Stir-fried noodles

Serves 4
Preparation: 10 minutes
Cooking: 20 minutes
*Carbohydrate: 35 g, Protein: 12 g,
Fat: 12 g, Fibre: 2 g, Calories: 285 kcal,
Sodium: 547 mg (per portion)*

What you need:

- 4 tablespoons vegetable oil
- 2 garlic cloves, crushed
- 125 g/4 oz medium-sized egg noodles
- 2 teaspoons dark soy sauce
- 125 g/4 oz mixed sliced chicken breast, prepared squid and shelled prawns
- ½ teaspoon black pepper
- 2 tablespoons nam pla (fish sauce)
- 125 g/4 oz shredded cabbage and broccoli florets
- 300 ml/½ pint chicken stock
- 1 tablespoon cornflour
- 1 tablespoon salted soya bean flavouring
- 2 tablespoons sugar

1 Heat half the oil in a work or large, deep frying pan. Add half the garlic and then stir-fry for 1 minute until golden brown. Add the noodles and soy sauce and cook, stirring constantly, for 3–5 minutes. Transfer to a warm serving dish and keep warm.

2 Heat the remaining oil in the wok and add the rest of the crushed garlic. Stir-fry for about 1 minute until golden brown. Add the chicken breast, squid, prawns, black pepper and nam pla. Stir-fry for 5 minutes.

3 Add the shredded cabbage and the broccoli florets to the meat mixture in the wok and stir-fry for 3 more minutes.

4 Stir in the chicken stock. Mix the cornflour with 2 tablespoons of water and stir into the wok. Add the soya bean flavouring and sugar, and bring to the boil. Lower the heat and cook for 3 minutes, stirring all the time. Pour the sauce over the noodles and serve immediately.

Left: *Farfalle alla napoletana*

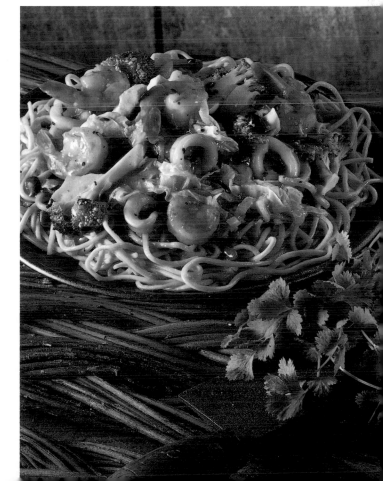

blanched
- 2 red peppers, cored, deseeded and chopped finely
- 4 large tomatoes, chopped
- 150 ml/¼ pint red wine
- 1 x 400 g/13 oz can of chopped tomatoes with herbs
- 375 g/12 oz dried farfalle
- salt and pepper
- 1 bunch of basil, to garnish

1 Heat the oil in a large frying pan. Add the chopped onion and garlic and fry for about 3 minutes until softened but not coloured.

2 Add the carrots and the red peppers to the frying pan and fry for a further 3 minutes. Stir in the chopped fresh tomatoes with the red wine and then add the canned tomatoes. Season with salt and pepper to taste and then simmer, partially covered, for about 15 minutes.

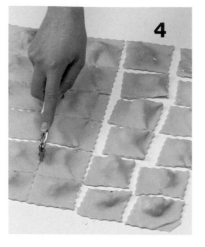

Spinach and ricotta ravioli

Serves 4–6
Preparation: 25 minutes
Cooking: 4–5 minutes
Carbohydrate: 57 g, Protein: 19 g,
Fat: 21 g, Fibre: 4 g, Calories: 473 kcal,
Sodium: 528 mg (per portion)

What you need:

- 300 g/10 oz homemade pasta dough

For the filling:
- 250 g/8 oz spinach leaves
- 125 g/4 oz fresh ricotta cheese
- 25 g/1 oz grated Parmesan cheese
- grated nutmeg
- 1 egg, beaten
- salt and pepper

To serve:
- 50 g/2 oz butter, melted
- 3–4 fresh sage leaves, torn
- grated Parmesan cheese

1 Begin by making the filling: thoroughly wash the spinach leaves and remove the stalks. Put the spinach in a saucepan without any water, cover with a lid and cook over very low heat for 5 minutes. Drain well and then place the spinach in a very large colander and press down firmly with a plate to squeeze out any excess moisture. Roughly chop the spinach.

2 Put the ricotta and Parmesan cheeses in a bowl and mix in the chopped spinach. Add the seasoning, to taste, grated nutmeg and beaten egg, mixing well until the mixture is like a paste.

3 Roll out the pasta as thinly as possible on a lightly floured surface and cut into 2 equal-sized pieces. Put teaspoons of the ricotta and spinach filling over one piece of pasta at intervals, about 5 cm/2 inches apart.

4 Cover with the other sheet of pasta and press gently around each little mound with your fingers. Using a pastry cutter wheel, cut the pasta into squares. Cook the ravioli in gently boiling water for 4–5 minutes until they rise to the surface. Drain and serve with melted butter, sprinkled with sage leaves and Parmesan cheese.

Cook's Tip

To make this dish even more delicious, add chopped walnuts and bake in a pre-heated moderate oven, 180°C (350°F), Gas Mark 4, for 10 minutes to crisp up.

Right: *Spinach and ricotta ravioli*

Linguine with mussels and tomato sauce

Serves 4
Preparation: 25 minutes
Cooking: 20 minutes
Carbohydrate: 41 g, Protein: 26 g, Fat: 11 g, Fibre: 4 g, Calories: 356 kcal, Sodium: 626 mg (per portion)

What you need:

- 2.25 litres/4 pints mussels
- 3 tablespoons olive oil
- 1 onion, chopped
- 3 garlic cloves, crushed
- 750 g/1½ lb tomatoes, skinned and chopped
- 500 g/1 lb linguine
- 3 tablespoons chopped parsley
- salt and pepper

Below: Linguine with mussels and tomato sauce

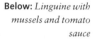

1 Prepare the mussels: wash them well and discard any that do not close tightly when tapped sharply against the work surface. Scrub the remaining mussels and remove the beards with a sharp knife. Place in a large saucepan with 125 ml/4 fl oz water, cover with a lid and cook over moderate heat for 5–6 minutes until the mussels open, shaking the pan constantly. Drain the mussels and remove their shells, reserving a few still in their shells to use for decoration later.

2 Heat the olive oil in a frying pan and add the onion and garlic. Sauté over a medium heat until golden and tender. Add the chopped tomatoes and seasonings, and cook gently over low heat until the mixture is thickened and reduced.

3 Add the shelled mussels and mix these gently into the tomato sauce. Simmer the mixture over a low heat for 2–3 minutes, or until the mussels are heated through.

4 Meanwhile, cook the linguine in salted boiling water until al dente. Drain well and gently toss with the tomato and mussel sauce. Transfer to a serving dish or 4 warm plates, sprinkle with chopped parsley and garnish with the reserved mussels.

Cook's Tip

Opening mussels either by cooking them or with a sharp knife often kills the mussel, it therefore must be eaten at once. Discard any fresh mussels which are open before you come to cook them or which do not open when cooked (see above).

Saffron rice

Serves 4
Preparation: 15 minutes, plus soaking
Cooking: 30 minutes
Carbohydrate: 54 g, Protein: 6 g, Fat: 24 g, Fibre: 1 g, Calories: 460 kcal, Sodium: 551 mg (per portion)

What you need:

- ½ teaspoon saffron threads
- 1 tablespoon boiling water
- 175 g/6 oz ghee or butter
- 2 large onions, sliced
- 375 g/12 oz Basmati or Patna rice
- 1 teaspoon cloves
- 4 cardamoms
- 1 teaspoon salt
- 1 teaspoon black pepper
- 750 ml/1¼ pints water
- silver leaf (varq), to garnish (optional)

cold water. Leave to soak overnight. The following day, rinse the kidney beans thoroughly and drain well.

2 Put the kidney beans in a large pan and add 900 ml/1½ pints boiling water. Cook for just about 30 minutes, until the kidney beans are almost tender.

3 Add the coconut milk, thyme, spring onions and chilli to the saucepan. Season with salt and pepper to taste and bring back to boiling point. Boil rapidly for 5 minutes.

5 Add the rice and stir well. Cover and simmer gently over a very low heat until the liquid has been absorbed. This will take about 20–25 minutes. If there is any remaining liquid left in the pan, drain the rice and beans. Transfer to a dish and serve hot.

Left: Saffron rice
Below: *Rice and beans*

1 Put the saffron threads in a small bowl with the boiling water and leave to soak for 30 minutes. Melt the ghee or butter in a heavy-based saucepan and then add the onions. Fry gently for 4–5 minutes until soft.

2 Put the rice in a sieve and wash thoroughly under cold running water to remove any milling and polishing dust. Drain well.

3 Add the rice to the onions in the pan, and stir in the cloves, cardamoms, salt and pepper. Fry for 3 minutes, stirring frequently.

4 Meanwhile, put the measured water in a kettle and bring to the boil. Add to the pan, together with the saffron and its soaking liquid, then lower the heat and simmer for 15–20 minutes until the rice is cooked. Drain well and transfer the rice to a serving dish. Serve hot, garnished, if liked, with silver leaf.

Rice and beans

Serves 6
Preparation: 5 minutes, plus overnight soaking
Cooking: 55 minutes
Carbohydrate: 95 g, Protein: 16 g, Fat: 1 g, Fibre: 7 g, Calories: 453 kcal, Sodium: 247 mg (per portion)

What you need:

- 250 g/8 oz dried red kidney beans
- 600 ml/1 pint coconut milk
- 2 sprigs of fresh thyme
- 2 spring onions, finely chopped
- 1 fresh green chilli, deseeded and finely chopped
- 500 g/1 lb long-grain rice
- salt and pepper

1 Put the dried red kidney beans in a large bowl and cover with

Right: *Nasi goreng*

Nasi goreng

Serves 4–6
Preparation: 15 minutes
Cooking: about 30 minutes
Carbohydrate: 30 g, Protein: 48 g,
Fat: 13 g, Fibre: 0 g, Calories: 419 kcal,
Sodium: 1539 mg (per portion)

What you need:

- 375 g/12 oz long-grain rice
- 2 eggs
- 2 tablespoons vegetable oil
- 1 small onion, finely chopped
- 2 garlic cloves, roughly chopped
- 1 hot fresh red chilli, deseeded and roughly chopped
- 500 g/1 lb skinned chicken breast fillets, cut diagonally into thin strips
- 250 g/8 oz peeled cooked prawns
- 2 tablespoons soy sauce, or more to taste
- salt and pepper
- spring onions, to garnish

1 Rinse the rice and put in a large saucepan and cover with cold water. Bring to the boil with 1 teaspoon salt, stir well, lower the heat and simmer, uncovered, for 20 minutes or until the rice is al dente. Drain, rinse under cold running water and drain again thoroughly. Then set the cooked rice aside to cool.

2 Make an omelette: beat the eggs with salt and pepper. Heat 1½ tablespoons of oil in a small frying pan until hot but not smoking. Run the eggs over the base of pan, lift up the edges and let the unset egg run underneath. Cook until the underneath is golden and the top set. Slide out of the pan, then roll up carefully into a cigar shape. Leave to cool, seam side down.

3 Crush the onion, garlic and chilli to a paste, then fry the remaining oil in a wok or deep frying pan, for 1–2 minutes until fragrant. Add the chicken and stir-fry for 3–4 minutes until it changes colour all over. Add the prawns and soy sauce. Stir-fry until the chicken is tender.

4 Mix the cold rice with the chicken and prawns. Toss over a high heat until the rice is piping hot. Add salt, pepper and more soy sauce to taste.

5 Turn the rice into a serving dish and garnish with spring onions and the omelette cut into rings.

Cook's Tip

This famous Indonesian rice dish can be made with different meats besides chicken. Duck or turkey breasts can be used, as can pork or beef. The authentic version includes a nugget of terasi – a dried shrimp paste, mixed in with the onion, garlic and chilli. It is available at Oriental speciality shops.

Chicken couscous

Serves 6–8
Preparation: 40 minutes
Cooking: about 2¾ hours
Carbohydrate: 80 g, Protein: 39 g,
Fat: 22 g, Fibre: 8 g, Calories: 640 kcal,
Sodium: 233 mg (per portion)

What you need:

- 125 g/4 oz chickpeas, soaked in cold water overnight, then drained
- 2 onions, finely chopped
- 3 garlic cloves, finely chopped
- 2 teaspoons ground coriander
- 2 teaspoons cumin
- 2 teaspoons turmeric
- 2 teaspoons chilli powder
- ½ teaspoon ground cinnamon
- 2 tablespoons extra-virgin olive oil
- 2 tablespoons tomato purée
- 12 skinned and boned chicken thighs, cut into large, bite-sized pieces
- 4 carrots, thickly sliced
- 2 parsnips, thickly sliced
- 2 potatoes, cut into chunks
- 50 g/2 oz butter
- 4 courgettes, thickly sliced
- 2 tablespoons raisins
- 500 ml/17 fl oz water
- 2 tablespoons olive oil

- 500 g/1 lb ready-prepared 'quick' couscous
- a large knob of butter
- harissa sauce, to taste
- salt and pepper
- fresh coriander, to garnish

1 Simmer the chickpeas for 1 hour in a pan, half-covered.
2 Gently fry the onions, garlic and ground spices in the oil in the bottom of a couscousière or large pan for 5 minutes until softened.
3 Stir in the tomato purée, drained chickpeas and seasoning. Cover with water and bring to the boil, stirring. Simmer, stirring occasionally, for 1 hour. Top up with water to keep the chickpeas covered. Add the chicken and simmer, covered, for about 20 minutes. Stir occasionally.
4 Add the carrots, parsnips and potatoes, stir, cover with water and bring to the boil. Cover and cook for 30 minutes or until the chicken and vegetables are tender, adding the courgettes and raisins halfway through.
5 Prepare the couscous: put the measured water in a saucepan, add the olive oil and 2 teaspoons of salt, and bring to the boil. Remove from the heat. Stir and

pour in the couscous, and allow to swell for 2 minutes, or according to the packet instructions. Add the butter and heat over low heat for 3 minutes, while stirring with a fork to separate the grains.
6 Remove the couscous, check the chicken for seasoning, add the harissa sauce and stir well.
7 Fork the remaining butter into the couscous. Arrange the couscous in a ring with chicken and vegetables in the centre. Garnish with coriander and serve with some extra harissa sauce separately.

Tabbouleh with raisins, pistachios and cracked pepper

Serves 4
Preparation: 10 minutes, plus 1 hour chilling
Carbohydrate: 64 g, Protein: 10 g, Fat: 38 g, Fibre: 2 g, Calories: 626 kcal, Sodium: 858 mg (per portion)

What you need:

- 250 g/8 oz bulgar wheat
- 1 small red onion, finely chopped
- 2 tablespoons chopped fresh coriander
- 2 tablespoons chopped fresh mint
- 75 g/3 oz raisins
- 125 ml/4 fl oz extra-virgin olive oil
- 50 ml/2 fl oz lemon juice
- 1 tablespoon cracked black pepper
- 2 teaspoons ground coriander
- 1 teaspoon ground cinnamon
- 50 g/2 oz pistachio nuts, chopped
- 50 g/2 oz stoned black olives, chopped
- salt

1 Place the bulgar wheat in a bowl and add plenty of cold water. Set aside the bulgar wheat to soak for 30 minutes then drain off any remaining water.
2 Mix the bulgar wheat with the red onion, herbs, raisins, olive oil, lemon juice, pepper and spices, stirring well until all the ingredients are evenly blended. Allow the bulgar wheat to cool and then chill for 1 hour in the refrigerator for the flavours to develop fully.
3 Remove the salad from the refrigerator and then allow to return to room temperature. Stir in the nuts and the stoned black olives, making sure that they are evenly distributed. Season with salt and pepper to taste and serve at once.

Above: Tabbouleh with raisins, pistachios and cracked pepper
Below left: Chicken couscous

Vegetables

It wasn't for nothing that your mother told you to eat your greens! But vegetables aren't only good for you, they're also relatively inexpensive, highly versatile, and absolutely delicious – provided, of course, that they are imaginatively cooked. Which is what these recipes are all about: from the humble potato to the glossy aubergine, there are hundreds of exciting and unusual things you can do with them all. Vegetable dishes should never be boring. They should both complement and enhance the meat or fish dish that they are intended to accompany.

Below: *Potato cakes*
Right: *Gratin dauphinois*

Potato cakes

Serves 4
Preparation: 20 minutes
Cooking: 5–10 minutes
Carbohydrate: 49 g, Protein: 12 g, Fat: 16 g, Fibre: 4 g, Calories: 371 kcal, Sodium: 280 mg (per portion)

What you need:

- 1 kg/2 lb potatoes
- 3 eggs
- 125 g/4 oz onions, chopped
- 1 tablespoon flour
- 1 tablespoon chopped fresh parsley and chives
- 1 garlic clove, crushed
- freshly grated nutmeg
- 6 tablespoons oil
- salt and pepper

1 Grate the potatoes coarsely, using a grater or food processor, place in a sieve and rinse under cold running water. Drain and transfer the potatoes to a bowl.
2 Add the eggs to the bowl of grated potatoes and mix well. Add the chopped onions, flour, chopped parsley and chives and the garlic. Season with salt and pepper and grated nutmeg, then stir the mixture thoroughly.
3 Divide the potato mixture into equal-sized portions and, using a spoon, mould them into small cakes.
4 Heat the oil in a frying pan. When hot, add the potato cakes and fry until golden brown and crisp on both sides, turning them once during cooking. Serve the potato cakes very hot.

Gratin dauphinois

Serves 4–6
Preparation: 15–20 minutes
Cooking: 1¼–1½ hours
Carbohydrate: 50 g, Protein: 10 g, Fat: 30 g, Fibre: 3 g, Calories:495 kcal, Sodium: 725 mg (per portion)

What you need:

- 1 garlic clove, cut in half
- 75 g/3 oz softened butter
- 1 kg/2 lb waxy potatoes, peeled and thinly sliced
- freshly grated nutmeg
- 350 ml/12 fl oz hot milk
- 250 ml/8 fl oz single cream
- salt and pepper

1 Rub the cut garlic around the inside of a large earthenware baking dish to give flavour to the gratin. Brush the dish thickly with some of the softened butter.
2 Place a layer of the thinly sliced potatoes in the dish and sprinkle with salt, pepper and nutmeg. Continue layering all the potatoes in this way, seasoning each layer as you go.
3 Mix the milk and cream, then pour over the potatoes, so they are almost covered by the liquid.
4 Dot the remaining butter over the top, then bake in a preheated oven, 180°C (350°F), Gas Mark 4, for 1–1¼ hours or until tender when pierced with a skewer. Increase the oven heat to 200°C (400°F), Gas Mark 6 for the last 15 minutes of cooking time to brown the top layer. Serve hot, straight from the baking dish.

Carrots with ginger and orange butter

Serves 4–6
Preparation: 10 minutes
Cooking: 10–12 minutes
Carbohydrate: 21 g, Protein: 2 g, Fat: 11 g, Fibre: 6 g, Calories: 189 kcal, Sodium: 355 mg (per portion)

What you need:

- 1 kg/2 lb carrots, sliced, or whole baby carrots

For the ginger and orange butter:

- 50 g/2 oz butter, softened
- 1 teaspoon grated root ginger
- ½ teaspoon grated orange rind
- ½ tablespoon orange juice
- ½ teaspoon clear honey
- 1 tablespoon chopped fresh chervil
- salt and pepper

1 Steam or boil the carrots for 10–12 minutes until tender.

2 Meanwhile, make the ginger and orange butter. Place all the ingredients in a food processor and blend until smooth and evenly combined.

3 Transfer the cooked carrots to a warmed serving dish, add the butter and toss well together until the carrots are thoroughly coated with the butter, then serve at once.

Roasted autumn vegetables with a garlic sauce

Serves 4–6
Preparation: 25 minutes
Cooking: 1¼ hours
Carbohydrate: 49 g, Protein: 8 g, Fat: 13 g, Fibre: 8 g, Calories: 331 kcal, Sodium: 353 mg (per portion)

What you need:

- 1 large head of garlic
- 2 large onions, cut into wedges
- 8 small carrots, quartered
- 8 small parsnips
- 12 small potatoes, halved if large
- 2 heads fennel, sliced thickly
- 4 sprigs of rosemary
- 4 sprigs of thyme
- 6 tablespoons extra-virgin olive oil

For the garlic sauce:

- 1 large slice of day-old bread (about 75 g/3 oz)
- 4 tablespoons milk
- 75 ml/3 oz extra-virgin olive oil
- salt and pepper

1 Blanch the head of garlic in boiling, salted water for about 5 minutes. Drain and pat dry on absorbent kitchen paper.

2 Put all the vegetables and herbs in a large roasting pan, placing the garlic in the middle. Season well and stir in the oil to coat the vegetables. Cover the tin with foil and bake in a preheated oven, 220°C (425°F), Gas Mark 7, for 50 minutes. Remove the foil and bake for 30 minutes.

Cook's Tip

Roasting vegetables in a hot oven draws out their natural sweetness and intense flavour. It is important to cut the vegetables into similar-sized pieces so they will cook evenly.

3 Remove the garlic. Carefully peel and discard the skin and mash the garlic flesh with a fork. Put the bread in a bowl, add the milk and soak for 5 minutes.

4 Place the bread and garlic flesh in a blender and process to form a smooth paste. Gradually blend in the oil, adding a little at a time, until evenly combined, then season to taste.

5 Serve the roasted vegetables accompanied by the garlic sauce to dip.

Roasted Jerusalem artichokes

Serves 4
Preparation: 10 minutes
Cooking: 30 minutes
Carbohydrate: 22 g, Protein: 5 g, Fat: 288 g, Fibre: 7 g, Calories: 2687 kcal, Sodium: 203 mg (per portion)

What you need:

- 750 g/1½ lb Jerusalem artichokes, scrubbed but not peeled
- 4 tablespoons walnut or extra-virgin olive oil
- 12 whole garlic cloves
- 1 tablespoon chopped fresh sage leaves
- 25 g/1 oz walnuts, toasted and chopped
- salt and pepper

1 Cut any larger artichokes in half so they are all roughly the same size, then blanch in lightly salted water for 5 minutes.

2 Drain well and toss them immediately with the oil, garlic, sage, salt and pepper.

3 Place in a roasting tin and bake in a preheated oven, 200°C (400°F), Gas Mark 6, for about 30 minutes, turning occasionally, until they are golden and tender.

4 Transfer the artichokes to a warmed serving dish, scatter over the chopped walnuts and serve at once.

Cook's Tip

The Jerusalem artichoke is a very underrated vegetable, perhaps due to its anonymity: it could easily be mistaken for just another variety of the potato family. However, it has a flavour all of its own – somewhere between turnip and potato with a nutty, almost peppery taste. When cooking by this method there is no need to peel the artichokes.

Below: *Roasted Jerusalem artichokes*

Variation

Roasted parsnips with thyme butter

Toss 625 g/1¼ lb baby parsnips with 1 tablespoon olive oil, 1 clove of garlic, 2 thyme sprigs and sea salt and place in a roasting pan. Bake in a preheated oven at 200°C (400°F), Gas Mark 6, for about 40–45 minutes, stirring occasionally.

Meanwhile, melt 25 g/ 1 oz butter in a small pan, add 1 tablespoon chopped fresh thyme, 1 teaspoon grated lemon rind, a pinch each of salt and cayenne pepper, and fry gently for 3–4 minutes until softened.

Remove the parsnips from the oven, discard the thyme and dot with thyme butter. Toss well and serve at once.

Mixed bean sauté with almonds and chives

Serves 4
Preparation: 10 minutes
Cooking: 6–7 minutes
Carbohydrate: 10 g, Protein: 9 g,
Fat: 1 2 g, Fibre: 6 g, Calories:177 kcal,
Sodium: 200 mg (per portion)

What you need:

- 750 g/1½ lb mixed beans, trimmed and sliced (e.g. broad beans, runner beans, French beans, flat beans, yellow string beans, etc.)
- 2 tablespoons almond or extra-virgin olive oil
- 1 small leek, trimmed, cleaned and sliced
- 2 garlic cloves, sliced
- 50 g/2 oz flaked almonds
- 2 tablespoons chopped fresh chives
- salt and pepper

Below: Mixed bean sauté with almonds and chives
Above right: *Fried chilli cabbage*

1 Blanch all the beans in lightly salted boiling water for 1 minute. Drain, refresh under cold water and pat dry on kitchen paper.
2 Heat the oil in a wok or large frying pan, add the leek, garlic and almonds and fry gently for 3 minutes until softened.
3 Add the beans, stir-fry for 3–4 minutes until tender, add the chives, salt and pepper and serve.

Fried chilli cabbage

Serves 4–6
Preparation: 20 minutes
Cooking: 35 minutes
Carbohydrate: 21 g, Protein: 7 g,
Fat: 39 g, Fibre: 6 g, Calories: 459 kcal,
Sodium: 577 mg (per portion)

What you need:

- 125 g/4 oz ghee or butter
- 1 small onion, chopped
- 6 garlic cloves, crushed
- 1 teaspoon white cumin seeds
- 1 teaspoon turmeric
- 1 cabbage, coarsely chopped
- 125 g/4 oz potatoes, chopped
- 125 g/4 oz shelled peas
- 125 g/4 oz carrots, sliced
- salt
- 250 g/8 oz tomatoes, skinned and sliced
- 1 teaspoon aamchoor (mango powder)
- 1 green chilli, chopped
- 15 g/½ oz root ginger, grated
- 1 teaspoon garam masala
- 1 tablespoon chopped coriander leaves
- 2 tablespoons melted butter

Cook's Tip

Garam masala is a mixture of spices used in Indian cooking. The ingredients and their proportions vary from one region of India to another, but a typical mixture would probably include black cumin seeds, cloves, cinnamon, cardamom and peppercorns. You can make up a mixture yourself at home, or you can buy it ready-made in most supermarkets.

1 Melt the ghee or butter in a large saucepan and fry the onion, garlic and cumin seeds for about 5 minutes until golden brown. Add the turmeric and shake the pan for a few seconds.

2 Add the chopped cabbage, potatoes, peas, carrots and salt. Cook, stirring continuously, for 5 minutes. Cover the pan and cook gently over a low heat for a further 10 minutes.

3 Add the tomatoes, aamchoor (mango powder), the chilli and ginger. Stir well, then replace the lid and continue cooking for another 10 minutes.

4 Add the garam masala and chopped coriander and stir well. Heat through over a low heat for about 5 minutes, then serve hot with the melted butter poured over the top.

Morel mushrooms with wild rice

Serves 2
Preparation: 10 minutes
Cooking: 3 minutes
Carbohydrate: 51 g, Protein: 6 g, Fat: 42 g, Fibre: 0 g, Calories:627 kcal, Sodium: 204 mg (per portion)

What you need:

- 150 g/5 oz fresh morel mushrooms, rinsed, trimmed and halved lengthways, or 15 g/½ oz dried morels plus 5 g/¼ oz dried horn of plenty mushrooms and 125 g/4 oz mixed fresh mushrooms, such as shiitake, yellow and grey oyster, trimmed
- 125 g/4 oz cup raw wild rice, well rinsed
- 50 g/2 oz butter
- 6 tablespoons double cream
- 1 tablespoon brandy
- salt and pepper

1 If you are using the dried mushrooms, soak them in warm water for 20–30 minutes, then drain. Cook the wild rice in a saucepan of salted boiling water for 18–20 minutes until the grains begin to split. Drain well.

2 Meanwhile, melt half of the butter in a heavy-based frying pan. Add all of the mushrooms and sauté over a moderately high heat for about 2–3 minutes. Season to taste.

3 Add the cream and brandy and reduce the heat. Continue cooking until the liquid has almost all evaporated. Transfer the mushrooms to a bowl, cover and keep warm.

4 Melt the remaining butter in the pan, add the wild rice and reheat, stirring to coat well. Season to taste and serve topped with the mushrooms.

Stir-fried garlic mushrooms

Serves 4
Preparation: 5 minutes
Cooking: 5 minutes
Carbohydrate: 5 g, Protein: 2 g, Fat: 7 g, Fibre: 1 g, Calories: 103 kcal, Sodium: 258 mg (per portion)

What you need:

- 2 tablespoons olive oil
- 1 tablespoon butter
- 250 g/8 oz mixed mushrooms, such as shiitake and chestnut, rinsed, trimmed and thickly sliced
- 3–4 garlic cloves, crushed
- 125 g/4 oz oyster mushrooms, rinsed, trimmed and thickly sliced
- 2–3 tablespoons dry sherry or vermouth
- salt and pepper
- 4 tablespoons chopped fresh parsley

1 Heat a wok or large frying pan until hot. Add the oil and butter and heat over a moderate heat until foaming.

2 Add the shiitake and chestnut mushrooms, the garlic, salt and plenty of pepper. Increase the heat to high and stir-fry for about 2 minutes.

3 Add the oyster mushrooms, sprinkle over the dry sherry or vermouth and stir-fry for another 3 minutes, or until tender.

4 Taste, adjust the seasoning, then remove the pan from the heat and stir in the chopped fresh parsley. Serve at once.

Above left: *Morel mushrooms with wild rice*
Below: *Stir-fried garlic mushrooms*

Ratatouille

Serves 6
Preparation: 15 minutes
Cooking: 1¾ hours
Carbohydrate: 12 g, Protein: 4 g,
Fat: 34 g, Fibre: 5 g, Calories: 379 kcal,
Sodium: 350 mg (per portion)

What you need:

- 5 courgettes, peeled and sliced
- 2 aubergines, sliced
- 200 ml/7 fl oz olive oil
- 3 onions, finely chopped
- 2 large green peppers, grilled, skinned and sliced
- 1 kg/2 lb tomatoes, skinned and quartered
- 6 garlic cloves, finely chopped
- 1 teaspoon coriander seeds, crushed
- 75 ml/3 fl oz dry white wine
- salt and pepper
- 1 tablespoon chopped basil
- 2 tablespoons chopped fresh parsley

1 Place the sliced courgettes and aubergines in a colander and lightly salt. Set aside for about 15 minutes to allow them to drain, and then rinse and pat dry with absorbent kitchen paper.
2 Heat a little of the oil in a large frying pan, add the onions and fry gently over low heat for about 15 minutes, until soft and golden, and then transfer to a flameproof casserole dish.
3 Fry the peppers, tomatoes, courgettes and aubergines for 15 minutes each. When cooked, drain and add to the casserole. Replenish the pan with the remaining olive oil as necessary.
4 Mix all the vegetables in the casserole, and add the garlic, coriander and wine. Season to taste, then simmer gently for about 30 minutes. Add the basil and parsley just before serving.

Okra with chillies

Serves 4
Preparation: 10 minutes
Cooking: 5–10 minutes
Carbohydrate: 8 g, Protein: 5 g,
Fat: 16 g, Fibre: 6 g, Calories: 189 kcal,
Sodium: 217 mg (per portion)

What you need:

- 3 tablespoons ghee or butter
- 1 large onion, sliced
- 3 garlic cloves, sliced
- 2.5 cm/1 inch fresh root ginger, peeled and grated
- 2 fresh red chillies, finely chopped
- ½ teaspoon chilli powder
- 500 g/1 lb okra
- 250 g/8 fl oz water
- salt
- 2 teaspoons unsweetened desiccated coconut

1 Melt the ghee or butter in a heavy saucepan, then add the onion, garlic, ginger, chillies and chilli powder. Fry gently for about 5 minutes, until softened. Stir occasionally.

2 Top and tail the okra, then add to the pan with the measured water and salt to taste. Bring to the boil, lower the heat, cover and simmer for 5–10 minutes, until the okra are just tender, but still firm to the bite. Sprinkle with the coconut and serve hot.

Sicilian-style aubergines

Serves 4
Preparation: 40 minutes
Cooking: 1 hour
Carbohydrate: 7 g, Protein: 6 g,
Fat: 18 g, Fibre: 4 g, Calories: 214 kcal,
Sodium: 2062 mg (per portion)

What you need:

- 3 aubergines, cut into 1 cm/½ inch dice
- salt
- 50 g/2 oz anchovy fillets
- 1 onion, thinly sliced
- 4 tablespoons olive oil
- 2 celery sticks, diced
- 150 ml/¼ pint passata (sieved tomatoes)
- 3 tablespoons white wine vinegar
- 1 yellow pepper, deseeded and thinly sliced
- 1 red pepper, deseeded and thinly sliced
- 50 g/2 oz capers, roughly chopped
- 50 g/2 oz black olives, pitted and sliced
- 50 g/2 oz green olives, pitted and sliced
- 2 tablespoons pine nuts
- 2 tablespoons chopped fresh parsley

1 Put the diced aubergine in a colander, sprinkle with salt and leave for 15–20 minutes to exude the bitter juices. Rinse off the salt under cold running water, then pat dry with kitchen paper.

2 Soak the anchovies in a little warm water in a bowl to remove some of their saltiness. Remove, pat dry and cut the anchovies into thin strips. Set aside.

3 Sauté the onion in the oil until soft and golden. Add the celery and cook for 2 minutes. Add the aubergine, cook for 3 minutes until golden, stirring from time to time. Add the passata and cook gently until absorbed. Add the vinegar, cook for 1 minute, then add the peppers, anchovies, capers and olives and cook for about 3 minutes.

4 Transfer to an ovenproof dish and bake, covered, in a preheated oven at 180°C (350°F), Gas Mark 4 for 40 minutes. Stir in the pine nuts and cook for another 20 minutes. Serve warm or cold, sprinkled with parsley.

Above left: *Ratatouille*
Left: *Okra with chillies*
Below: *Sicilian-style aubergines*

Desserts

The dessert provides the finishing touch to a meal. It is important to plan your menu so that you choose the appropriate dessert for the meal. Try, for example, to balance a rich main course with a light dessert, such as a fruity concoction or a refreshing sorbet. The time of year plays a part, too, in your choice of dessert. The winter months demand something hot, warming and satisfying, allowing you to forget the big freeze outside, while hot summer days call for ice creams, sorbets and frozen desserts to help you make the most of the sunshine. Make generous amounts of your desserts so that everyone can enjoy them to the full.

Below: *Warm chocolate pots*
Right: *Chocolate tartlets*

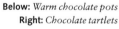

Warm chocolate pots

Serves 8
Preparation: 5 minutes, plus cooling and setting
Carbohydrate: 20 g, Protein: 4 g, Fat: 14 g, Fibre: 0 g, Calories: 223 kcal, Sodium: 28 mg (per portion)

What you need:

- 175 g/6 oz chocolate, chopped
- 250 ml/8 fl oz strong expresso coffee
- 2 tablespoons whisky
- 50 g/2 oz sugar
- 6 egg yolks
- 50 ml/2 fl oz double cream
- grated nutmeg, to decorate

1 Place the chocolate in a pan with the coffee and whisky. Heat until the chocolate has melted. Add the sugar and stir until dissolved. Remove from the heat.
2 Beat in the egg yolks until thickened. Pour through a fine sieve into 8 expresso cups. Cool and chill until set.
3 Whip the cream until it holds its shape and spoon a little on to each pot. Sprinkle with nutmeg. Pour boiling water into a dish to a depth of 1 cm/½ inch. Sit the pots in the boiling water for 1 minute, remove and serve.

Chocolate tartlets

Makes 10–11
Preparation: 25 minutes, plus cooling
Cooking: 20 minutes

Carbohydrate: 36 g, Protein: 6 g, Fat: 30 g, Fibre: 1 g, Calories: 431 kcal, Sodium: 224 mg (per portion)

What you need:

For the pastry:
- 250 g/8 oz plain flour
- 250 g/4 oz chilled butter, diced
- 50 g/2 oz caster sugar
- 1 egg, beaten

For the filling:
- 175 g/6 oz dark chocolate, broken into squares
- 2–3 tablespoons water
- 15 g/½ oz unsalted butter, diced
- 1 tablespoon brandy
- 3 eggs, separated
- icing sugar, for dusting

1 Place the flour in a bowl, add the butter and rub in until the mixture resembles breadcrumbs. Stir in the sugar, then add the egg and mix to a firm dough, adding a little water if necessary.

2 Knead the dough on a floured surface. Roll out and line 8 x 7 cm/3 inch deep tartlet tins. Re-roll trimmings and line 2–3 more tins. Fill each with crumpled foil and place on a baking sheet. Bake in a preheated oven, 200°C (400°F), Gas Mark 6, for 15 minutes. Remove the foil and return to the oven for 5 minutes. Cool.

3 Make the filling: place the chocolate in a bowl. Add the water. Set over a pan of hot water until the chocolate has melted.

4 Remove the bowl from over the water and stir in the butter until melted. Add the brandy and the egg yolks. Whisk the egg whites until they are stiff and dry; fold into the chocolate mixture.

5 Spoon the mixture into the cases, then set. Dust the tartlets with icing sugar before serving.

207

Peach, apricot and blueberry gratin

Serves 6
Preparation: 10 minutes
Cooking: 5–6 minutes
Carbohydrate: 21 g, Protein: 7 g,
Fat: 7 g, Fibre: 2 g, Calories: 169 kcal,
Sodium: 46 mg (per portion)

What you need:

- 4 firm ripe peaches, halved, stoned and very thinly sliced
- 6 firm ripe apricots, halved, stoned and very thinly sliced
- 175 g/6 oz blueberries
- 250 g/8 oz mascarpone cheese
- 250 g/8 oz Greek yogurt
- 3 tablespoons light muscavado sugar
- 1 teaspoon ground cinnamon

Below: Peach, apricot
and blueberry gratin
Right: *Peach granité*

1 Spoon the peaches and apricots into a gratin dish with the blueberries.
2 Beat the mascarpone and yogurt together and spread over the fruit.
3 Combine the sugar and cinnamon, sprinkle over the gratin to cover the surface and cook under a hot grill for 5–6 minutes until the sugar is caramelized. Cool for a few minutes and serve.

Peach granité

Serves 4
Preparation: 15 minutes, plus cooling and freezing
Cooking: 5 minutes
Carbohydrate: 109 g, Protein: 1 g,
Fat: 0 g, Fibre: 1 g, Calories: 494 kcal,
Sodium: 14 mg (per portion)

What you need:

- 4 ripe but firm peaches
- 250 ml/8 fl oz rosé wine
- 250 ml/8 fl oz water
- 250 g/8 oz caster sugar
- a pinch of cinnamon
- 4 fresh mint sprigs, to decorate

For the granité:

- 250 ml/8 fl oz rosé wine
- 125 ml/4 fl oz fresh orange juice
- 125 g/4 oz caster sugar

1 Blanch the peaches for 30 seconds only in boiling water. Remove with a slotted spoon and allow to drain. Place under cold running water for a few seconds to cool them. Cut each in half, peel them and remove the stones.

Variation

Amaretti fruit gratin

Crumble 125 g/4 oz of amaretti biscuits into a gratin dish. Add fruit and 4 tablespoons Kirsch and cook as in the main recipe.

Above left: *Poached figs in cassis with cinnamon sauce*

Variation

Poached pears

Replace the 12 figs in the main recipe with 6 firm, ripe pears. Peel the pears and cook them in the syrup for about 40 minutes until cooked through but not mushy. Remove the pears from the syrup and place in a serving dish. Bring the poaching liquid to the boil and simmer until reduced and thickened. Pour over the pears and leave to cool. Make the sauce as in the main recipe.

2 Put the rosé wine, water, sugar and cinnamon into a large saucepan and bring to the boil. Add the peach halves and poach gently for 4–5 minutes. Remove from the heat and allow the peach halves to cool in the poaching liquid. When cool, transfer them to a plate and reserve the poaching liquid. Slice the peach halves thinly using a sharp knife.

3 Meanwhile, make the granité. Add the rosé wine, orange juice and sugar to the cooled, reserved poaching liquid, and then boil the liquid fast to reduce by about one-third. Set to one side and allow to cool. When cool, pour into a shallow plastic tray and place in the freezer until well frozen.

4 Remove the granité from the ice tray with a spoon, scraping it to make it look like shattered glass. Place the peach slices in 4 glass serving glasses or dishes, pile the granité on top and decorate each with a sprig of mint. Serve immediately.

Poached figs in cassis with cinnamon sauce

Serves 4
Preparation: 10 minutes, plus chilling
Cooking: 10 minutes
Carbohydrate: 23 g, Protein: 5 g, Fat: 4 g, Fibre: 3 g, Calories: 191 kcal, Sodium: 39 mg (per portion)

What you need:

- 300 ml/½ pint red wine
- 150 ml/¼ pint cassis
- 2 cinnamon sticks
- 2 strips lemon peel
- 2 strips orange peel
- 300 ml/½ pint water
- 12 large firm ripe figs, washed

For the sauce:

- 150 g/5 oz Greek yogurt
- 2 tablespoons Greek honey
- 1 teaspoon ground cinnamon

1 Place the red wine, cassis, cinnamon sticks, citrus peel and water in a saucepan and bring to the boil.

2 Add the figs, cover the pan and simmer gently for 10 minutes until the figs are dark red and softened. Do not overcook.

3 Remove the figs with a slotted spoon and place in a serving dish. Bring the poaching liquid to a rolling boil and simmer until it is reduced by half and is thick and syrupy. Pour over the figs and leave to cool.

4 Meanwhile, combine all the sauce ingredients together and set aside for the flavours to develop. Serve the figs at room temperature with a spoonful of sauce for each serving.

Cook's Tip

This delicious warm pudding is ideal as an autumn dessert. However, to make a cool finish to a summer meal, serve the figs fresh. For each person, simply cut 2 figs in half and serve with the sauce.

Peach tart

Serves 6
Preparation: 25 minutes
Cooking: 50–55 minutes
Carbohydrate: 40 g, Protein: 8 g,
Fat: 19 g, Fibre: 2 g, Calories: 357 kcal,
Sodium: 121 mg (per portion)

What you need:

For the pastry:
- 175 g/6 oz plain flour
- 75 g/3 oz chilled butter, diced
- 2 egg yolks

For the filling:
- 2 tablespoons bramble jelly
- 2 egg whites
- 75 g/3 oz caster sugar
- 50 g/2 oz ground almonds
- 25 g/1 oz chopped toasted almonds
- a few drops almond essence
- 4 small peaches, halved, stoned and sliced thickly

1 Place the flour in a bowl, add the butter and rub in with the fingertips until the mixture resembles fine breadcrumbs. Stir in the egg yolks and a little cold water if necessary to make a firm dough.
2 Turn the dough out on to a floured surface and knead briefly. Roll out and line a 23 cm/9 inch deep flan tin. Chill for 30 minutes, if time permits.
3 Fill the pastry case with crum-pled foil and bake in a preheated oven at 200°C (400°F), Gas Mark 6, for 15 minutes, then remove the foil and bake the pastry case for a further 5 minutes. Lower the oven temperature to 180°C (350°F), Gas Mark 4.
4 Spread the bramble jelly over the pastry case. In a grease-free bowl, whisk the egg whites until stiff and dry. Whisk in 1 table-spoon of the sugar, then fold in the remainder with the ground almonds, toasted almonds and almond essence. Spread the filling over the pastry case.
5 Arrange the peaches over the filling. Bake for 30–35 minutes, or until the filling is set and golden brown. Serve either warm or cold, as you prefer.

Lemon tart

Serves 6–8
Preparation: 15 minutes, plus 30 minutes chilling
Cooking: 30 minutes
Carbohydrate: 70 g, Protein: 13 g,
Fat: 38 g, Fibre: 3 g, Calories: 658 kcal,
Sodium: 340 mg (per portion)

What you need:

- 250 g/8 oz plain flour
- pinch of salt
- 125 g/4 oz butter
- 1 egg yolk
- 2–3 tablespoons iced water

For the filling:
- grated rind and juice of 3 lemons
- 75 g/3 oz caster sugar
- 2 eggs plus 1 egg white
- 75 ml/3 fl oz double cream
- 125 g/4 oz ground almonds
- a good pinch of ground cinnamon

For the topping:
- 2 lemons, thinly sliced
- 125 g/4 oz caster sugar

1 Make the pastry: sift the flour and salt into a bowl and rub in the butter until the mixture resembles fine breadcrumbs. Stir in the egg yolk and sufficient iced water to make a soft and pliable dough. Chill in the refrigerator for 30 minutes.
2 Make the filling: put the lemon rind and juice, and sugar in a mixing bowl. Break in the eggs and add the egg white. Beat well together and then beat in the cream, ground almonds and cinnamon. The mixture should be thick and smooth.
3 Roll out the pastry on a lightly floured surface, and line a 25 cm/10 inch loose-based flan tin. Prick the base with a fork and pour in the filling mixture. Bake in a preheated oven at 190°C (375°F), Gas Mark 5, for 30 minutes, or until it is set and golden. Set aside to cool.
4 Heat the lemon slices in a little water over low heat for 10 minutes, or until tender. Remove and drain the lemon slices, keeping about 75 ml/3 fl oz of the liquid. Add the sugar and stir over gentle heat until dissolved. Bring to the boil, add the lemon slices and cook rapidly until they are well coated with thick syrup. Remove and use to decorate the tart. Leave to cool and serve.

Above left: Peach tart
Below: Lemon tart
Right: Exotic fruit clafoutis

Exotic fruit clafoutis

Serves 4–6
Preparation: 15 minutes
Cooking: 25–30 minutes
Carbohydrate: 35 g, Protein: 9 g,
Fat: 8 g, Fibre: 2 g, Calories: 259 kcal,
Sodium: 207 mg (Per portion)

What you need:

- 500 g/1 lb fresh pineapple and mango, peeled
- 2 tablespoons dark rum
- 3 eggs
- 20 g/¾ oz plain flour
- pinch of salt
- 50 g/2 oz caster sugar, plus extra for sprinkling
- 300 ml/½ pint milk
- 1 vanilla pod

1 Cut the fresh pineapple and mango flesh into 1 cm/½ inch chunks. Put the prepared fruit in a bowl and sprinkle with the rum. Set aside while you make the batter.

2 Break the eggs into a bowl and beat lightly together. Sift the flour and salt and blend well with the beaten eggs. Whisk in the sugar until smooth.

3 Heat the milk with the vanilla pod but do not allow to boil. Remove from the heat and allow to infuse for 5 minutes. Remove the vanilla pod and strain into the egg mixture, a little at a time, beating well until thoroughly blended. Beat in the rum from the soaked fruit.

4 Arrange the pineapple and mango in a shallow, greased ovenproof dish. Pour the batter mixture over them and bake in a preheated oven at 200°C (400°F), Gas Mark 6, for 25–30 minutes, until risen and set. Cool a little and serve warm, sprinkled with caster sugar.

Strawberry and lychee sorbet

Serves 4
Preparation: 15 minutes, plus freezing
Cooking: 15 minutes
Carbohydrate: 75 g, Protein: 2 g, Fat: 0 g, Fibre: 3 g, Calories: 291 kcal, Sodium: 15 mg (per portion)

What you need:

- 1 x 425 g/14 oz can lychees in light syrup
- 175 g/6 oz caster sugar
- 125 ml/4 fl oz water
- 750 g/1½ lb strawberries, hulled
- 1 tablespoon lemon juice

Below: *Strawberry and lychee sorbet*
Above right: *Mango ice cream*
Right: *Apple sorbet*

1 Strain the lychee juice into a saucepan. Halve the lychees, cut away any brown shell that remains and add the flesh to the pan. Heat through gently for about 5 minutes and then process in a blender until fairly smooth.
2 Put the sugar and water in a clear pan and heat gently until the sugar is dissolved. Bring to the boil and simmer for about 3 minutes. Remove from the heat and allow to cool.
3 Process the hulled strawberries in a blender with the lemon juice, add the cooled sugar and water syrup as you blend. Pass this through a sieve to remove the pips and stir into the lychees.
4 Transfer the mixture to a plastic container and freeze for about 1 hour. Remove from the freezer and beat the mixture to break up all the ice crystals that have formed. Return to the freezer once again, and freeze until firm.
5 Remove from the freezer about 15 minutes before serving to allow the sorbet to soften slightly, and serve it in scoops.

Mango ice cream

Serves 8
Preparation: 20 minutes, plus freezing
Carbohydrate: 14 g, Protein: 4 g, Fat: 40 g, Fibre: 1 g, Calories: 425 kcal, Sodium: 63 mg (per portion)

What you need:

- 1 x 425 g/14 oz can of mango pulp
- 3 tablespoons clear honey
- 600 ml/1 pint double cream
- 50 g/2 oz ground almonds
- 4 egg whites
- a few mint leaves, to decorate

1 Warm the mango pulp in a saucepan over a gentle heat and then stir in the honey until melted. Remove from the heat and stir in the double cream and the ground almonds until they are evenly mixed through. Set aside until cool.
2 Pour the mango ice cream mixture into a freezer container and place in the freezer. Freeze for about 4 hours, or until the mango mixture is just beginning to freeze around the edges and to become slushy.
3 Remove the container from the freezer and turn out the mango ice cream into a bowl. Carefully break up the mixture with a fork.
4 Whisk the egg whites in a clean, grease-free bowl until stiff, and then fold them gently into the half-frozen mixture. Return to the freezer container and freeze for a further 4 hours, or until solid.
5 Remove from the freezer 20 minutes before serving to soften slightly. Serve in scoops decorated with mint leaves.

Apple sorbet

Serves 4
Preparation: 30 minutes, plus
freezing
Cooking: 10 minutes
Carbohydrate: 24 g, Protein: 2 g,
Fat: 0 g, Fibre: 2 g, Calories: 125 kcal,
Sodium: 36 mg (Per portion)

What you need:

- 150 ml/¼ pint dry white wine
- 50 g/2 oz soft light brown sugar
- a thin strip of lemon rind
- 2 tablespoons lemon juice
- a small piece of fresh root ginger, peeled
- 500 g/1 lb cooking apples, peeled, cored and sliced
- 2 egg whites
- small herb leaves such as lemon geranium, to decorate

1 Put the wine, sugar, lemon rind and juice and ginger into a saucepan and stir over a low heat until the sugar dissolves. Increase the heat and bring to the boil. Add the apple slices, poach them for 8–10 minutes, or until soft. Remove from the heat and leave to cool.
2 Discard the lemon rind and ginger and purée the fruit in a liquidizer or food processor, or rub through a sieve. Pour into a freezer container, cover and freeze for 1 hour.
3 Beat the egg whites until stiff. Turn the frozen mixture into a chilled bowl and beat it to break down the ice crystals. Fold in the egg whites. Return the mixture to the freezer for about 3–4 hours, until firm.
4 To serve, transfer the sorbet to the refrigerator for about 30 minutes, scoop out and decorate with the herb leaves.

Crème caramel

Serves 4–5
Preparation: 15 minutes
Cooking: 45 minutes
Carbohydrate: 32 g, Protein: 12 g,
Fat: 12 g, Fibre: 0 g, Calories: 271 kcal,
Sodium: 155 mg (per portion)

What you need:

- 500 ml/17 fl oz milk
- 1 vanilla pod, split in half
  lengthways
- 4 eggs
- 50 g/2 oz sugar

For the caramel:

- 50 g/2 oz sugar
- 1 tablespoon water
- 1 teaspoon lemon juice

1 Put the milk and vanilla pod
in a heavy saucepan and bring to
the boil. Remove from the heat
and set aside for 5 minutes to
infuse. Whisk the eggs and sugar
together in a bowl until well
combined. Remove the vanilla
and whisk the milk into the egg
and sugar mixture.

2 While the milk is infusing,
make the caramel. Put the sugar,
water and lemon juice in a small
saucepan and cook over moderate heat, stirring well, until the
sugar dissolves. Continue cooking slowly and when it turns a rich
golden caramel colour, remove
from the heat immediately.

3 Pour the caramel into 6 small
moulds or alternatively 1 large 1
litre/1¾ pint charlotte mould.
Rotate the moulds quickly so
that the caramel coats the base
and sides evenly.

4 Strain the custard through a
fine sieve. Pour into the moulds
and stand them in a roasting pan
half-filled with water (bain-
marie). Cook in a preheated oven
at 150°C (300°F), Gas Mark 2
for about 45 minutes, or until set.

5 Leave to cool and chill in the
refrigerator before unmoulding.

To unmould, dip the base of the
moulds into a bowl of hot water
for 30 seconds and then turn out
on to a serving plate.

Baked lemon and bay custards

Serves 8
Preparation: 5 minutes, plus
2 hours infusing and chilling
Cooking: 55–60 minutes
Carbohydrate: 21 g, Protein: 5 g,
Fat: 13 g, Fibre: 0 g, Calories: 216 kcal,
Sodium: 52 mg (per portion)

What you need:

- 12 bay leaves, bruised
- 2 long strips lemon rind
- 150 ml/¼ pint double cream
- 4 eggs
- 1 egg yolk

Below: *Crème caramel*

- 150 g/5 oz caster sugar
- 100 ml/3½ fl oz lemon juice

1 Put the bay leaves, lemon rind and cream in a small saucepan and heat gently until it reaches boiling point. Remove from the heat and set aside for about 2 hours to infuse.

2 Whisk the eggs, egg yolk and sugar together until the mixture is pale and creamy and then whisk in the lemon juice. Strain the cream mixture through a fine sieve into the bowl and stir until well combined.

3 Pour the custard equally into 8 individual ramekin dishes and place on a baking sheet. Bake in a preheated oven at 120°C (250°F), Gas Mark ½ for 50 minutes, or until the custards are almost set in the middle.

Allow to go cold, and then chill in the refrigerator until required. Return to room temperature before serving.

Cook's Tip

This recipe is a variation of the old classic, lemon tart. Here, the lemon custard is infused with bay leaves, giving it a heady scent. The custard is poured into ramekin dishes and baked in a very low oven: if the oven is too hot the custard will curdle. Check the custards after 40 minutes, the centres should be almost set but still move a little, they will firm up as they cool.

Champagne syllabub and strawberries

Serves 4
Preparation: 5–10 minutes, plus
1–2 hours chilling
Carbohydrate: 11 g, Protein: 2 g,
Fat: 36 g, Fibre: 1 g, Calories: 400 kcal,
Sodium: 33 mg (per portion)

What you need:

- 150 ml/¼ pint Champagne or dry sparkling wine
- 2 tablespoons caster sugar
- finely grated rind and juice of ½ lemon
- 300 ml/½ pint double cream
- ripe strawberries, to serve

1 Mix the Champagne, sugar, lemon rind and juice together in a large bowl.
2 Add the cream and whisk the mixture until it forms soft peaks.
3 Spoon into glasses and chill for 1–2 hours before serving.
4 Serve with some fresh, ripe strawberries. Best of all, if you can find them when in season, is a mixture of wild and cultivated strawberries.

Above left: *Baked lemon and bay custards*
Below: *Champagne syllabub and strawberries*

Crêpes Suzette

Serves 6–8
Preparation: 25 minutes plus
1 hour standing
Cooking: 6–8 minutes
*Carbohydrate: 45 g, Protein: 8 g,
Fat: 21 g, Fibre: 1 g, Calories:415 kcal,
Sodium: 517 mg (per portion)*

What you need:

For the batter:
- 125 g/4 oz plain flour
- ¼ teaspoon salt
- 3 eggs
- 2 tablespoons oil
- 50 g/2 oz melted butter
- 1 tablespoon caster sugar
- 2 teaspoons vanilla sugar
- 350 ml/12 fl oz milk
- 25 g/1 oz butter, for frying

For the sauce:
- 125 g/4 oz softened butter, diced
- 125 g/4 oz caster sugar
- grated rind and juice of 1 orange
- 6 tablespoons Cointreau or Grand Marnier
- 3 tablespoons brandy

1 Make the batter: sift the flour and salt into a bowl and make a well in the centre. Tip in the eggs, oil, melted butter and sugars. Blend thoroughly, drawing in the flour from the sides, until the mixture is smooth.

2 Gradually add the milk, a little at a time, beating well between each addition. The batter should be smooth and the consistency of single cream. Add a little more milk if necessary and then leave to stand for 1 hour.

3 Melt a little butter in a small frying pan and when it is really hot, ladle some of the batter into the pan. Tilt the pan so that the batter covers the base evenly and fry until golden on the underside. Flip the crêpe over and cook the other side. Slide on to a warm plate and keep warm while you cook the others.

4 Make the sauce: put the butter and sugar in a bowl and beat together until smooth and creamy. Beat the orange rind and juice into the creamed mixture, and then beat in 3 tablespoons of the orange liqueur and 1 tablespoon of the brandy.

5 Transfer the orange mixture to a large frying pan and heat gently. Once boiling, boil rapidly for 1–2 minutes, and reduce the heat. Add the crêpes, one at a time, folding each one in half and then in half again.

6 Warm the remaining liqueur and brandy in a small saucepan. Taking great care, set alight and pour the alcohol flaming over the crêpes just before serving, or set alight at the table.

Cook's Tip

Pancake batter is such a versatile mixture. For instance, adding a splash of alcohol will lift it to new heights. Add 1 tablespoon of dark rum, brandy or apricot brandy to the quantity in this recipe. To enhance this addition, fill each cooked pancake with a spoonful of lightly whipped cream which has been flavoured with the appropriate alcohol and a small amount of sugar. Add 2 tablespoons of alcohol and 2 teaspoons caster sugar to 300 ml/½ pint lightly whipped double cream.

Left: *Crêpes Suzette*

Saturday night
fever

Cocktail know-how

As a pre-dinner drink, a reward after a hard day's work, or the basis for a get-together with friends, cocktails are meant to be fun.

● Instant eye-appeal comes from bright colours, a quirky glass, a decoration of fruit – or, for a bloody Mary, a stick of celery or a fresh chilli on a cocktail stick.

● Cocktail recipes are usually given in parts or measures: the jigger is a generous measure of 45 ml/1½ fl oz – about 3 tablespoons – but as long as you keep the proportions right it doesn't matter what you use.

● Many cocktails are shaken with ice to cool them, then strained before the ice dilutes the alcohol. A shaker with its own strainer is ideal, but a lidded jar and a clean tea strainer will do.

● Ice cubes can be crushed in a food processor, or in a strong polythene bag with a rolling pin.

● Add fizz with soda water or sparkling mineral water.

● To sweeten cocktails, make a sugar syrup by boiling 2 parts sugar with 1 part water for 5 minutes. Cool, bottle and keep in the refrigerator. This gives a clearer cocktail than dry sugar.

Far left: Margarita
Left: Sangria
Below: Singapore sling

Cocktail nibbles

Olives and salted nuts are the classic accompaniments to cocktails, but to make your drinks party into an occasion, prepare a selection of snacks. Easy to eat with one hand, crostini are ideal.

Crostini

- French or Italian bread, sliced
- garlic cloves, halved
- extra-virgin olive oil

Toast the bread lightly, then rub with the cut side of the garlic and drizzle with olive oil. Serve at once or add one of the following toppings.

Grilled pepper and frisée

Serves 4
- 1 red and 1 yellow pepper, deseeded and quartered
- 2 tablespoons hazelnut oil
- 2 garlic cloves, sliced
- grated rind of ½ lemon
- 25 g/1 oz sultanas
- 25 g/1 oz flaked hazelnuts
- 175 g/6 oz frisée lettuce
- salt and pepper

1 Grill the peppers until charred and soft. Place in a polythene bag to cool. Peel off the skin and slice the peppers.
2 Heat the oil in a frying pan, add the garlic, rind, sultanas and

nuts and fry gently for 5 minutes. Add the lettuce and cook over a low heat for 5 minutes. Season well with salt and pepper.
3 Place the lettuce on the toasted bread and top with the grilled, sliced peppers.

Mixed mushrooms

Serves 4
- 15 g/½ oz dried ceps
- 10 ml/3½ fl oz boiling water
- 2 tablespoons extra-virgin olive oil
- 1 garlic clove, crushed
- 375 g/12 oz mixed fresh mushrooms, sliced
- 1 tablespoon chopped fresh thyme
- 1 tablespoon chopped fresh parsley
- grated fresh Parmesan cheese
- salt and pepper

1 Soak the ceps in the boiling water for 20 minutes. Drain, reserving the liquid. Slice the ceps.
2 Heat the oil in a pan, add the ceps, garlic, mushrooms and thyme and stir-fry for 3–4 minutes. Add the ceps soaking liquid, cover and cook over a low heat for 5 minutes. Season to taste with salt and pepper.
3 Spoon the mixture on to the toasted bread and top with the parsley and Parmesan.

Aubergine and rocket

Serves 4
- 1 tablespoon cumin seeds
- 75 ml/3 fl oz extra-virgin olive oil
- 1 teaspoon grated lemon rind
- 2 small aubergines, sliced
- 125 g/4 oz rocket leaves
- salt and pepper

1 Dry-fry the cumin seeds in a small frying pan until they start to pop and give off a rich aroma.

Add all but 1 tablespoon of the oil and the lemon rind. Remove from the heat and leave to infuse for several hours. Strain the oil.
2 Brush the aubergine slices lightly with the cumin-flavoured oil and place under a medium-hot grill for 6–8 minutes, until charred. Turn the aubergines, brush with more oil and grill the other side. Leave to cool.
3 Place the aubergine slices on the toasted bread and drizzle over a little more cumin oil.
4 Toss the rocket leaves with the reserved olive oil, season and arrange over the aubergines.

Grilled tomato and olive paste

Serves 4
- 2–4 well-flavoured ripe but firm tomatoes
- extra-virgin olive oil
- 2 tablespoons olive paste
- a few basil leaves
- salt and pepper

1 Depending on their size, cut the tomatoes into wedges or quarters. Drizzle with olive oil and then place the tomatoes under a hot grill for 5–10 minutes, until tender and beginning to blacken at the edges.
2 Spread the olive paste over the toasted bread and top with the grilled tomato wedges and basil leaves. Season to taste with salt and pepper.

Above: marinated olives are delicious served with cocktails. Buy them from delicatessens or make your own by bringing to the boil 4 tablespoons olive oil, 4 tablespoons water, and chopped garlic, dried herbs or chillies. Leave to cool, then mix with plain olives – green or black, as you prefer – and leave to marinate in the refrigerator for 2–5 days.
Right: Crostini with a selection of vegetable toppings. You could also spread crostini with meat or fish pâté.
Left: Planter's punch (recipe on previous page)

Wine

Some of the world's finest – and most expensive – wines are best enjoyed after 30 or more years in the bottle, but the great majority are designed to be drunk young, usually with food. Spirits and liqueurs are too strong or too sweet to make good partners for food, but they too have a big part to play in cooking. In some countries, notably Germany and Belgium, beer plays the same role, being made in several styles and drunk as an important part of the meal.

Below: *A table in Provence, where Mediterranean shellfish is accompanied by a glass of good local white wine*

Wine is made in more than 50 countries round the world, from well over 1,000 grape varieties. The choice is much greater than that between red and white. There are many different white wines, including still and sparkling, dry and sweet, light-bodied and full-bodied. Much the same applies to red wines, with a full range of light-, medium- and full-bodied wines.

Which wine with which food?

Many serious words have been written about finding the perfect food and wine partnership, but while it is true that some foods go particularly well with certain wines, there are often other, less obvious possibilities.

In general, simple dishes demand straightforward un-complicated wines, while more elaborate dishes ask for the more expensive classics. A richly sauced dish goes extremely well with a wine that has enough natural acidity to cut through the sauce and balance it.

The basic principle of white wine with fish and red wine with meat is a sound one but it is not an exciting one and – as with all the best rules in life – there are many exceptions. Fish is sometimes better accompanied by a rosé wine, and even a red wine can on occasions be better still. The colour of the meat is usually best matched by the colour of the wine – a full-bodied claret or Burgundy with roast beef, say, a light white wine to complement the light flavours of chicken or turkey, and a full-flavoured wine to match the high intensity of goose, duck, pheasant and other game birds.

How much wine?

Half a bottle of wine per person is a good rule of thumb, but a whole bottle is probably a safer estimate as it ensures that you will not run short – which is one of the most embarrassing things that can happen at a party!

Above all, though, don't worry about it – as long as the food is good and the company genial, the wine will always slip down with remarkable ease!

Spirits and liqueurs

Spirits are strong drinks, distilled from grains e.g. whisky, gin, vodka; wine e.g. brandy, Cognac, Armagnac, fruit e.g. fruit brandies and eaux-de-vie such as Kirsch and other things such as rum from sugar cane. Liqueurs are spirits that have been lightly or heavily sweetened, and flavoured by the maceration of fruits, herbs or spices; sweeter liqueurs are usually lower in alcohol than spirits, but have a much higher alcohol content than wine. Some of the most widely known spirits and liqueurs are briefly described below, along with their percentage of alcohol by volume.

Percentage of alchohol by volume	Description
Advocaat (15–18%)	Yellow liqueur made from egg yolks and brandy
Amaretto (28%)	Amber-coloured liqueur made from almonds and apricot kernels
Apricot brandy (21–24%)	Not a brandy, but an amber-coloured liqueur
Calvados, applejack (40–45%)	Apple brandies, aged in wood, which gives them an amber colour
Cassis (15–25%)	Blackcurrant liqueur
Chartreuse, Izarra (green 50–55%, yellow 40%)	Herbal liqueurs
Crème de cacao (24%)	Brown or clear chocolate-flavoured liqueur
Crème de menthe (24–30%)	Bright green or clear peppermint-flavoured liqueur
Curaçao (30–40%)	Orange, blue, green or colourless liqueurs made from the rind of bitter oranges. **Triple sec** is a slightly sweeter type of Curaçao; **Cointreau** is the best-known triple sec. **Grand Marnier** is a special orange liqueur in which the orange rind is macerated in genuine French Cognac.
Galliano (40%)	Bright yellow, sweetish, herbal liqueur
Kahlúa, Tia Maria (26%)	Brown coffee-flavoured liqueurs
Kirsch (43%)	Clear spirit distilled from cherries and their kernels, which give a hint of almond flavour
Maraschino (30%)	Clear cherry liqueur; cherry brandy (22–25%) is also a liqueur, usually deep red
Mirabelle, Quetsch, Slivovitz (43–45%)	Plum brandies
Ouzo, Pernod, pastis (e.g. **Ricard**) (37–45%)	Unsweetened, aniseed or liquorice-flavoured spirits; clear, but turn cloudy when water is added
Poire William, Williamine (43–45%)	Pear brandies
Southern Comfort (43%)	Amber-coloured liqueur based on whiskey, flavoured with peaches and other fruit
Tequila (38%)	Clear spirit distilled from a Mexican plant

Cooking with alcohol

Besides flambéeing, alcohol can be put to many good uses in the kitchen. The alcohol evaporates during cooking, leaving the essential flavours of the wine or spirits in the dish. Sherry or brandy adds richness to clear soups and creamy shellfish bisques; a wine marinade for meat will tenderize it as well as adding flavour; using dry white wine or vermouth in the poaching liquid for fish or chicken forms the basis for a good sauce; red wine is often used to poach pears or peaches; a good cheese fondue contains dry white wine and a dash of Kirsch.

To create an almost instant sauce for fried fish or meat, first transfer the fish or meat to a warm plate, then pour off excess fat from the pan. Add a little wine, dry vermouth, sherry, madeira or brandy to the pan, and place over high heat for a few minutes, stirring constantly to deglaze the pan. Increase the amount of sauce with a little stock or water, bring back to a rapid boil, then, if you like, whisk in a little butter, cream or chopped fresh herbs.

When the alcohol is not cooked, it lends not only flavours but also a warming kick. Rum-soaked raisins are a good addition to baked apples or cheesecakes; use sherry, brandy or apricot brandy to soak the sponge for trifles; orange liqueurs go particularly well with strawberries and chocolate desserts.

Flambéeing

Setting light to alcohol and pouring it, flaming, over food is the traditional way to serve Christmas pudding, crêpes Suzette, and some savoury dishes. Besides looking spectacular, it imparts the flavour of the spirit at the last minute, while the alcohol burns away.

It is best to use spirits with a high alcohol content, although a flavoured liqueur can be mixed with spirits. The food must be hot, or the flames will die out, leaving the alcohol to soak into the food. The spirits should first be heated gently, so that the alcohol begins to evaporate; it can then be ignited with a match and poured, flaming, over the food.

Chilled claret cup

Serves 10–15
Preparation: 5 minutes, plus chilling

What you need:

- 1 bottle young Bordeaux red wine
- ½ bottle ruby port
- 150 ml/¼ pint brandy
- 5 tablespoons orange juice
- 3 tablespoons lemon juice
- 50 g/2 oz icing sugar
- 2 oranges, thinly sliced
- 1 lemon, thinly sliced
- 350 ml/12 fl oz soda or sparkling mineral water
- sprigs of fresh mint, to decorate

Below: Chilled claret cup
Above right: Mulled wine

1 Put the wine, port and brandy in the refrigerator and chill for about 2 hours.

2 Fill a large jug with crushed ice, then add the wine, port and brandy and stir well.

3 Put the orange and lemon juice in a small bowl with the icing sugar and stir until the sugar dissolves. Add to the jug with the slices of orange and lemon.

4 Then add the soda or mineral water and stir well. Serve immediately, decorated with a sprig of mint in each glass.

Mulled wine

Serves 8–12
Preparation: 20 minutes

What you need:

- 8 cloves
- pinch of ground ginger
- pinch of grated nutmeg
- 2 cinnamon sticks, plus extra to serve (optional)
- 1–2 tablespoons soft brown sugar
- 150 ml/¼ pint boiling water
- 1 bottle red wine
- 150 ml/¼ pint port

1 Put the spices, sugar and boiling water into a saucepan over a low heat and simmer gently for 15 minutes.

2 Strain the spiced liquid and add to the wine. Then heat gently for 5 minutes, to just below simmering point.

3 Add the port and serve the mulled wine hot, in warmed glasses or mugs, with a stick of cinnamon in each one, if liked.

Variation

Riesling cup

Use a good, fruity dry or medium-dry white wine: Reisling is an ideal wine for this.

Chill the bottle of wine, 75 ml/3 fl oz brandy and 75 ml/3 fl oz Cointreau for 2 hours. Pour the chilled drinks over ice cubes in a large jug and stir well. Still stirring, add 2 tablespoons fresh lime juice and 400 ml/14 fl oz soda or sparkling mineral water. Add 125 g/4 oz fresh raspberries, 1 peach, peeled, stone and finely sliced, and a few fresh mint or lemon balm leaves.

Baking

There is nothing quite like the satisfaction of baking your own bread. Home-baked bread tastes out of this world, and the aroma it creates in the kitchen is one of the most wonderful smells in the world. Baking bread is not as time-consuming as you might think, particularly if you use all the latest kitchen gadgetry. Get into the habit of knocking up a quick loaf between having a cup of tea and cooking the supper, and tomorrow's breakfast will never be the same again!

Millet and cumin loaf

Makes 1 x 1 kg/2 lb loaf
Preparation: 15 minutes, plus rising
Cooking: 35 minutes
Carbohydrate: 18 g, Protein: 4 g, Fat: 3 g, Fibre: 1 g, Calories: 109 kcal, Sodium: 218 mg (per slice)

What you need:

- 50 g/2 oz millet
- 150 ml/¼ pint boiling water
- 15 g/½ oz fresh yeast
- 250 g/8 oz plain strong flour, plus extra, for dusting
- 1 teaspoon sugar
- 150 ml/¼ pint warm water
- 250 g/8 oz wholemeal bread flour
- 2 teaspoons sea salt
- 1 teaspoon cumin seeds
- 125 g/4 oz Cheddar cheese, grated
- vegetable oil, for oiling

1 Soak the millet in the boiling water for 20 minutes. Combine the yeast, 4 tablespoons of the plain flour and the sugar with the warm water in a small bowl and leave in a warm place for 10 minutes till frothy. Drain the millet, reserving any liquid left over.

2 In a large bowl, mix together the remaining plain flour with the wholemeal flour, soaked millet, salt, cumin seeds and cheese. Make a well in the centre and gradually work in the frothed yeast, reserved millet liquid and enough extra warm water to form a stiff dough.

3 Transfer to a lightly floured surface and knead for 8–10 minutes until smooth and elastic. Place in an oiled bowl, turning once to coat the dough, cover and leave in a warm place for 1 hour, or until doubled in size.

4 Knock back the dough by kneading gently. Shape into an oval and press into an oiled 1 kg/2 lb loaf tin. Brush with a little oil and bake in a preheated oven, 220°C (450°F), Gas Mark 8, for 35–40 minutes until golden. It should sound hollow when tapped on the bottom.

Left: *Millet and cumin loaf*

Tomato bread

Makes 2 x 500 g/1 lb loaves
Preparation: 30 minutes, plus rising
Cooking: 35 minutes

Carbohydrate: 26 g, Protein: 4 g, Fat: 3 g, Fibre: 1 g, Calories: 137 kcal, Sodium: 125 mg (per slice)

What you need:

- 4–5 sun-dried tomatoes, very finely chopped
- 750 g/1½ lb strong flour
- 1 teaspoon salt
- 1 teaspoon sugar
- 25 g/1 oz butter or margarine, or 1 tablespoon olive or sunflower oil
- 20 g/¾ oz fresh yeast, or 7 g/¼ oz sachet fast-action dried yeast

1 Place the sun-dried tomatoes in a small bowl. Add enough boiling water to cover and set aside for 2–3 minutes.

2 Sift the flour and salt into a large bowl and stir in the sugar. Rub in the fat or add the oil. If using fresh yeast, put it into a separate bowl. If using fast-action dried yeast, add it to the flour in the bowl.

3 Drain the sun-dried tomatoes, reserving the soaking liquid in a measuring jug. Make it up to 450 ml/¾ pint with lukewarm water. The temperature of the liquid should be about 43°C/110°F. Cream the fresh yeast, add the liquid, top with a sprinkling of flour and leave for about 10 minutes, or until the surface is covered with bubbles. Blend with the flour. If using fast-action dried yeast, stir the liquid into the yeast and flour and blend to a dough.

4 Turn the dough out on to a lightly floured working surface and knead thoroughly until the dough is firm and elastic and no longer feels sticky. Knead in the chopped tomatoes.

5 Return the dough to the mixing bowl and cover the bowl with clingfilm. Leave in a warm place for about 1 hour or until the dough has doubled in bulk. Then knock back the dough again and shape it.

6 To make two loaves; grease and warm 2 x 500 g/1 lb loaf tins. Divide the dough in half. Press out each half to form a neat rectangle, the same length and three times the width of each tin. Fold the dough to fit the loaf tins and place it in the tins with the fold underneath.

7 To make two bloomer loaves; form the dough into two large sausage shapes and place on lightly greased baking sheets. Make equally spaced shallow cuts along the top of each.

8 Cover the dough lightly and leave until nearly doubled in bulk. This will take about 20 minutes or so.

9 Bake the loaves in a preheated oven, 220°C (425°F), Gas Mark 7, for about 35 minutes or until cooked. When they are cooked, the loaves should sound hollow when tapped lightly on the base. Finally, turn the loaves out of the tins and allow to cool.

Cook's Tip

If the loaves are not as crusty as you like, simply place on a flat baking sheet and return to the oven for a few minutes.

Left: *Tomato bread*
Right: *Roquefort bread*

Roquefort bread

Makes 1 x 500 g/1 lb loaf
Preparation: 15 minutes, plus rising
Cooking: 30 minutes
Carbohydrate: 39 g, Protein: 9 g, Fat: 7 g, Fibre: 2 g, Calories: 242 kcal, Sodium: 576 mg (per slice)

What you need:

- 500 g/1 lb strong white flour
- 2 teaspoons salt
- 25 g/1 oz butter
- 7 g/¼ oz sachet fast-action dried yeast
- 150 ml/¼ pint lukewarm milk
- 250 g/8 oz cooked potato, sieved
- 125 g/4 oz Roquefort or blue cheese, crumbled
- beaten egg, to glaze

1 Sift the flour with the salt into a warmed bowl. Rub in the butter until the mixture resembles fine breadcrumbs. Stir in the dried yeast.

2 Stir the milk into the sieved potato in a bowl. Work this mixture into the flour to make a soft but not sticky dough. Knead on a floured board for 5 minutes, then knead in the crumbled cheese.

3 Grease a 500 g/1 lb loaf tin. Shape the dough to fit the tin, or shape into a round cob shape and place on a greased baking sheet. Cover with oiled polythene and leave to rise in a warm place for 30 minutes, or until the loaf has doubled in bulk.

4 Brush with beaten egg and bake in a preheated oven, 200°C (400°F), Gas Mark 6, for 15 minutes. Reduce the heat to 180°C (350°F), Gas Mark 4, and bake for 15 minutes more. Turn the loaf out of the tin and leave to cool on a wire rack.

Naan

Makes 6
Preparation: 30 minutes, plus
rising
Cooking: 10 minutes
Carbohydrate: 67 g, Protein: 10 g,
Fat: 10 g, Fibre: 3 g, Calories: 370 kcal,
Sodium: 725 mg (per ⅙ of a bread)

What you need:

- 15 g/½ oz fresh yeast
- ¼ teaspoon sugar
- 2 tablespoons warm water
- 500 g/1 lb self-raising flour
- 1 teaspoon salt
- 150 ml/¼ pint tepid milk
- 150 ml/¼ pint natural yogurt
  (at room temperature)
- 2 tablespoons melted butter
  or cooking oil
- 2–3 tablespoons melted butter
- 1 tablespoon poppy or sesame
  seeds

1 Put the yeast in a small bowl with sugar and water. Mix well until yeast has dissolved. Leave in a warm place for 15 minutes.
2 Sift the flour and salt into a large bowl. Make a well in the centre and add the yeast, milk, yogurt and fat. Mix well to a

Below: *Naan*
Right: *Soda bread*

smooth dough and knead on to a floured surface. Knead for 10 minutes, till smooth and elastic.
3 Place in a bowl, cover with clingfilm and leave to rise in a warm place for 1 to 1½ hours, or until doubled in size.
4 Turn on to a floured surface, knead for a few minutes, then divide into 6 pieces. Pat or roll each piece into a round.
5 Place on a warmed baking sheet and bake in a preheated very hot oven, 240°C (475°F), Gas Mark 9, for 10 minutes. Brush with butter and sprinkle with the poppy or sesame seeds. Serve warm.

Soda bread

Makes 2 x 500 g/1 lb loaves
Preparation: 15 minutes
Cooking: 25–30 minutes
Carbohydrate: 37 g, Protein: 5 g,
Fat: 3 g, Fibre: 1 g, Calories: 183 kcal,
Sodium: 266 mg (per slice)

What you need:

- 1 kg/2 lb plain flour
- 2 teaspoons salt
- 1 teaspoon bicarbonate of
  soda
- 1 teaspoon cream of tartar
- 50 g/2 oz butter or margarine
- 600 ml/1 pint buttermilk
- flour for sprinkling

1 Sift dry ingredients in mixing bowl and rub in the fat. Add the buttermilk and mix quickly to a soft dough. Turn on to a floured surface, knead and divide in half.
2 Shape into 5cm/2 inch thick rounds and place on a floured baking sheet. Cut a deep cross on top and sprinkle with flour.
3 Bake in a preheated hot oven, 220°C (425°F), Gas Mark 7, for 25–30 minutes. Cool on rack.

Nutrition

Much research has been done in the past few years into the effects of food on health as a result of which some foods which, years ago, were regarded as healthy and energy giving – full-fat milk and sugar, for example – are now regarded as things that should be drunk and eaten in moderation. Other foods which were once regarded as fattening – bread and potatoes, for example – are now considered to be healthy and, provided they are not smothered in high-fat additions, unlikely to add to weight.

A balanced diet

So what is the best way to develop a balanced diet? First bear in mind that no food is of itself bad for you. The occasional helping of chips, packet of crisps or secretly consumed box of chocolates is not going to lead to instant heart disease or cancer, provided that, for most of the time, you eat foods that positively contribute towards health in sensible quantities for your height and weight. Foods are made up of a number of different elements and it is worth knowing more about what these are.

Protein

Protein is found in meat, poultry, fish, eggs, dairy products, beans, pulses and nuts. Most people need only around 50–75 g/ 2–3 oz per day but tend to take in around 50 per cent more than that. Protein should make up around 10 per cent of your daily food intake in order to ensure growth in children and young adults and the maintenance of body tissue at all ages.

Carbohydrates

These come in two forms – simple and complex.

Simple carbohydrates are the sugars group – dextrose, fructose, glucose and sucrose – which tend to be added to foods rather than eaten alone. Complex carbohydrates are an integral part of starches such as cereals and rice and are automatically consumed when you eat these foods. Simple carbohydrates provide energy in the form of calories and should be consumed in moderation, if at all.

Complex carbohydrates contain many other nutritional benefits. As long as they are eaten without the addition of simple carbohydrates, they are not, in themselves, fattening.

Fats

Fats are found in oils, nuts, avocadoes, dairy products and most processed foods. While a small amount of fat is essential for maintaining a healthy body, most people eat too much. It is estimated that a large proportion of people have a fat intake of around 40 per cent. It is interesting to note, too, the success rate of the low-fat diets which have come into fashion in the past decade or so – far more successful than the 'starve yourself into slimness' regimes that

Good nutrition is about eating the right food to maintain good health. It doesn't necessarily mean avoiding any particular food but it does mean eating more of the foods that do you good and less of the ones that can, in excess, do you harm. Poor nutrition in the western world tends to be the result of over- rather than under-eating. Another contributory factor is the large proportion of processed food in most people's diets – it is estimated that as much as 70 per cent of all the food that is eaten in the West today has been processed.

Below: *A colourful market stall not only looks good – it also does you good*

formerly held sway. Recent Government recommendations suggest that a maximum fat intake should be no more than 35 per cent of the diet and that less will do no harm.

Fats consists of units of fatty acid which fall into three types with different chemical structures. All whole fats consist of all three types but in different proportions, some of which are healthier than others.

Saturated fats consist mainly of saturated fatty acids and come in the form of dairy products and meat. They are mainly solid when at room temperature.

Polyunsaturated fats consist mainly of polyunsaturated fatty acids and tend to be liquids such as vegetable oils (though not coconut and palm oils which are saturated fats).

Monounsaturated fats are also found in vegetable oils, notably grapeseed, groundnut and olive, and in avocados.

Evidence shows that eating a lot of saturated fats raises the blood cholesterol which, in turn, leads to coronary heart disease (see Cholesterol section, below). Polyunsaturated fats help lower cholesterol but not to the degree in which saturated fats raise it.

Less is known about what monounsaturated fats do to cholesterol but looking at Mediterranean diets, which are high in olive oil and where the incidence of heart disease is considerably lower than in the UK, it is likely that they also help to lower cholesterol.

All fats are heavily loaded with calories, which is another good reason for cutting down the amount in a diet.

Cholesterol

Cholesterol occurs naturally in the human body and also in some foods, such as eggs, fish, offal and shellfish. Some cholesterol is essential for good health. Too much leads to a furring up of the arteries (atherosclerosis), which restricts blood flow and leads to coronary heart disease.

People whose doctor's or home tests indicate a high level of cholesterol should avoid foods containing it. Cholesterol level can also be reduced by not getting fat, giving up smoking, and taking plenty of exercise.

Fibre

Dietary fibre is also known as non-starch polysaccharides (NSP) and comes in two forms; soluble and insoluble

Fibre is found in cereals, fruit and vegetables and their derivatives such as brown rice, pasta and wholemeal bread. The soluble variety found in cereals (especially oats) and vegetables (especially dried beans) is thought to help lower cholesterol levels.

Non-soluble fibre is found also in cereals (especially wheat bran) and vegetables, and absorbs water during the digestion process, creating large soft stools which are easy to pass through the system. Research has shown that apart from the benefits of avoiding constipation and piles, this also reduces the likelihood of bowel cancer.

High-fibre foods are filling and pass through the system easily so are good for those trying to lose weight.

Sugar

Sugar, like carbohydrates, falls into two groups – intrinsic and extrinsic. Intrinsic sugars are a natural part of foods like fruit, cereals, potatoes and rice while extrinsic sugars are not part of cellular structure but exist alone. Examples are glucose, honey and sucrose. It is extrinsic sugars that lead to tooth decay.

Sugar is not essential for human health. It provides energy in the form of calories but nothing else. Experts recommend consumption of as little as possible extrinsic sugar and certainly no more than around 10 per cent of daily food intake (about 50 g/2 oz per day). Doing without it certainly helps reduce the calories.

Salt

Salt (correct name sodium chloride but usually referred to as sodium) is essential for the health of body cells and occurs naturally in many foods.

Top left: seafood is full of nutrients
Above left: stir-frying uses very little fat
Right: sugar has no nutritional benefits

Because of the salt added to virtually all processed foods (including some sweet ones) and the salt liberally sprinkled by many people on foods that already contain it, most people consume at least 10 times more salt than their body requires.

Cutting down on salt helps reduce high blood pressure (hypertension), which is a risk factor for coronary heart disease and stroke. If you want to cut down on salt, do not add it at table and avoid salty foods such as bacon and cheese.

Vitamins

Vitamins cannot be synthesized by the body and most must therefore be taken in, on a daily or regular basis, from the diet. The body can store Vitamins A, D, E, K and B 12 but not the rest. Each of the 20 known vitamins performs a different function and is therefore required in different quantities.

Vitamins divide into two types: fat soluble (main ones A, D, E and K) and water soluble (main ones B complex and C).

Fat soluble vitamins are less affected than the water soluble type by cooking; water soluble vitamins tend to leach out into the cooking water and to be destroyed by heat.

People who eat a well-balanced diet should not need to take any of the vitamin supplements that crowd the shelves of health food shops and supermarkets. Too much of some vitamins (notably A, D, E, and K, which are stored in the body and not excreted) can be harmful if toxic levels are reached.

However, if you have been ill. or if your doctor pinpoints a particular deficiency or need, you

Above: *carrots are particularly rich in Vitamin A*
Right: *the humble potato is actually a very good source of Vitamin C*

may need to take certain vitamin supplements for a period of time.

Vitamin A

Also known as retinol, this is found mainly in dairy products such as butter, cheese and milk, offal (particularly liver), eggs, oily fish and the substance beta carotene which is found in green, orange and yellow vegetables such as spinach and carrots.

Vitamin A is essential for growth, healthy skin and being able to see in poor light.

Vitamin B complex

There are several B vitamins. The best-known of these are probably B1 (thiamin), B2 (riboflavin) and B3 (niacin). They are all discussed in detail below.

Vitamin B1 (thiamin)

This is found in fortified and wholegrain cereals, milk, meat (especially pork), nuts, potatoes and pulses. This vitamin is also present in yeast, yeast extract and wheatgerm.

The need for Vitamin B1 is increased when people drink alcohol and caffeine or are on all types of antibiotics and/or the contraceptive pill.

This vitamin is useful because it aids the release of energy from both types of carbohydrate.

Vitamin B2 (riboflavin)

Vitamin B2 is found in cheese, eggs, fortified breakfast cereals, meat, milk, offal and is also found in yeast extract.

It tends to leach out into cooking water so try to use cooking water in gravy, sauces and soups. Don't leave milk bottles standing on the doorstep as it is also destroyed by ultra-violet light.

Vitamin B2 is essential for growth, healthy eyesight and skin and for helping release energy from carbohydrates.

Vitamin B3

This is found in most fish, fortified breakfast cereals, meat, offal and pulses.

It leaches out into the cooking water, so it is a good idea to use it when cooking other things.

Vitamin B3 is essential as it assists in the release of energy within the body cells.

Vitamin B5 (pantothenic acid)

This is present in lots of foods, notably eggs, fish roe, nuts, offal, pulses, vegetables and yeast.

It is destroyed by cooking above boiling point.

Vitamin B5 helps you produce energy, and it also aids other metabolic tasks.

Vitamin B6 (pyridoxine)

This is present in lots of foods, notably eggs, fish, liver, meat, pulses, vegetables, wholegrain cereals and yeast extract.

Vitamin B6 helps the the body to form new red blood cells and also to utilise proteins. Extra B6 supplements can sometimes help with PMT (pre-menstrual tension) symptoms.

Vitamin B12 (cobalamin)

This is found only in foods of animal origin such as cheese, eggs, meat, milk, offal and oily fish. Like other B vitamins, it leaches out into the cooking water. It is essential for growth, developing red blood cells and repairing the nervous system.

People who are following a

standard diet will get enough through eating a variety of animal foods. Vegetarians who eat sufficient dairy products should also be all right, but vegans – who don't include any dairy products at all in their diet – may need to take a supplement.

Biotin

This is a water soluble member B vitamin without a number. It is found in brown bread and rice, eggs, offal, oily fish and yeast.

Biotin protects bone marrow, hair and the nervous system.

Folic acid

This is a water soluble member of the B group, also without a number. It is found in eggs, green leafy vegetables, liver, nuts, pulses, wholemeal cereals, wheat bran and germ, and yeast.

A lack of folic acid can cause anaemia, depression, tiredness and insomnia. It helps produce red blood cells and amino acids. Pregnant women are in particular need of folic acid to prevent foetal malformation. They may need to take supplements.

Vitamin C

Ascorbic acid is easily lost during cooking, both leaching out into the water and being destroyed by heat. Ideally, microwave or steam foods containing Vitamin C to preserve as much of the vitamin as possible. Use any cooking liquid in other ways. Vitamin C is found in fruit and vegetables.

It is vital for growth, development of the collagen essential for strong bones, gums, teeth and body tissues. It acts as an antioxidant and may help prevent certain illnesses, but there is no firm evidence that it protects against, or cures, colds and flu.

Vitamin D

Cholecalciferol is found in only a few foods (mainly eggs, liver and oily fish) and most of that stored in the liver is made by the body from sunlight on the skin.

Vitamin D is required for developing healthy bones, general growth and the absorption of calcium from foods. A lack of vitamin D can cause brittle bones in the elderly and rickets in young children.

Vitamin E

Vitamin E is mainly found in avocados, eggs, nuts, oily fish, all polyunsaturated spreads, spinach, sunflower seeds and wholegrain cereals.

Vitamin E consists of a group of compounds called tocopherols which work as antioxidants at protecting the body from damage by free radicals which can cause cancer.

Vitamin K

Vitamin K is found in alfalfa, cauliflower, cereals, green vegetables, liver and kelp.

Vitamin K helps in blood clot-

Above: *Tomatoes are a good source of Vitamin C. Their vitamin content is highest when they are eaten raw*

ting and the development of certain proteins. In addition to being present in many foods, it can also be synthesized by bacteria in the gut.

Minerals

Minerals, also known as trace elements, are essential for a number of bodily functions, in particular the development of bones and teeth, regulation of body fluid composition and enzyme control. Minerals come from the soil via animals and plants.

Calcium

Calcium is found mainly in cheese, milk, sardines, white flour (which is fortified with it by law) and yogurt.

Calcium is essential for forming healthy bones and teeth but is not deposited in bones after the age of around 35. It is important to have had a good intake of calcium before this age in order to combat osteoporosis.

Fluoride

Fluoride is found mainly in drinking water which has been fluoridated, and also in sea-weed (though not the chopped cabbage that masquerades as such) and tea.

Fluoride helps build strong bones and teeth and forms some protection against tooth decay. Taken in excessive quantities, it can cause erosion of tooth enamel and give a mottled look to the teeth.

Iodine

Iodine's richest source is kelp. Other sources include dairy products, fish, milk and meat.

Iodine is essential for producing thyroid hormones.

Iron

Iron is found in the greatest quantities in liver and red meat, although it is also present in eggs, pulses, some vegetables and wholegrain cereals. Vegetarians and vegans need to take particular care that they are getting sufficient iron in their diet as the quantities in the latter foods are not as readily absorbed as those from liver and meat.

Iron is a vital component of the haemoglobin in red blood cells that transports oxygen round the body. Anaemia is the result of insufficient iron.

Magnesium

Magnesium is found in many foods, notably cocoa, green vegetables, nuts, other vegetables and wholegrain cereals.

Like calcium, magnesium plays an important part in the development of bones and teeth but is also involved in muscle and nerve functions and the release of energy.

Phosphorus

Phosphorus is found in a wide variety of foods including cheese, eggs, fish, lentils, liver, meat, milk, wholegrain cereals and yeast extract.

Phosphorus is also important for bones and teeth and in the release of energy.

Potassium

Potassium is found in virtually all foods, especially fruit and vegetables, but not in fats, oils or sugar. Bananas are particularly rich in potassium.

Potassium, along with salt, regulates levels of acidity and alkalinity in the body and control the balance of water.

A lack of potassium may occur after heavy bouts of diarrhoea or vomiting as well as in people taking diuretics.

Zinc

Zinc is found in cheese, eggs, fish, liver, meat, milk, shellfish (especially oysters) and yogurt.

Zinc plays a major part in the healing of cuts and wounds and is essential for growth and sexual development.

Calories

Calories are the energy derived from eating foods. The term refers to the amount of heat required to raise the temperature of 1 gram of water by 1°C.

A kilocalorie equals 1,000 Calories but, in practice, the word calorie is usually used to describe a kilocalorie. Kilojoule is a term little used in the UK although it frequently appears on food labels and is more widely known in Continental Europe. One kilocalorie (better known as a calorie) equals 4.183 kilojoules. You can see which measurement is easier to work in!

To lose weight – bear in mind that in the UK approximately 21 million people are overweight – you need to consume fewer

Below: *Fruit is high in fibre and vitamins*
Right: *Cheese is rich in Vitamins A, B2, B12, and in calcium and phosphorus*

calories. Aim for a weight loss of around 1kg/2lb a week until you reach your target.

Don't crash diet – you'll only put the weight on again quickly, as most of what you have lost is water. Simply reduce your calorie intake by 500 to 1,000 calories a day depending on how many you consume, but don't go below about 1,200.

Once you have reached your target you will need to make permanent changes to your diet to stay there. Reduce your intake of fat and sugar (there's no need to cut them out altogether) and increase your consumption of fruit and vegetables.

Fish and poultry (skin removed) are low in calories and lean meat with all the fat removed is also good. Plenty of starchy foods like bread, cereals, pasta and potatoes will fill you up without putting on weight, provided, of course, that you don't dress them with fatty toppings or sauces.

Don't fry foods. Try boiling, grilling, microwaving or steaming, none of which needs much, if any, added fat. Use lower fat alternatives where possible: yogurt rather than of cream, reduced-fat cheese instead of full-fat cheese, and skimmed or semi-skimmed milk.

Don't deprive yourself of all the treats that you enjoy which are high in calories. Just ration them a little.

And don't make your companions lives a misery when you go out for meals. Stick to what guidelines you can and vow to cut out a treat or two over the next couple of days.

Lastly, remember that alcohol is high in calories. Drink it only in moderation.

Microwave

Think of your microwave as an extra pair of hands in the kitchen. Above all, don't be frightened of it. If you're new to using a microwave and you are nervous of it, begin by using it for simple tasks until you build up your confidence. By using it for the foods that it cooks best, and by pairing it with traditional methods of cooking, you will achieve the best of both worlds. This form of cooking also enables you to reduce the amount of salt, fat and sugar that you might normally use.

Below: *Baking an elaborate cake becomes child's play*
Right: *A microwave turns out a soup in minutes*

Two methods of cooking, steaming and poaching, both of which retain the food's flavour and moisture, give perfect results in the microwave. Fish is particularly suited to these forms of cooking, and vegetables keep their colour, flavour, crispness and a high proportion of their vitamin content. Small quantities of jams and preserves can be cooked quickly, fruit can be poached in minutes, eggs scrambled in no time at all, and porridge can be prepared for breakfast leaving no messy pans.

Roasting needs more attention and you will need to use either a roasting bag, or a microwave roasting rack and be prepared to baste often during the cooking time. To get the brown finish on a roast joint, you can add soy sauce, tomato purée, paprika or turmeric to the juices, or you can brush the meat or poultry with redcurrant jelly or honey.

A browning dish or skillet will give a grilled appearance to steaks, chops, bacon rashers, sausages, kebabs, hamburgers, fish and poultry pieces. To prevent bacon curling, snip the fatty edge. Sponge cakes cook in a very short time, rise well and stay moist inside, though the outside can harden as the cake cools. Disguise the pale colour of microwaved cakes with icing, or add chocolate, coffee, treacle, brown sugar, ginger or spices to the cake mixture.

Pastry needs to be rolled very thinly to help in crisping, and pastry cases should be baked blind to avoid them being soggy. You will not achieve the golden colour of conventionally cooked pastry, but the addition of wholemeal flour to the basic mix will give colour. Bread will not be crusty, so only cook baps and soft breads and crisp them under the grill or on a roasting rack.

A combination oven, which offers both microwave and conventional cooking, can be either table-top or built in and is a good choice for small kitchens.

Techniques

Microwave cooking has its own special methods which you need to employ for total success. They are very simple and extremely easy to follow.

Arranging: regular-sized food (scones, tomatoes, etc.) should be placed in circles, moving those on the outside to the centre during the cooking. Uneven-sized food (chops, chicken drumsticks, small fish, etc.) should be placed with their thinner parts towards the centre of the dish where they will cook more slowly.

Covering: this traps steam and thereby helps to tenderize food and speed up cooking time. Use an inverted plate, or pierced microwave film to allow some steam to escape. Foods that splatter, like sausages and bacon, can be covered with absorbent kitchen paper.

Shielding: cover bones that pro-trude with tiny pieces of foil (shiny side down) topped with microwave film, to prevent them from burning.

Standing: joints of meat, cakes and puddings, should be left to stand, covered, for the time spec-ified in recipes. This is because food continues to cook after it is taken out of the microwave.

Stirring: to distribute heat evenly, food cut into pieces and liquids should be stirred from the out-side, where food cooks first, towards the centre.

Turning: even ovens fitted with turntables or stirrer blades can have blind spots, so dishes that cannot be stirred, like cakes, joints of meat or poultry, should be rotated by a quarter or half turn during cooking.

Chicken stock

Break up a carcass, slice an onion and place in a large bowl with a bay leaf and mace blade. Cover with boiling water and cook on Full power for 15 minutes. Cool and strain.

Cook's Tip

Do not be frightened of your microwave: make friends with it and you will be richly rewarded.

Above: *Successful sauces like this succulent Apple sauce take just a few minutes to prepare* **Below right:** *The great advantage of scrambling eggs in the microwave is that there is no difficult pan to clean*

Fish stock

Put 500 g/l lb fish trimmings in a large bowl with a sliced onion, a carrot, a stick of celery and 2 bay leaves. Pour on 600 ml/1 pint of boiling water, then cover the bowl and cook on Full power for 15 minutes. Cool, strain and use within 24 hours.

Apple sauce

Peel, core and slice 500 g/l lb cooking apples into a bowl. Add 125 g/4 oz sugar, cover and cook on Full power for 7 minutes. Beat in 25 g/1 oz butter until smooth. Finally, add 2 tablespoons of chopped fresh herbs, such as thyme, parsley or sage, if you are serving the apple sauce with roast pork.

Béchamel sauce

Place 25 g/1 oz plain flour, a bay leaf and a blade of mace in a large basin. Slowly add 300 ml/½ pint milk, whisking all the time, season to taste and add 25 g/1 oz butter. Cook (whisking twice during the cooking time) on Full

power for 4–5 minutes. Whisk again, remove the bay leaf and mace, check seasoning and serve.

Fudge sauce

Place 250 g/8 oz sugar, ¼ teaspoon salt, contents of a 175 g/6 oz can evaporated milk in a bowl and mix well. Cook on Full power for 5–6 minutes, when the sauce should be boiling fast. Add 50 g/2 oz plain dessert chocolate, broken into pieces, 25 g/1 oz butter and 1 teaspoon vanilla essence. Stir until chocolate has melted and serve the sauce warm over ice cream.

Fruit poaching syrup

Put 50 g/2 oz sugar, 150 ml/¼ pint water and 1 tablespoon lemon juice in a bowl, cover and cook on Full power for about 5–6 minutes, stirring once. Poach any fruit halves in the syrup for 4–5 minutes, stirring once.

Béchamel sauce variations

Cheese: add 125 g/4 oz grated Cheddar cheese to the sauce, whisking until it melts. Cook for 1 minute. Mushroom: add 250 g/8 oz thinly sliced button mushrooms to the sauce and cook for 2 minutes. Parsley: chop a handful of fresh parsley and add to the sauce, stir well and serve. Onion: finely chop 1 large onion or 2 small onions and cook in 25 g/1 oz butter for 5 minutes on Full power. Then add the flour and milk, stir in the bay leaf and mace and cook as in the main recipe.

Toasted salted almonds

Spread 125 g/4 oz almonds (it is not advisable to use a smaller quantity because they will probably scorch) on a flat dish and cook on Full power for 5–7 minutes. As a finishing touch, sprinkle with sea salt. Serve with drinks.

Left: *Make Béchamel sauce with absolutely no trace of lumps*

Croûtons

Cube 2 thick slices of bread (you can use white, brown or granary, as you prefer), discarding the crusts. Arrange the cubes of bread in a single layer on absorbent kitchen paper and then cook in the microwave on Full power for 3–4 minutes. Melt 25 g/1 oz butter in a medium bowl on Full power for about 20–30 seconds, add the croûtons and stir until all the butter has been absorbed.

Scrambled eggs

Whisk 4 eggs with 4 tablespoons of milk in a bowl, using a balloon whisk. Season and add 25 g/1 oz butter, diced. Cook, whisking every 30 seconds during the cooking time, on Full power for 1½ minutes, until the eggs are light and creamy. The eggs will continue to cook when you take the bowl out of the oven, so it is important that you remove them before they have finished cooking, otherwise you will end up with rubbery tasting eggs. Serve on hot buttered toast.

Utensil tips

● Container test: to see if something is safe to use, place a tumbler half full of water in it. Cook on Full power for 1 minute. If the water is warm and the container remains cool, then it can be used in the microwave oven.
● For a lighter, less greasy result when cooking meat in a roasting bag, place the meat joint on a microwave rack or upturned saucer so that it does not sit in the fat as it cooks.
● Keep small rubber bands and use them to secure the neck of roasting bags.
● Pottery that is unglazed and porous tends to overheat and slows down cooking time, so avoid using in the microwave.
● Roasting bags, or boil-in-bags, should be pierced to allow steam to escape.
● Round, shallow, straight-sided containers allow quick, even cooking and give the best results.
● Sterilize jars by half filling each one with water and heating until boiling. Remove the hot jars carefully, pour away the water and drain them upside-down before filling.

● The bigger the dishes used in your microwave the better. They allow plenty of room for stirring and prevent spillage.
● Utensils can be a choice of ceramics, glass, paper, plastic or wood, so check what you have in your kitchen before being tempted to spend money on something that you may not really need.
● Wood and wicker can be used for warming bread rolls, but make sure metal wire or staples have not been used, and that they are not bonded with glue.
● Vegetables cooked in roasting bags retain flavour and moisture and can easily be stirred or shaken during cooking time. Seal the bags with rubber bands, string or cut a plastic strip from the top of the bag.

Food tips

● Alcohol for flambéed fruit or puddings can be heated in a jug for 15 seconds. Pour the warm alcohol over the pudding immediately and set alight.
● Blanch almonds by heating 250 ml/8 fl oz water in a measuring jug on Full power for 2½ minutes. Add almonds, cook for 30 seconds, strain and remove skins.
● Chocolate for decorative piping should be broken into small pieces, put in a bowl and melted on Defrost. Then put it in a greaseproof paper piping bag and snip off the end.
● Chocolate for sauces can be melted in about 1½–2 minutes. Simply break into small squares, place in a bowl and cook on Full power.
● Citrus fruit will yield more juice if you prick the skin and warm it for 15–20 seconds on Full power. Halve and squeeze.

Warnings

● Microwaves are deflected by metal so you cannot use the following: cast-iron flameproof casseroles, roasting pans, cake and pie tins, china with metallic decoration and lead crystal. Food will not cook in them, and they may damage the magnetron and cause arcing (sparking) which can pit the oven walls.

● Thermometers should never be left in a bowl when cooking jams or preserves.

● Glass tumblers and small dishes can be used, but if they are not designed for the microwave, do not cook food with a high proportion of sugar or fat in them because they can overheat and make the glass crack.

● Always check foods after the minimum suggested cooking time has elapsed. It is easy to extend the cooking time but impossible to rescue dishes that have been overcooked.

● Clingfilm designed for the microwave should be used rather than ordinary food wrap film.

● Never try to hard-boil eggs in the microwave. Pressure inside the shells will make them explode.

● Use only wooden skewers – metal ones can cause arcing (sparking), which will damage the appliance; plastic ones will melt!

● Clarify crystallized honey by placing the open, wide-neck jar of honey in the microwave oven and warm it on Full power for 1–2 minutes.

● If you are entertaining with pasta, it is easier to cook it in advance, using a conventional method, then drain and turn into a bowl. Before eating, dot with butter (do not mix), cover and heat for a few minutes in the microwave. Stir and serve.

● Herbs are good dried in the microwave oven. Rinse 25 g/1 oz fresh leaves under cold water, drain and dry. Spread between two sheets of absorbent kitchen paper and cook on Full power for 2 minutes. Remove the top sheet and cook for further 1–2 minutes or until all the moisture has been extracted from the leaves. Crush and store in an airtight container.

● If you are partial to marrow, it is useful to know that this vegetable responds particularly well to microwave cookery. First make sure it fits the oven, then slip it in a roasting bag and secure

the neck of the bag. Cook a stuffed 2 kg/4 lb marrow on Full power for 10 minutes.

● Meat needs to be evenly marbled with fat to ensure even cooking. Boned, rolled and carefully tied joints cook very well.

● Pastry can be given an extra touch of colour by adding wholemeal flour.

● Peeling tomatoes is easy. Place around the rim of a plate lined with absorbent paper and heat on Full power for 10–15 seconds. Leave for 5 minutes, slit skins with a knife and slip them off.

Above: *Preserves and jams made easy*
Below: *Fish is well suited to this method*
Right: *Vegetables retain colour and flavour*

- All portions need to be evenly cooked, so it is a good idea to, place them as far apart as possible in a dish or on a plate, turning and repositioning them several times during the cooking process to ensure even cooking.
- Poultry should be securely trussed to retain its shape while cooking in the microwave.
- Rind from oranges and lemons can be saved for flavouring: place it on a glass plate and cook on Full power until all the moisture has evaporated. Cool, then crumble and store in an airtight container until you are ready to use it.
- Salt has a toughening effect on meat, so always add it after your microwave cooking. Use unsalted butter for cooking any meat.
- Scrambling eggs in the microwave works brilliantly, but it is vital to beat or stir the mixture frequently and not overcook it. The eggs should be really very moist when removed from the oven as they will continue to cook for 2–3 minutes.
- Skin surrounding any food must be pierced before microwave cooking, to prevent pressure build-up causing the skin to burst.
- Spices and herbs should be used in moderation, to taste in microwave cooking, because it brings out their flavour.
- Sugar that has hardened is very easily softened. Place 175 g/ 6 oz in a bowl with a chunk of apple, cover and cook on Full power for about 30 seconds. Leave to stand for 5 minutes.
- Unmould jellies and other moulded desserts by placing in the oven on Full power for 30 seconds or so. (Remember not to use metal moulds.)

Microwave to freezer to microwave

The modern-day combination of microwave and freezer makes it possible to lead a busy life and still afford to be hospitable! You can cope with unexpected visitors, cook ahead for entertaining, prepare batches of food for the family, and shop in advance for holidays.

The defrost control on the microwave makes it possible to thaw food automatically by repeatedly giving short bursts of microwave energy followed by rest periods. If your oven is without defrost, this can be achieved by microwaving on Full power for 30-second bursts, with 1½ minute intervals. In this way, you will have even thawing, without the food cooking before the remainder of the food is thawed.

Thawing and freezer tips

- Blanch vegetables in the microwave in preparation for putting them in the freezer.
- Chops and steaks should be separated; fruit and vegetables should be shaken or forked apart; and liquids and dishes such as casseroles and stews should be stirred and broken up at the beginning of thawing.
- Foil freezer containers should not be used in the microwave, so transfer the contents into a suitable dish.
- Freezer- and microwave-proof containers enable you to freeze food that can later be thawed and/or reheated in the microwave, saving you both time and trouble.
- Reheat sliced meat, and vegetables such as broccoli and asparagus, in a sauce.

Microwave cooking times Fresh vegetables

Fresh vegetables and weight	Preparation	Water to be added	Cooking time
Artichokes 4 medium	Wash and trim	150 ml (¼ pint)	10–20 mins
Aubergines 500 g (1 lb)	Peel and dice	2 tablespoons	5–6 mins
Beetroot 500 g (1 lb)	Wash, skin and cut in half	None	7–8 mins
Broad beans 500 g (1 lb)	Remove from pods and wash	2 tablespoons	7–10 mins
Broccoli 250 g (8 oz)	Slice into spears	3 tablespoons	4–5 mins
Brussels sprouts 250 g (8 oz)	Trim	3–4 tablespoons	8 mins
Cabbage 500 g (1 lb)	Trim and shred	3 tablespoons	7–8 mins
Carrots 250 g (8 oz)	Scrape and slice	2 tablespoons	7 mins
Cauliflower 500 g (1 lb)	Trim and cut into florets	4 tablespoons	9–10 mins
Celery 1 head	Trim and dice	None	10–13 mins
Corn on the cob (2)	Trim and wash	4 tablespoons	7–8 mins
Courgettes 500 g (1 lb)	Trim, slice and sprinkle with salt	None	7–9 mins
Fennel 500 g (1 lb)	Slice	2 tablespoons	9–10 mins
Leeks 500 g (1 lb)	Trim and slice	3 tablespoons	7–9 mins
Mushrooms 125 g (4 oz)	Peel or wash whole	2 tablespoons	2½–3 mins
Onions 250 g (8 oz)	Peel and slice	3 tablespoons	4–6 mins
Parsnips 500 g (1 lb)	Peel and slice	3 tablespoons	6–8 mins
Peas 250 g (8 oz)	Remove from pods	3 tablespoons	6–8 mins
Potatoes 500 g (1 lb)	Peel and cut into evenly sized pieces	3 tablespoons	6–7 mins
Potatoes 250–300 g (8–10 oz)	Scrub and prick well	None	9 mins
Runner beans 250 g (8 oz)	String and slice	2 tablespoons	5 mins
Spinach 250 g (8 oz)	Wash and shred	4 tablespoons	7 mins
Swede 250 g (8 oz)	Peel and dice	None	6–8 mins
Tomatoes 250 g (8 oz)	Slice	None	2–3 mins
Turnips 250 g (8 oz)	Peel and dice	2 tablespoons	6–7 mins

Microwave cooking times Joints of meat

Joint and weight	Approx. cooking time	Standing time (wrapped tightly in foil)
Beef 500 g (1 lb)	Rare: 4–5 mins. Medium: 7 mins Well done: 9 mins	20–30 mins
Lamb 500 g (1 lb)	7–9 mins	25–30 mins
Pork 500 g (1 lb)	7–9 mins	20–25 mins
Gammon joints 500 g (1 lb)	7 mins	15–20 mins
Chicken 500 g (1 lb)	6–7 mins	15–20 mins
Turkey up to 3.5 kg (8 lb)	6–7 mins	25–30 mins

Microwave cooking times Fish

Fish and weight	Approx. cooking time	Standing time (covered)
Cod fillets and steaks 500 g (1 lb)	4 mins	5–10 mins
Plaice, gutted and filleted 500 g (1 lb)	3 mins	5–10 mins
Sole, filleted 500 g (1 lb)	3–4 mins	5–10 mins
Haddock, gutted and filleted 500 g (1 lb)	3 mins	5–10 mins
Mackerel (2), gutted but whole 250 g (8 oz)	2 mins each side	5–10 mins
Kipper fillets 250 g (8 oz)	3 mins	5 mins

Microwave cooking times Small cuts of meat

Cut or type of meat and weight	Special points	Approx. cooking time	Standing time
Mince 500 g (1 lb)	Cook covered	5 mins	2 mins
Steak: rump or fillet 250 g (8 oz)	----	3–4 mins	2 mins
Chops, loin: lamb or pork 2 portions 150 g (5 oz) each	Cook covered	6 mins	2 mins
Fillet: lamb or pork 375 g (12 oz)	Cook on roasting rack	6 mins	5 mins
Breast of lamb 625 g (1 lb 4 oz)	Cook on rack	6 mins	3 mins
Bacon 250 g (8 oz)	Cook on a rack, allow fat to drain.	4 mins	2 mins
Chicken: 2 portions 425 g (14 oz)	Cook covered	10 mins	10–15 mins
Gammon steaks 200 g (7 oz)	Cook covered	2½–3 mins	5 mins
Gammon joints 500 g (1 lb)	Slice before cooking	7 mins	10 mins
Liver 500 g (1 lb)	----	4 mins	5 mins
Kidneys 2 or 3	----	3–5 mins	5 mins

Microwave defrosting times Joints of meat

Type	Approx. time per 500 g (1 lb) on LOW setting	Special instructions
Beef Boned (sirloin, topside)	8–10 mins	Turn over regularly during thawing and rest if the meat shows signs of cooking. Stand for 1 hour.
Joints on bone (rib or beef)	10–12 mins	Shield bone end with small, smooth pieces of foil and overwrap with microwave film. Turn the joint during thawing. The meat will still be icy in the centre but will thaw completely if you leave it to stand for 1 hour.
Minced beef	8–10 mins	Stand for 10 mins
Cubed steak	6–8 mins	Stand for 10 mins
Steak (sirloin, rump)	8–10 mins	Stand for 10 mins
Beefburgers Standard (50 g/2 oz)	2 burgers: 2 mins 4 burgers: 2–3 mins	Can be cooked from frozen, without thawing, if preferred.
Quarter-pounder	2 burgers: 2–3 mins 4 burgers: 5 mins	
Burger buns	2 buns: 2 mins	Stand burger buns for 2 mins.
Pork and Bacon Boned rolled joint (loin, leg)	7–8 mins	As for boned roasting joints of beef above. Stand for 1 hour.
On the bone (leg, hand)	7–8 mins	As for beef joints on bone above. Stand for 1 hour.
Tenderloin	8–10 mins	Stand for 10 mins.
Chops	8–10 mins	Separate during thawing and arrange 'spoke' fashion. Stand for 10 mins.
Bacon rashers	2 mins per 250 g (8 oz)	Remove from pack; separate after thawing. Stand for 6–8 mins.
Lamb/Veal Boned rolled (loin, leg shoulder)	5–6 mins	As for boned roasting joints of beef above. Stand for 30–45 mins.
On the bone (leg, shoulder)	5–6 mins	As for beef joints on bone above. Stand for 30–45 mins.
Minced lamb or veal	8–10 mins	Stand for 10 mins.
Chops	8–10 mins	Separate during thawing. Stand for 10 mins.
Offal: Liver	8–10 mins	Separate during thawing. Stand for 5 mins.
Kidneys	6–9 mins	Separate during thawing. Stand for 5 mins.

Microwave defrosting times Fish

Type	Approx. time per 500 g (1 lb) on LOW setting	Special instructions
White fish fillets or cutlets, e.g. cod, coley, haddock, halibut, whole plaice or sole	3–4 mins per 500 g (1 lb), plus 2–3 mins	Stand for 5 mins after each 2–3 mins.
Oily fish, eg, whole and gutted mackerel, herring, trout	2–3 mins per 250 g (8 oz), plus 2–3 mins	Stand for 5 mins after each 2–3 mins and for 5 mins afterwards.
Lobster tails, crab claws, etc.	3–4 mins per 250 g (8 oz), plus 2–3 mins	As for oily fish above.
Crab meat	2–3 mins per 250 g (8 oz), plus 2–3 mins	As for oily fish above.
Prawns, shrimp, scampi	2½ mins per 125 g (4 oz) 3–4 mins per 250 g (8 oz)	Pierce plastic bag, if necessary. Stand for 2 mins. Separate with a fork after 2 mins. Stand for 5 mins then plunge into cold water and drain.

Microwave defrosting times Poultry and game

Type	Approx. time on LOW setting	Special instructions
Whole chicken or duckling	6–8 mins	Remove giblets. Stand in cold water for 30 mins.
Whole turkey	10–12 mins	Remove giblets. Stand in cold water for 2–3 hours.
Chicken portions	5–7 mins	Separate during thawing. Stand for 10 mins.
Poussin, grouse, pheasant, pigeon, quail	5–7 mins	----

Microwave defrosting times Baked goods

Type	Quantity	Approx. time on LOW setting	Special instructions
Bread Loaf, whole	1 large	6–8 mins	Uncover and place on absorbent kitchen paper. Turn over during thawing. Stand for 5–15 mins. Defrost in original wrapper but remove any metal tags. Stand for 5–15 mins.
Loaf, whole	1 small	4–6 mins	
Loaf, sliced	1 large	6–8 mins	
Loaf, sliced	1 small	4–6 mins	
Slice of bread	25 g (1 oz)	10–15 seconds	Place on absorbent kitchen paper and time carefully, stand for about 1–2 mins.
Bread rolls, tea cakes, scones	2	15–20 seconds	Place on absorbent kitchen paper and time carefully, stand for about 2–3 mins.
	4	25–35 seconds	
Crumpets	2	15–20 seconds	Place on absorbent kitchen paper and time carefully, stand for about 2–3 mins.
Croissants	2	15–20 seconds	Place on absorbent kitchen paper and time carefully, stand for about 2–3 mins.

Microwave defrosting times Cakes and pastries

Type	Quantity	Approx. time on LOW setting	Special instructions
Cakes	2 small	30–60 seconds	Place on absorbent kitchen paper and stand for 5 mins.
	4 small	1–1½ mins	
Sponge cake	500 g (1 lb)	1–1½ mins	Place on absorbent kitchen paper and test and turn after 1 min. Stand for 5 mins.
Jam doughnuts	2	45–60 seconds	Place on absorbent kitchen paper and stand for 5 mins.
	4	45–90 seconds	
Cream doughnuts	2	45–60 seconds	Place on absorbent kitchen paper. Check after half the thawing time. Stand for 10 mins.
	4	1¼–1¾ mins	
Cream éclairs	2	45 seconds	Stand for 5–10 mins.
	4	1–1½ mins	Stand for 15–20 mins.
Choux buns	4 small	1–1½ mins	Stand for 20–30 mins.
Pastry Shortcrust and puff	250 g (8 oz) packet	1 min	Stand for 20 mins.
	425 g (14 oz) packet	2 mins	Stand for 20–30 mins.

Freezing

Freezing food whether it is fresh or cooked is a wonderful solution for today's busy lives. When you freeze food do be certain that you prepare and store it correctly so you can be sure that all the ingredients for your meals have retained their original qualities and nutrients.

Cooling

Food must be as cool as possible before being packaged for the freezer, otherwise moisture in the form of steam will be retained. This, and the food's warmth, will cause large ice crystals to form between the food's tissues which will damage them. The best method is to stand pans and dishes of food in bowls of ice cubes or ice-cold water.

Ice glazing

Use for whole fish to protect skin and prevent air getting to the flesh. Open freeze it until solid, then dip quickly in cold water and refreeze. Repeat this process again and again until the ice is about 6 mm/¼ inch thick, then wrap in a double layer of foil for storing.

Overwrapping

To prevent cross-transference of flavours and odours from one food to another or to give added protection. Wrap the food to be frozen in a double thickness of foil, or with rigid containers, double wrap and seal in a polythene bag.

Interleaving

Separating portions of food so that they freeze individually. Place sheets of cling film or foil between each chop, steak or hamburger, etc., then freeze together in one container or package. Portions can be taken out and the package resealed and stored again.

Open freezing

Keeps individual pieces separate so they do not freeze in a solid mass, or delicate, decorative and soft-texture foods intact. Line baking sheets with foil or greaseproof paper, spread food on top without pieces touching. Freeze until solid, then remove from tray and pack in bags.

Discoloration

Apples, apricots, peaches and pears turn brown when cut. Prevent this by adding juice of 1 lemon to 1 litre/1¾ pints water. Slice the fruit into solution, leave for about 15 minutes and rinse before puréeing or freezing as slices. For fruit packed in syrup, dissolve ½ teaspoon ascorbic acid powder in 1 tablespooon cold water and add to 600 ml/1 pint syrup.

Headspace

The space between the surface of the food and the lid of a rigid container. Liquids expand during freezing and will force off a container lid if packed to the brim. Food then becomes exposed to the air and will spoil during their freezing time. Roll or crumple greasproof paper into small balls and place on top of stews, casseroles, fruit, etc., to keep contents submerged in the liquid.

Sugar syrup

To 1.2 litres/2 pints water use 250 g/8 oz sugar for light syrup; 500 kg/1 lb for medium; or 1 kg/2 lb for heavy. Bring the ingredients slowly to the boil, water must not boil before the sugar dissolves or it may crystallize into lumps. Boil hard for about 2 minutes to get a clear syrup and leave it to cool.

Warnings

As a general rule, once food has thawed it should not be refrozen. Raw meat, poultry, fish, fruit and vegetables can only be frozen if they are cooked first before returning to the freezer. Thawed food should be cooked as quickly as possible, and not kept for longer than one would keep fresh food before cooking or eating it.

Packaging

Use bags for small fruit and vegetables; and rigid containers for food that might be knocked, crushed or broken during storage. To exclude air and cover surfaces, regularly shaped and sturdy food can be enclosed in foil or film using the techniques of druggist's and butcher's wrap.

● Druggist's wrap: place awkwardly shaped food on a large square of foil. Slice one corner so that it covers food. Turn in one side, then the other so food is nearly hidden. Fold foil back on itself and bring fourth corner to top. Press to exclude air.

● Butcher's wrap: place reguarly shaped food on a large foil triangle. Lift up the two long sides, bring to the top. With edges meeting, make one sharp fold. Continue to fold foil until it reaches food. This will press out air. Fold in foil at both sides, seal on top with freezer tape.

To blanch vegetables

This is essential to prevent the loss of vitamin C. Place 250 g/8 oz vegetables in a blanching basket and immerse completely in 4 litres/7 pints boiling water. Return to the boil quickly, then calculate blanching time from moment water reboils. (Times are given on pages 245–246). Plunge basket of vegetables into ice-cold water for same length of time as boiling to prevent further cooking and drain well before packing. Water can be re-used 6 or 7 times.

Preparing fruit

● Free flow pack: for soft fruits which make their own juice and can be used partially frozen. The fruit keeps it shape and small amounts can be removed without having to thaw the whole quantity. Open freeze the fruit until frozen solid. Pack in rigid containers or polythene bags.

● Dry sugar pack: for soft, juicy, whole or sliced fruit. The fruit juice combines with sugar to make a natural syrup. Place in a large shallow dish, sprinkle over sugar and allow to stand until fruit juice begins to flow and sugar dissolves. Allow 500 g/1 lb caster sugar to 2 kg/4 lb fruit. Stir fruit gently until evenly coated with syrup and pack in rigid containers, allowing 1 cm/½ inch headspace.

● For small quantities: place fruit in freezer container, sprinkle with sugar, layer with fruit and sugar until full. In thawing, fruit sugar will make its own syrup.

● Packing in sugar syrup: for non-juicy fruits and those which discolour quickly. Use a really light syrup for delicately flavoured fruit, medium and heavy for other types of fruit, depending on the fruit's natural sweetness. Make the syrup a day in advance so that it is cold before use. Pack the fruit to be frozen into rigid containers, pour over the cold syrup covering the fruit but leaving about 1–2 cm/ ½–1 inch headspace. Fruit must be fully submerged in the syrup before freezing, if necessary push several pieces of crumpled greasproof or wax paper down into the syrup before sealing the container.

● Purée: for well-ripened or slightly damaged fruit. This is a good and really effective method for fruit which might otherwise go to waste. Wash and dry the fruit. Lightly cook all of the hard fruits, such as apples, purée and then add the sugar. (The quantities to use are: 50–125 g/2–4 oz sugar per 500 g /1 lb fruit.) Pack the fruit into rigid containers, allowing 1 cm/½ inch headspace between the purée and the top of the container, and seal securely.

A–Z of freezing fruit

	Preparation	Packing	To use
Apples	Peel, core, slice or chop. For purée, cook in the minimum of water with or without sugar. Sieve and cool.	Free flow/light syrup/puréed	Thaw in the unopened containers. For pies and tarts thaw enough to separate the slices for stewing. Used for mousses, soufflés and sauces.
Apricots	Wipe and leave whole; skin fruit by plunging it in boiling water for 30 seconds, rub off skins, stone, halve or slice.	Heavy syrup with ascorbic acid/puréed	Thaw in their containers for 3 hours or at room temperature and serve cold. Frozen in syrup: tip into a saucepan and heat gently. Storage: sugar syrup packs – 1 year; purée – 4 months.
Blackberries	Pick on a dry day for best results. Avoid blackberries with large woody pips. Wash in iced water. Dry well and remove stalks.	Dry sugar/free flow/light syrup	Thaw in their containers. Use while partially frozen to serve cold or in pies. Frozen in syrup: tip into a saucepan and heat gently.
Cherries	Red varieties are better for freezing than black. Wash and dry well, remove stalks and stone.	Free flow/ medium syrup	Thaw unopened in their containers for 3 hours at room temperature for pies and fruit salads. Tip frozen into a saucepan and heat gently.
Currants – red, black and white	Remove from stalks, wash, dry well, top and tail and leave whole. If preferred, freeze currants on the stalks which can be removed when thawing. OR Stew in the minimum of water, sweeten to taste. Cool.	Free flow/light syrup/puréed	Thaw unopened in their containers for 3 hours at room temperature for pies and cold desserts. Frozen in syrup: tip into a saucepan and heat gently.
Damsons	Wash, dry and cut in halves. Remove the stones, which can flavour the fruit.	Syrup/puréed	Thaw unopened in the container for 3 hours at room temperature. Use in jams and pies, or sauces and mousses.
Figs	Wipe, dry and snip off stems. May be peeled or left unpeeled.	Free flow/light syrup	Leave to stand in wrappings or containers for 1½ hours at room temperature.
Gooseberries	Wash and drain, top and tail and leave whole.	Medium syrup/puréed and sieved	Thaw unopened at room temperature before using in jams and pies. Frozen in syrup, tip into a saucepan and stew gently. Use partially thawed purée in fools and mousses.
Grapes	Wash and drain, top and tail and leave whole.	Medium syrup	Thaw unopened in the container for about 2 hours at room temperature. Use while partially frozen from pies and fruit cocktails.
Guavas	Peel, halve and remove seeds Leave as halves or slice.	Dry sugar/light syrup/puréed	Thaw in their containers to use in pies or flans. Cook from frozen until tender, stirring frequently.
Kiwifruit	Peel carefully and leave whole.	Free flow	Thaw in containers until partially frozen then slice to serve.
Lemons	Wipe over the fruit and leave whole, or cut into slices, grate peel, or extract juice.	Whole: freeze wrap in a polythene bag. Slices: free flow. Peel: grate before extracting juice, pack in small cartons. Juice: freeze in ice-cube trays. Pack cubes in polythene bags.	Thaw in wrapping for about 3 hours at room temperature and use as required.
Lychees	Choose fresh fruits with a reddish-brown hue. Remove outer husk and squeeze out central stones.	Heavy syrup	Thaw in the refrigerator for 1 hour. Use partially frosted in fruit salads.
Mangoes	Peel and slice the flesh away from the stone.	Medium syrup with lemon juice	Thaw in the container for 1½ hours at room temperature.
Melon	Peel, cut in half and remove the seeds. Slice, cube or cut into balls.	Dry sugar/medum syrup	Thaw unopened in the container for about 3 hours at room temperature. Serve while still frosty.
Nectarines	Skin if liked, halve and stone.	Medium syrup	Thaw in containers in the refrigerator for 3–4 hours.

	Preparation	Packing	To use
Oranges	Scrub skins and dry. Peel, remove pith and cut into segments or slices. Remove membrane and pips. Leave Sevilles whole (the bitter type used for marmalade).	Light syrup/dry sugar	Thaw sliced fruit in its container for about 3 hours and serve chilled. Use whole fruit frozen for marmalade.
Papayas	Peel, halve and scoop out the seeds. Cut into thin slices.	Medium syrup/puréed with lemon juice	Thaw in their containers for 1–2 hours.
Passionfruit	Choose firm ripe fruits with soft, purple, wrinkled skins. Halve and scoop out the seeds.	Weigh and mix with half its weight of sugar. Stir to dissolve and pack in rigid containers	Thaw in the container for 1½ hours.
Peaches	Peel with a knife or plunge into boiling water for 30 seconds and then into cold water, this will loosen the skin. Cut into halves or slices and remove stone.	Heavy syrup with ascorbic acid or lemon juice	Thaw in the container for about 4 hours. Serve chilled.
Pears	Wash, peel and core. Halve or slice. Best frozen lightly cooked as they tend to lose flavour and crispness if frozen raw.	Poach for 1½ minutes in heavy syrup with ascorbic acid or lemon juice	Thaw in the container for about 4 hours.
Persimmons	Peel and leave whole or slice, removing any seeds.	Whole: wrap in foil Slices: syrup with a little lemon juice	Thaw in the wrappings or container for 3 hours.
Pineapple	Peel, core and slice or dice.	Medium syrup/dry sugar	Thaw unwrapped in containers for 3 hours. Serve chilled.
Plums	Wash, halve and remove stones.	Free flow/medium syrup	For pies: thaw for about 3 hours before using. Otherwise tip frozen in a pan and heat gently in their own syrup.
Raspberries	Wash in iced water, gently and leave whole, or sieve fruit to a purée.	Free flow/medium syrup/dry sugar	Thaw unopened in containers for 3 hours at room temperature, use just before the fruit has completely thawed.
Rhubarb	Wash firm but tender and cut into required lengths.	Blanch in boiling water for 1 minute. Drain and pack in polythene bags or rigid containers without sugar.	Thaw partially in containers. Frozen fruit: tip enough water just to stop it catching, add sugar to taste and heat gently.
Strawberries	Remove stalks. Wash in iced water and dry gently on absorbent kitchen paper. Leave whole or purée with sugar to taste. Note: frozen whole strawberries do show a loss of texture and flavour on thawing. They are best used for decoration or in fruit salad.	Free flow/dry sugar/medium syrup/puréed	Thaw in containers for about 3 hours at room temperature and use just before fruit has completely thawed.

A–Z of freezing vegetables

	Preparation	Blanching time	Packing	To use
Artichokes, globe	Remove outer leaves, trim and wash.	Up to six at a time – 7 minutes	In polythene bags or rigid containers, leaving 1 cm/½ inch headspace.	Thaw overnight in the refrigerator or 4 hours at room temperature. Eat with vinaigrette dressing.
Artichokes, Jerusalem	Only worth freezing as a purée. Scrub, peel, then simmer in water until tender.	Nil	In rigid containers, leaving 2½ cm/1 inch headspace. (Storage: 3 months).	Reheat gently from frozen with a little milk to prevent it catching, or use for soup.
Asparagus	Clean, trim off woody ends. Grade by thickness of stems. Cut to fit container, but don't tie.	Thin – 2 minutes. Medium – 3 minutes Thick – 4 minutes	Pack closely in rigid containers head to tail or tie in bundles and freeze in a polythene bag.	Plunge in boiling water for 5–8 minutes.
Aubergines	Wash and cut in 1 cm/½ inch slices. Blanch immediately to avoid discoloration.	4 minutes.	Open freeze, pack in polythene bag.	Plunge in boiling water for 3–5 minutes.

A–Z of freezing vegetables

	Preparation	Blanching time	Packing	To use
Beans, broad	Choose small young beans. Shell and grade into sizes.	2 minutes	Open freeze, then pack into polythene bags.	Plunge into boiling water for 5–10 minutes.
Beans, French and runner	Choose young tender stringless beans. Cut off ends and tips, leave whole if small, or cut into 2½ cm/1 inch lengths.	Whole or cut – 2 minutes	Open freeze, then pack into polythene bags.	Plunge in boiling water for 8–10 minutes.
Beetroot	Choose young beetroot not more than 7 cm/3 inch in diameter. Twist off tops leaving about 5 cm/2 inch attached.	Nil	Skin, dice or slice or leave whole. Pack into polythene bags or rigid cartons (Storage: 6 months.)	Thaw in refrigerator and use in salads. To serve cook in boiling water for about 25–45 minutes or until tender.
Broccoli	Choose compact heads, cut off woody stalks and trim to an even length.	Thin stalks – 3 minutes Thick stalks – 4 minutes	Pack head to tail in polythene bags or rigid containers, or open freeze, then pack as above.	Plunge frozen into boiling water and cook for 5–8 minutes.
Brussel sprouts	Choose small even-sized sprouts. Trim off outside leaves.	Small – 3 minutes Medium – 4 minutes	Open freeze. Then pack in polythene bags.	Plunge frozen into boiling water and cook for 5–8 minutes.
Cabbage – red, white	Wash and shred.	1½ minutes	Pack in polythene bags. (Storage: blanched, 1 year; braised, 6 months.)	Plunge in boiling water for 3–5 minutes; braise red cabbage, when it can be re-frozen.
Carrots	Choose small young carrots. Scrub and leave whole. If using large carrots scrape and slice or dice.	Small, whole – 5 minutes Diced or sliced – 3 minutes	Pack in polythene bags or rigid containers.	Plunge frozen into boiling water and cook for 5–10 minutes.
Cauliflower	Choose compact white cauliflower. Break into florets of an even size not larger than 2½ cm/1 inch across.	3 minutes	Open freeze then pack in polythene bags (Storage: 6 months).	Plunge frozen into boiling water and cook for 5–8 minutes. Serve with a sauce.
Celeriac	Choose firm, small roots. Peel and wash then cut into cubes or slices. Alternatively grate.	1–2 minutes for cubes and slices; 1 minute for grated.	Open freeze then pack into rigid containers or polythene bags.	Plunge frozen cubes or slices into boiling water for 5 minutes. Toss in butter or a sauce. Use grated from frozen in soups and casseroles or cook as above for 3 minutes.
Celery	Choose tender young stalks. Scrub and cut into even lengths	Nil	Pack in polythene bags	Do not use raw after freezing. Reheat in the oven or in boiling water for 3–5 minutes.
Chicory	Choose firm specimens with tightly packed conical heads. Remove base and any damaged outer leaves	4 minutes	Pack into polythene bags	Plunge into boiling water for 8 minutes. Or thaw in wrappings at room temperature for 2 hours. Squeeze to remove excess moisture then use as required.
Corn on the cob	Choose young, tender corn. Remove husk and silk and grade according to size.	Small – 4 minutes. Medium – 6 minutes Large – 8 minutes	Pack individually in polythene bags, or scrape off kernels, open freeze, then pack as above.	Thaw cobs before cooking, about 4 hours at room temperature. Plunge whole cob into boiling water for 15 minutes, or cook from frozen in boiling water for about 5 minutes.
Courgettes	Pick even-sized young courgettes, cut in half or into 1 cm/½ inch slices.	1 minute	Open freeze, then pack in polythene bags or rigid containers.	Plunge while frozen into boiling water for 3 minutes or thaw and sauté in butter.

	Preparation	Blanching time	Packing	To use
Fennel	Choose firm, tight heads with white leaf bases. Trim and scrub the outer leaves. Cut into quarters.	3–5 minutes	Pack into polythene bags.	Plunge into boiling water for 7 minutes. Use from frozen in stews.
Leeks	Remove outer leaves. Trim ends and wash well.	Nil	Pack in polythene bags (Storage: 6 months.)	Plunge from frozen in boiling water for 7–10 minutes.
Marrow	Peel and remove the seeds. Chop into large pieces.	3 minutes	Pack in polythene bags or rigid containers. (Storage: 10 months.)	Plunge in boiling water for 3–5 minutes.
Mushrooms	Choose fresh cultivated mushrooms. Wash and dry thoroughly. Leave whole if button, or slice.	Do not blanch in water but sauté in butter allowing 6 tablespoons of melted butter to ½ kg/1 lb mushrooms, for 4–5 minutes	Pack in rigid containers, with cooking liquid. (Storage: raw 1 month; cooked: 3 months.) Open freeze buttons if wished, pack in polythene bags.	Add while frozen to soups. sauces, stews, etc., or if packed in melted butter, reheat gently in the oven or under a grill.
Onions	Choose whole small onions or slice or chop larger onions. Open freeze unblanched for short storage: 3 months.	Nil	Pack in polythene bags or rigid containers and over-wrap to prevent cross-flavouring (Storage: 6 months.)	Add while frozen to soups, sauces, casseroles and stews.
Parsnips	Choose small young parsnips. Trim and peel. Cut into strips or dice.	2 minutes	Open freeze then pack in polythene bags.	Plunge into boiling water for 10 minutes.
Peas	Choose young, sweet tender peas. Pod and sort carefully.	1 minute	Open freeze, then pack in polythene bags or rigid containers.	Plunge into boiling water for 4–7 minutes.
Peppers – red or green	Choose firm glossy peppers. Wash, remove seeds and stem, slice or dice.	Nil	Pack in polythene bags or rigid containers.	Plunge frozen into boiling water for 5–10 minutes.
Potatoes – new boiled	Choose small even-sized ones. Scrape or scrub the potatoes. Slightly undercook until just tender.	Nil	Pack in polythene bags or boiling bags. (Storage: 3 months.)	Plunge into boiling water for 3–5 minutes, or put boiling bag in boiling water, remove from the heat and stand for 10 minutes.
Potatoes– chipped	Prepare in the normal way. Deep fry in hot oil 180°C/350°F until just tender, not brown. Drain well, cool.	Nil	Open freeze, then pack into polythene bags or rigid containers. (Storage: 6 months.)	Fry in shallow or deep frying pan, take care as spitting can occur.
Potatoes – mashed	Cook and mash old potatoes in the normal way. Make into duchesse or croquette potatoes.	Nil	Open freeze, then pack into polythene bags or rigid containers (Storage: 3 months.)	Reheat as directed in the recipe used.
Spinach	Choose young, fresh spinach, wash very thoroughly. Quicker to cook first, then freeze as a leaf or as a purée.	Blanch in small quantities only – 2 minutes	Pack into polythene bags or polythene containers.	Plunge frozen into boiling water, cook for 2–3 minutes. Drain well and toss in a little butter.
Swedes	Trim, peel and dice.	3 minutes	Pack in polythene bags or rigid containers.	Cook from frozen in boiling water for 8–10 minutes or add to soups, stews and casseroles.
Tomatoes	Choose firm tomatoes, skin and leave whole or purée.	Nil	Pack whole skinned tomatoes in polythene bags or rigid containers. Freeze purée in rigid containers.	Not suitable for eating raw as they collapse. Add to stews, soups and casseroles, or fry or grill whole or halved.
Turnips	Choose small turnips. Trim, peel and dice, if large. Or cook and purée.	Small, whole – 4 minutes Diced – 2 minutes	Pack in polythene bags. Pack purée in rigid containers.	Cook from frozen in boiling water for 8–10 minutes or add to soups and stews.

Glossary

Acidulated water Water with added acid, such as lemon juice or vinegar, which prevents discoloration.

Al dente The Italians say that pasta is ready to eat when it is *al dente* which when literally translated means 'firm to the bite'.

Antipasti Italian hors d'oeuvres. The literal Italian translation is 'before the meal' and it usually denotes an assortment of cold meats, vegetables and cheeses which are often marinated.

Arborio The Italian rice used in making risotto. It is similar in shape to pudding rice, but never quite softens in the middle.

Au gratin A cheese and breadcrumb topping, browned under the grill.

Bain-marie A large, water-filled pan in which smaller dishes are set for cooking when an indirect, gentle heat is required.

Bake blind To part-bake an unfilled pastry case by pricking the base with a fork, covering with greaseproof paper or foil and filling with ceramic or dried beans.

Ballotine Boned, rolled and stuffed meat, usually poultry, served hot.

Balsamic vinegar Italian vinegar that has been aged for anything up to 20 years in oak casks. It is dark in colour with an intense, slightly sweet flavour.

Barbecue To cook over glowing coals, often of charcoal.

Bard To cover or wrap lean meats in a sheet of fat to prevent drying out.

Baste To spoon pan juices (usually fat-based) over meat or vegetables to moisten during cooking.

Beignets Fritters

Beurre manié Flour and butter worked into a paste, then used to thicken soups, stew juices, etc.

Beurre noir Butter heated to a light brown colour, usually served with fish.

Bind To hold dry ingredients together with egg or liquid.

Bisque Smooth and thickened shellfish soup.

Blanch To immerse food briefly in boiling water to soften, remove skin, par-cook, set a colour, or remove a strong taste.

Bouillon Broth or unclarified stock obtained from boiling meat or vegetables.

Bouquet garni Classically made up of a bay leaf, a sprig of thyme and 2-3 sprigs of parsley, which are either bound together with string or tied into a small muslin bag. It is used to flavour almost any savoury dish that needs long cooking, and is removed before the dish is served.

Braise To cook food very slowly in a small amount of liquid in a pan or pot with a tight-fitting lid, after initial browning.

Brochette Grilled and served on a skewer.

Buckwheat Small, triangular-shaped grain, milled into either flour or grains.

Bulgar wheat Cracked wheat that has been partially processed. Sometimes sold as cracked wheat or pourgouri, and used extensively in Middle Eastern cooking.

Butterfly To slit a piece of food in half horizontally, almost cutting through so that when opened it resembles butterfly wings. Often used for king prawns, chops and thick fillets of fish.

Canapé Small appetizer of pastry, biscuits, etc. with a savoury topping.

Capers Small buds of a flowering shrub grown in the Mediterranean. As they are normally pickled in brine or salted, they should be washed and dried before use.

Casserole Ovenproof cooking pot with a lid.

Cassis A fruit liqueur or syrup made from blackcurrants.

Cassoulet A French dish which consists of haricot beans cooked in a stewpot with pork, other meat and poultry, seasoning and a gratin topping. Sausages and duck and goose portions are often added.

Caramelize To cook sugar or sugar syrup to the caramel stage. The term is also used when grilling a sugar topping until brown.

Ceps (dried) Dried mushrooms that need reconstituting in boiling water before using. Also known as porcini, which is their Italian name.

Clarify To melt and strain butter of its milk particles and impurities; to clear stocks, etc. by filtering.

Cocotte A small ovenproof dish without a lid.

Compôte Fresh or dried fruit served cold in a syrup.

Consommé Concentrated clear meat or poultry stock.

Coulis A thin liquid purée, usually of fresh or cooked fruit or vegetables, which can be poured.

Court-bouillon Aromatic liquid generally used for poaching fish or shellfish.

Couscous This is actually a type of pasta though it is treated like a grain and is pre-soaked before cooking to soften it. It is often used in North African or Middle Eastern cooking.

Crackling The crisp cooked rind of a joint of pork.

Cream To beat fat and sugar together to a pale consistency.

Croustade Small bread cases, brushed with melted butter and baked or deep-fried until crisp.

Croûte A slice of fried or toasted bread on which food is served.

Croûton Small shapes (usually dice) of fried or occasionally toasted bread used as a garnish.

Crudités Raw vegetables such as carrot, cucumber and celery, usually cut into sticks or slices and used with a dipping sauce.

Curdle To cause milk or sauce to separate into solid and liquid. Often used to describe any mixture that separates.

Dariole A small castle-shaped mould, for cakes, mousses, etc.

Deglaze To free congealed cooking juices and sediments from the bottom of a roasting tin or pan by adding water, stock or wine and stirring over heat. The juices may be used to make gravy or added to a sauce.

Degorge To sprinkle with salt or to soak to remove indigestible or strong tasting juices from meat, fish or vegetables.

Degrease To skim grease from the surface of liquid.

Demi-glace A rich brown sauce.

Devilled A food seasoned with a hot-tasting sauce and grilled or fried.

Draw To remove the innards of birds.

Dredge To sprinkle the surface of food with flour, icing sugar, etc.

Dress To pluck, draw and truss poultry or game birds; or to put dressing on a salad and toss.

Dropping consistency The stage reached when a spoonful of a mixture held upside down will drop off the spoon reluctantly.

Duxelles A stuffing of finely chopped mushrooms, often with shallots or ham.

Empanada A South American pastry turnover stuffed with a mixture of chopped meat, onions, etc.

Emulsion A milky liquid prepared by mixing liquids that are not soluble, such as oil and water or other substances.

En croûte To cook food in a pastry case.

En papillote To cook food enclosed in paper.

Entrée In Europe a dish served before the main course, now often referring to the main course itself.

Escalope A thin slice of meat from the fillet or leg.

Farce Stuffing.

Fines herbes A mixture of finely chopped fresh herbs. Traditionally these are fresh chervil, chives, parsley and tarragon.

Flake To separate cooked meat or fish into very small pieces.

Flamber To pour warmed spirit, often brandy, over food and set it alight.

Florentine A dish that is made with spinach.

Flute To make decorative indentations in the edges of pastry pies.

Fold in To combine two mixtures gently with a metal spoon to retain their lightness.

Freezer burn Appears as brown or greyish-white patches on the surface of frozen food. It is caused by extreme dehydration and is often seen on meat, poultry and fish.

Fumet A strong, well-reduced stock made from fish or meat.

Galantine Boned, rolled and stuffed meat, usually poultry, served cold.

Galette Any sweet or savoury mixture that is shaped in a flat round.

Garam masala A ready-made spice powder made up of several different Indian spices.

Garnish To decorate a savoury dish.

Glaze A mixture that is brushed on the surface of food to give colour and shine.

Gnocchi These are little Italian dumplings made from mashed potatoes, potato flour, polenta or wheat flour. They are usually poached in boiling water to cook.

Goujons Small strips of meat or fish, coated and deep-fried.

Hard ball A stage of sugar boiling used in jams, etc.

Hollandaise A rich emulsion sauce made with egg yolks and butter.

Hors d'oeuvres the first course or savoury morsels served with drinks.

Hull To remove the green calyx from fruit.

Infuse To extract flavour by steeping food in hot liquid.

Jardinière A garnish of neatly cut, separately cooked vegetables.

Julienne Matchstick strips of vegetables, citrus rind or meat, used as a garnish.

Kibbled Coarsely chopped, used particularly for wheat.

Knead To work dough by stretching and folding it to distribute the yeast and give a springy consistency.

Knocking back To punch or knead air from yeast dough after rising.

Knock up To slightly separate the layers of raw puff pastry with the blade of a knife, to help rising during cooking.

Lard To thread strips of fat (usually pork) into lean meat to moisten it.

Lardons Small cooked strips or cubes of pork or bacon fat, used to flavour or garnish a dish.

Liaison Ingredients used to bind or thicken.

Macédoine A mixture of diced vegetables or fruit.

Macerate To steep raw food, usually fruit, in sugar syrup or alcohol.

Magret A boned breast of duck, presented with the skin and underlying layer of fat attached.

Marinade The liquid in which food is marinated.

Marinate To soak raw food (usually meat, poultry or game) in liquid, often wine or oil, to tenderize and give flavour.

Médallions Small rounds of meat, evenly cut.

Mesclun This is a French salad using wild salad leaves and grasses.

Millet A small pinhead grain with a nutty flavour.

Mirepoix A bed of diced vegetables (usually carrot,